0613

C000233257

CONTEMPT, SYMPATHY AN

14.95 £5-00

(8.98

CONTEMPT, SYMPATHY AND ROMANCE

*Lowland Perceptions of the Highlands
and the Clearances
During the Famine Years, 1845–1855*

Krisztina Fenyő

TUCKWELL PRESS

First published in Great Britain in 2000 by
Tuckwell Press
The Mill House
Phantassie
East Linton
East Lothian EH40 3DG
Scotland

Copyright © Krisztina Fenyő, 2000

ISBN 1 86232 089 6

The Publishers acknowledge subsidy
from the Scottish Arts Council toward the publication of this volume

British Library Cataloguing in Publication Data
A catalogue record for this book is available
on request from the British Library

The right of Krisztina Fenyő to be identified
as the author of this work has been asserted by her
in accordance with the Copyright, Design and Patent Act 1988

Typeset by Hewer Text Ltd, Edinburgh
Printed and bound by Cromwell Press, Trowbridge, Wiltshire

To the Memory of My Grandparents

Acknowledgements

I would like to express my gratitude to the staff of the National Library of Scotland, the Glasgow Mitchell Library, the Glasgow University Library, and especially the Colindale Newspaper Library of the British Museum, for their patience with my newpaper searches and their invaluable help with massive photocopy orders.

My sincerest thanks are due to my two supervisors at the University of Glasgow, Professor Ted Cowan and Professor Douglas Gifford, for their understanding support and inspiring supervision. I owe special thanks to Dr David Lloyd-Jones whose magnificent house provided me with the most inspirational environment to work in.

My thanks are due to Andrew Malcolm who first took me to the Highlands many years ago. I would also like to say thank you to my friends, in the department and in the wider world, who helped and encouraged me during the writing of this book: to Heather Anderson, Meriel Beattie, Marianna Birkeland, Caroline Hoare, Lucy Hooker, Irene Maver, Kirsty Reid, and many friends on the 'Eorpa' team of BBC Scotland Television.

My thanks are also due to my parents for their encouragement, and I promise that I will translate this book for them.

Krisztina Fenyő, Budapest

Contents

Illustrations

Introduction

Lowland readers of the *Scotsman* were becoming annoyed in 1847. Since the outbreak of the Potato Famine in the Highlands in the late summer of 1846 they had been constantly beseeched to subscribe to relief for their starving Highland neighbours. At first their charity was generous, but as newspaper reports started to flow in with 'revelations' about the exaggeration of the famine and of the 'inherently idle character' of the Highland Gaels many Lowlanders lost their patience.

Why should they support with their own hard and industrious work the habitually 'lazy' and 'barbarous' Highlanders, who were clearly an 'inferior race' to them? They were angry and appalled, and insisted that charity must have its limits, and if the starving people did not manage to help themselves they had better remove themselves from the land. Letters expressing such sentiments were frequent in the pages of the *Scotsman* and several other newspapers during the years of the Highland Famine. And this was only the beginning of an upsurge of views of contempt, and at times even sheer hatred, for the Highland Gaels in the Lowland press.

There were, however, other voices expressing sympathy towards the Highlanders. The picture emerging from contemporary Scottish news-papers shows that when Lowlanders judged the Highlanders they basically formed three camps. One regarded the Gaels as an 'inferior race' deserving only deep contempt; another looked at them with sympathy and pity, vowing 'to lift them from the dust'; and the third had very romantic notions about the 'inherent poetic' nature of this 'noble' people. In short, these were views of contempt, sympathy and romance. There were very few neutral voices.

These three different views were simultaneously present in public opinion, often running in parallel columns in the same newspaper. While the romanticisation of the Highlands was persistent and considerable, and sympathy towards the Highlanders was slowly growing, by far the most prevalent and most strongly expressed view was that of contempt.

The prevalence of contemptuous views was ensured because most of the major papers with the biggest circulations belonged to this group. The leading *Scotsman* was one of the firmest members of this camp with its average 2500 copies in the period.[1] The largest circulation paper, the

Glasgow Herald with an average of 4000 copies, also belonged here, along with the *Inverness Courier* (average 1900), and several smaller papers such as the *Fifeshire Journal* (c.600) and the *Perthshire Constitutional* (c.800). These papers taken together simply dwarfed the sympathetic ones. The only large paper with sympathetic views was the *Witness* with similar average circulation to the *Scotsman*. For the 1840s and early 1850s at least, then, the forum of contempt was the dominant one on the Scottish newspaper scene.

The views of one reader of the *Scotsman* in 1847 were characteristic of many who regarded the Gaels with contempt. These following lines were to be echoed and repeated with a growing sense of hatred in pamphlets, press reports and readers' letters throughout the years of the Great Famine:

> Will you allow me to make another suggestion through your paper! It is that a short pamphlet in the Gaelic language should be prepared and extensively circulated among the Highland population, denouncing in stern terms the indolent habits that prevail among them – contrasting the steady industry of the Saxon with the scarcely occasional labour of the Celt – tracing the consequence of this in the respective conditions at present of the Lowlander and the Highlander – enforcing the necessity of their working regularly throughout the year, and if they cannot find employment where they are, of migrating elsewhere in search of it – and giving a hint, that unless they do so, they cannot expect to be again compassionated and relieved –[2]

There was growing impatience and annoyance not only on the part of certain Lowland newspaper readers and editors but also among those landowners and government officials who were intent on 'improving' and 'civilising' the Gael. This mission was often a failure, for which mostly the Gaels themselves were blamed. Highland destitution was linked directly to the 'character' of the Gaels, and their perceived 'inherent' sloth and 'abhorrence' of regular work came to be seen as the main reason for the famine and the general destitute state of the Highlands. 'The great cause of the destitution is – not the failure of the potato crop last year, but – the intense and abominable idleness of the inhabitants',[3] contended the editor of the *Fifeshire Journal*.

The firmly established stereotype of the lazy Highlander was soon carried further, especially in the *Scotsman* and the *Fifeshire Journal*, when their correspondents embarked on a tour around the Western Isles in 1847. These articles conveyed a very strong sense of hatred. They denounced the Gaels as an 'inferior race to the Lowland Saxon', a 'dirty race', 'vicious', 'perverse' and 'degraded'. The remedies these journalists suggested were to 'improve' the 'race' by 'Lowland intermixture', and to change the 'Celtic character in great measure' by breaking up the old system and actually forcing them into the new one.

Such strong views were not confined to the journalists of the *Scotsman* and the *Fifeshire Journal.* A flood of readers' letters followed their reports expressing full agreement. Such letters along with numerous editorials and correspondents' reports reflected a marked sense of Lowland superiority arising from the conviction that their Highland neighbours belonged to an 'uncivilised, inferior race' with inherent habits of 'sloth and laziness'. The Highland Celts were seen as useless and burdensome in a developed modern age. The future clearly belonged to the 'industrious' and 'Saxon' Lowlanders, these writings suggested, and if the Highlanders wanted to improve their situation they must change their old ways and habits. Throughout the 1840s there were still considerable 'improvement hopes' around, in the belief that there was a solution for the Highland problem if only the Highlanders were capable of shaking off their lazy habits.

By the early 1850s, however, a strong sense of giving up on the Highlanders and Highland improvement set in. A large section of public opinion as well as government officials concluded that the only permanent solution to the Highland problem was to transport the Highlanders from their native land, where they grew up in 'habitual indolence', to other parts of the British Empire where they would learn industry and find plenty of work available. The large-scale emigration scheme of the Highland Desti-tution Board was widely judged by public opinion as beneficial both for the country and the Highlanders themselves. By this change of environment the Highlanders would finally become 'improved' and become part of the modern civilised world, many thought. However, there were people who considered the Celtic Highlanders so inherently inferior a race that no improvement could help them, and again, the only solution for the problem was to get rid of them and send them off their land.

Ten years after the outbreak of the Highland Famine the firm opinion of the majority of the public was that the best route for the destitute Gaels lay outside the country. They had to go, not only because of the poverty of the land but also because they belonged to the 'inferior' Celtic race. Such a people was better sent to a remote colonial land instead of being a permanent burden and drain on the 'superior' and developed Anglo-Saxon Lowlanders. They were seen as a 'diseased' and 'damaged' part, which had to be removed from the 'healthier' body of the nation.

While most of the big Scottish newspapers waged a war of contempt against the Highland Gaels, by the late 1840s a few journalists had gone into battle on the other side. Many of them represented a new type of journalist, who considered the cause of defending the Highlanders as a duty. They were crusaders of the press with a missionary zeal.

Imbued with sympathy, they regarded the Gaels as victims of vicious landlord oppression and the objects of an 'exterminating policy'. Most of them considered themselves much more than mere journalists. They behaved like fighting men brandishing their pen as the main weapon in the battle against a 'tyrannical' system. The power of the press, they believed, was all-important in stopping landlord abuses:

> What is to hinder a combination of landowners, backed by a sufficient military force, to extirpate and root out the Celtic race forever? Nothing, whatever, but the fear of the press. Had it not been for the press we would have houses burning, the military parading, and the work of demolition going on in every strath and valley throughout the whole Highlands.[4]

In their missionary zeal to save the Highlanders, many writers sharpened their fighting pens and often used very strong language. In describing the plight of the Gaels, the most widely used expressions were 'extermination', 'deportation', 'rooting out', 'annihilation' and 'expulsion'. One journalist simply stated: 'Extermination is the order of the day, *pur et simple*, . . .'[5]

Language became a weapon here, a means to achieve a higher goal. It primarily served the aim of shaking up public opinion and making it do something for the ill-fated Gaels. At the start of the battle, most crusading journalists believed that it was indeed possible to achieve this goal.

This new type of journalist also differed from their contemporaries in giving their names and personalities to their cause. While the various commissioners and correspondents of the *Scotsman, Inverness Courier* or *Glasgow Herald* remained anonymous, the Highlanders' champions made sure their names were printed in full. They certainly took great pride in their mission and stood open to any counter-attacks.

But the sympathetic newspapers were not united. There were essentially two main groups of journalists divided by their basic attitudes towards the Highlanders. While all of them were fundamentally sympathetic to the suffering of the Gaels, they differed in how they saw the causes and remedies of the Highland problem. They were also very different in the heat of their indignation and the style of their writing.

One group was that of the 'true crusaders', the most radical of all journalists. This included Thomas Mulock, Donald M'Leod and Donald Ross, all of them at various stages writing for the *Inverness Advertiser* and the *Northern Ensign*. Ross also wrote for the *North British Daily Mail.*

These men were the most uncompromising and most consistently radical critics of the landlords' policies.

The other main group of journalists were on the 'softer' side. They were very critical but fell far short of the radicalism of Mulock or Ross. And above all, they had a strongly patronising and paternalistic attitude towards the Highland Gaels. This group was mainly represented by Robert Somers, editor of the *North British Daily Mail*, and by Hugh Miller, editor of the *Witness*. While the most radical crusaders led a continuous campaign on behalf of the Gaels, these men would only occasionally speak out against Highland landlord policies. They were much more 'sober' and 'balanced' critics, and the tone of their language was less passionate. And they were also much more prone to romanticise the Highlanders.

Until the 1850s these more 'sober' views were dominant in the sympathetic camp of the Scottish press. The most radical and crusading paper, the *Northern Ensign*, only started in June 1850. In the 1840s, it was mainly the *Witness* and the *North British Daily Mail* which carried the banners of Highland sympathy. By the 1850s, however, the voice of the *Witness* had all but disappeared and the crusaders virtually took over the pro-Highlander press.

The sheer amount of articles these radical crusading papers carried was in itself impressive and indicative of the intensity of their campaign. While the *Witness* between 1850 and 1855 published some fourteen articles relating to the Highland crisis, the *Northern Ensign* ran over a hundred articles on the subject, usually devoting one third of the paper to the cause. The *Inverness Advertiser* was similarly active; between 1849 and 1855 it had over a hundred and twenty articles on Highland destitution. In comparison, the *North British Daily Mail* was dwarfed with its mere thirty-four articles.[6]

The first half of the 1850s therefore witnessed an exceptional flood of radical missionary journalism in the Scottish press. However, the journalists on these radical papers were fighting a lone battle. In their circulation and influence these papers were overshadowed by both the hostile press and the sympathetic but less radical papers. The *Inverness Advertiser* and the *Northern Ensign* both sold just over 1,000 copies per issue in the 1850s, while the *Witness* had over 2,500 copies. Meanwhile, the *Scotsman* stood at over 3,000 and the *Glasgow Herald* exceeded 5,000 by 1854.[7]

Small as their circulation was in comparison, these radical papers and their writers nevertheless made a noise out of proportion to their size. Thomas Mulock attained a reputation of being 'notorious' and Donald Ross was often mockingly referred to as the 'friend' of the Highlanders. Both of them also ensured reaching a wider audience by publishing series of letters or pamphlets. Their papers had very active readers who filled many pages with lengthy epistles.

It is difficult, therefore, to assess the true influence of these newspapers and their writers at the time, but they are invaluable sources of early radical and sympathetic writing on the Highlands.

Along with the two main currents of contempt and sympathy there was a third element present in the press: a romanticising trend. While the Highland Gaels were being physically cleared off the land, a strange kind of 'mental clearance' was taking place in Lowland public opinion.

The grim reality of the depopulated Highlands was disregarded and replaced by an imaginary landscape of romance and poetic beauty. Side by side with accounts of clearance and stern denunciations of the 'inferior' Gaels, newspapers ran romanticised diaries of tourist trips and popular poetry depicting the Highlands as a sort of reservation of grand romantic scenery. The real inhabitants of the Highlands were conspicuously missing here, yielding to an imaginary poetic land given over to poets and tourists.

The Highlands had long been seen as a magical land of romantic scenery and sublime beauty, especially since the end of the eighteenth century. By the mid-nineteenth century, however, the emptier the Highlands became, the more romantic they seemed. And while the inhabitants were cleared or emigrated from the land, their cultural traditions and garb were appropriated by Lowland and London mock Highland societies in a new fashion of 'Highlandism'.

Meanwhile, in popular poetry in the press and in some of the sympathetic accounts a strong sense of 'doom' and a concept of 'nation death' started to prevail. The Highland Gaels were now seen as a 'doomed' race, destined to vanish from their land with the advent of a new modern era. They were portrayed as children and romantic heroes of a distant past. Lament over the 'doom' and 'gloom' of the vanishing Celtic Highlands foreshadowed the Celtic Twilight of the late nineteenth century. The reality of the Clearances did appear in some popular poetry and literary work but it was the exception.

The romantics did not form such a well-defined 'camp' as did the representatives of contempt and sympathy. Rather they just coloured the two main trends, and they often overlapped them, reflecting some of the elements of the other two. One such element was the belief in 'inherent' or 'racial' characteristics.

Those who despised the Gaels believed that they were 'inherently' lazy, those who romanticised them believed that they were 'inherently' poetic. These were, in fact, two sides of the same coin, both based on the assumption that the Highlanders were *racially different*. But for the romantics the difference was a positive thing. The Gaels were imaginative, poetic, more romantic than the Saxon Lowlanders could ever become, as Hugh Miller suggested in a review of the poetry of Evan M'Coll in the *Inverness Courier*.

> The Celt is essentially a different person from the Saxon in the very constitution of his mind . . . the Highlander is delighted by the external beauty of things, the Lowlander in diving into their secret causes . . . the Highlander is a descriptive poet, the Lowlander is a metaphysician . . . The Gaelic, as a language, is singularly rich in the descriptive, but comparatively barren in the abstract. Phrenologists remark nearly the same thing of the Celtic head – the reflective organs are always less prominently developed than the knowing ones.[8]

As opposed to the rational Saxon, the Celts were thought to be primarily a people of the imagination, emotions, or even irrationality, given to second sight, witchcraft and the like. They were also sometimes portrayed as a kind of idyllic and colourful peasantry.

Above all, it was their environment itself which was seen as a land of magic beauty. For the romantics, the Highlands were the ultimate paradise of grand scenery, but, intriguingly, mainly because they were so barren, so 'people-less'. Had the Highland mountains been covered with townships and people, it would have been perhaps more difficult to find them so mysterious and wild. Oddly, therefore, the very reality of the depopulating Highlands suited those who were romantically inclined. Even some of the sympathetic writers were not immune to such tendencies.

The attitudes of contempt, sympathy and romance, therefore, were not strictly divided. Although especially contempt and sympathy were quite clearly defined, there were a number of overlapping elements. Perhaps the most powerful of these was the sense of giving up on the Highlands. It was there in the forced emigration schemes and in the idea that the Gaels were irredeemably useless; it was there in the disillusionment of some of the sympathetic crusading journalists; and it was there in the doom and gloom of the pre-Celtic Twilight poetry.

Views and insights expressed through the newspapers attained a considerable audience and influence due to the unparalleled growth of the press itself by the mid-nineteenth century. Both circulation and readership had increased significantly, and by the 1840s the press came to be regarded as a powerful forum in public life.

Along with many scientific inventions and general improvements, the press was considered in the mid-nineteenth century as one of the wonders of Victorian progress. Newspapers had experienced unprecedented expansion since the 1830s. While in 1800 the number of newspapers in Britain was 92, and 302 in 1835, by 1845 the total number had risen to 502, a growth of 200 new titles within ten years.[9] And the number of copies rose at a similar pace: in 1842 over 50 million copies went on sale in England, and over five million in Scotland; by 1845, within three years, the number in England increased by seven million and in Scotland by one million.[10]

The press was becoming an industry of its own, and its expansion and significance filled many contemporaries with awe. Naturally, this undoubtedly rapid progress gave the newspapers a sense of self-importance and pride, as this article in the *Inverness Courier* well reflected in 1847:

> When the first metallic type issued shining from its matrice, Peter Schoeffer may have felt that the art of printing was on the right road to perfection; De Worde may have foreseen that a Bible for every church and a ballad for every romantic maid would in time be demanded; but that a Printing House Square should one day influence nations – throw off from its one press its twenty or thirty thousand sheets in a morning, each sheet containing the matter of a volume – was a speculation beyond the range of their imaginations. We have come to a time when the power of the press on public opinion is felt, and its position as one of the necessary social institutions recognised.[11]

What was the reason for this extraordinary expansion of the press and the extension of its role?[12] One of the most important factors was the gradual reduction of the various taxes on newspapers. Before the 1830s the 'taxes of knowledge' – the Advertisement Duty, the Stamp Duty and the Excise Duty on paper – weighed heavily on newspapers, putting their costs up so much that only the moneyed classes could afford to buy them. The tax revenue from the Advertisement Duty formed 'a nice item in the Budget',[13] and from the three greatest advertising media, the *Times*, the *Telegraph* and the *Glasgow Herald*, it alone amounted to above £130,000 in a year.

Even more than the Advertisement Duty, the Stamp Duty was seen at the time as the greatest obstacle. It was expensive – seven pence for an average weekly newspaper – and restrictive as publishers had to purchase, in advance, a special stamp for each copy of any paper defined as containing 'news'. This, of course, greatly limited circulation, and increased losses, since if the stamped paper was not sold, the publisher had to bear the loss.

And the tax on paper made raw material costs high, and further increased the price of newspapers. All of which made the newspaper of the early nineteenth century a luxury of the few, circulating mainly among the upper classes of society.

With the movement towards free trade, these taxes were gradually reduced and then repealed from the 1830s onwards. First, in 1833 the Advertisement Duty was reduced from 3s. 6d. to 1s. 6d, then in 1836 the Stamp Duty was lowered from 4d. to 1d., and in the same year the Excise Duty on paper was also reduced from 3d. to $1\frac{1}{2}$ d. The average price of a weekly paper thus dropped from 7d. to $4\frac{1}{2}$ d.

As a result of these reductions, advertisements and sales increased immediately, and the lower production and sales costs prompted further changes, including an increase in the size of newspapers and their staff. Meanwhile, education, literacy and the franchise were extended, which added to the numbers of the reading public. Technical innovations in printing technology and improved methods of distribution also helped the growth of the press. From 1845 the electric telegraph transformed news-gathering, and brought the provincial papers closer to the centres of news. In 1838 second editions became general, and in the second half of the 1840s supplements appeared.

The lower cost and price also produced an expansion of cheap, popular weekly papers, building on the tradition of the popular literature of the old chapbooks, broadsheets and penny serial novels. New types of papers appeared and spread, such as class papers representing the interest of particular professions and trades, and pressure group papers advocating such causes as Free Trade, temperance, religious freedom, Owenism, industrial reform, vegetarianism and hydropathy. By 1847 there were 555 different newspapers and journals, and the newspaper was increasingly regarded a 'necessary adjunct to every pursuit'.[14] And when the final barricades preventing the free flow of newspapers came down in the early 1850s with the abolition of Advertising Duty in 1853, and of Stamp Duty in 1855, there was indeed no stopping. Dailies and cheap penny papers proliferated, and coupled with the rise in general literacy they led to the extension of readership to the lower middle and upper working classes. As one contemporary chronicler of the press remarked, with some exaggeration: 'All men, now-a-days, who read at all, read newspapers'.[15]

This great expansion made the press a significant new power, perceived as 'The Fourth Estate', the 'guardian of liberties'. Contemporary observers spoke of the newspapers' 'unquestionable' and 'powerful' influence,[16] and the papers themselves stated that they were 'the surest bulwark of the people's liberties',[17] providing 'moral and political' safeguard'. By 1857, Alexander Andrews, writing *The History of British Journalism*, could enthusiastically say:

> The list of our public journals is a proud and noble list – the role of an army of Liberty, with a rallying point in every town. It is a police of public safety, and a sentinel of public morals. . . . For good or for evil, the Press must go on now: no power on earth can arrest it. Hundreds of thousands have been added to the number who look to it as a necessary of their existence.[18]

Many looked upon the press and its journalists not only as 'guardians of Liberty' but also as 'moral authorities'. This authority was largely corporate due to the anonymity of journalism, and to the growing reputations of the individual chief editors, such as John Delane of *The Times* and Alexander Russell of the *Scotsman*. From the second half of the 1840s newspapers had often become lively forums of public debate with an avalanche of 'Letters to the Editor' and forceful leaders on current issues, often with an openly stated intention to improve public morality. 'Investigative' and 'crusading' types of journalism were also becoming more widely used, with their great potential to influence public opinion.

During the period of the Highland Famine, newspapers were therefore already a powerful force in expressing and influencing public opinion. They provide an immense source of material by which to gauge Scottish public opinion at the time.

One indication of the amount of such material is the sheer number of articles unearthed in the preparation of this book. During the ten years between 1845 and 1855 the major newspapers which have been surveyed completely – *Scotsman, Glasgow Herald, Inverness Courier, Witness, Inverness Advertiser, North British Daily Mail* and *Northern Ensign* – contained well over 2000 articles on the Highlands.[19] On the actual topic of this book there were more than 600 articles, which have been directly or indirectly used.

Yet, so far this area of the Scottish press and public opinion has been largely neglected and unresearched. The press itself has not been used much as a valid historical source, but has been sometimes renounced as unreliable material.[20] The validity of sources, however, depends on what they are used for. The press is not examined here to establish historical data, or to make judgements on the debates about the economic state of the Highland estates. The press here is used as the most suitable means to analyse Scottish public opinion.

One notable treatment of the press as a significant source is Donald E.

Meek's anthology of Celtic poetry, which is drawn from the contemporary newspapers.[21] Meek stresses the importance of newspapers as sources, and points out that they have been much 'under-used' so far.[22] However, the newspapers Meek used in his anthology were those from the 1860s onwards.

The mid-nineteenth century press is still very much 'under-used', if not completely 'un-used'. Although some of the historians of the Clearances and the Famine have occasionally looked into newspaper files – mainly those of the *Inverness Courier* and the *Scotsman* – no systematic survey has so far been carried out on the press of this period. The material available in the newspaper files, however, not only presents a rich treasure-house but can also shed new light on attitudes to the Highlands and on the divisions in Scottish public opinion and identity at the time.

The extent of hostility, contempt and at times sheer hatred towards the Highland Gaels has not been appreciated or presented at any length so far. Most of this material has not been quoted or published so far, only at best slightly touched upon.[23] It has certainly not been presented as the major current view at the time, which could have had direct influence on actual landlord and government policies.

The sympathetic views are better known and better researched in comparison. Nevertheless, there is still much material lying unearthed in the sympathetic newspapers as well. The names of Thomas Mulock, Donald Ross, Donald M'Leod and Robert Somers are not unknown to historians of the Highlands and the Clearances, yet the newspapers these men were writing for have not been explored in any depth.

T.M. Devine in *The Great Highland Famine* mentions Mulock, Somers and Ross as occasional sources on evictions and remarks that they represented a different aspect of public opinion, being critical and arguing 'vehemently that the Highlands required more liberal aid and support'.[24] But he puts no great emphasis on their role and does not give any lengthier quotations from their writings. Newspapers such as the *Northern Ensign* receive only one mention in the book.

Even in James Hunter's seminal book, *The Making of the Crofting Community*, neither Robert Somers, nor the *Northern Ensign*, nor the *North British Daily Mail* are mentioned at all, and Donald Ross is referred to only once as 'the more outspoken critic of Highland landlordism'.[25] Thomas Mulock is entirely missing from the pages of Hunter's book. And in T.C.Smout's *A Century of the Scottish People* none of these names or newspapers receives even a passing reference. It is only John Prebble in his *The Highland Clearances* who gives Mulock, Ross, M'Leod and their newspapers any lengthier treatment and describes their battle in the Scottish press to any extent. But even Prebble seems unaware of Robert Somers' series of letters published in book form in 1848.

The early sympathetic and radical section of the press and public opinion in mid-nineteenth century Scotland has not yet been dealt with in a comprehensive survey. The abundant material in this period, however, can throw new light on the press at this time, and offer new perspectives on the roots of 1880s Highland radicalism.

Given such crusading radicals as Thomas Mulock or Donald Ross, writers like Hugh Miller and Robert Somers, who so far have usually been considered the 'radicals', should be re-evaluated. The writings of these journalists can also show that the radicalism of the 1870s and 1880s did not only feed on the influence of Ireland but also had its roots at home, in the battles which these early crusading journalists had fought in the 1850s.

The period between 1845 and 1855 has been chosen because it was a time of great crisis with the Famine and the ensuing destitution, when, as a result, public opinion was sharpened considerably. The end date of 1855 marks the period of the Crimean War (1854–56), during which the failure of recruitment from the Highlands highlighted the problems of depopulation again, and this time led to a shift towards much more sympathy than in the preceding decade.

Notes

1. Circulation figures are based here on the *Waterloo Directory of Scottish Newspapers and Periodicals*, Canada, 1989, and on T.C.Jack, *Scottish Newspaper Directory*, Edinburgh, 1855.
2. 'The Highland Destitution', Letter to the Editor. *Scotsman*, 20 January 1847.
3. 'Notes of a Winter Tour in the Western Isles', written by the editor, *Fifeshire Journal*, 11 February 1847.
4. 'Commissioner' to the *Inverness Advertiser*, 26 November 1850.
5. Thomas Mulock, 'Extension of Emigration from the Outer Hebrides', *Northern Ensign*, 3 July 1851.
6. These calculations are based on a comprehensive survey of these papers between 1845–1855. The articles counted in the list are those which directly dealt with the problem of Highland destitution and related issues, such as clearances and emigration. In the survey, every single issue of these main papers was searched.
7. Jack, *Scottish Newspaper Directory*.
8. 'The Mountain Minstrel, or Poems and Songs', in English, by Evan M'Coll, *Inverness Courier*, 10 October 1838.
9. Figures given in 'The British Press', *Inverness Courier*, 25 May 1847.

10. The figures given here are from the 'Stamps return', quoted in the *Inverness Courier*, 25 May 1847.

11. *Inverness Courier*, 25 May 1847.

12. This survey is based on the following works: Boyce-Curran, *Newspaper History* (London, 1978), Jack, *Newspaper Directory*, Mitchell's *Newspaper Press Directory* (London, 1846), Alexander Sinclair, *Fifty Years of Newspaper Life, 1845–1895* (Glasgow, 1898), R.M.W. Cowan, *The Newspaper in Scotland*, (Glasgow, 1946), W. Donaldson, *Popular Culture in Victorian Scotland* (Aberdeen, 1986).

13. Sinclair, *Fifty years . . .*, 15.

14. Mitchell, *Newspaper Press . . .*, 24.

15. Jack, *Scottish Newspaper Directory*, 21, quoting the words of F. Knight Hunt.

16. Jack, *Scottish Newspaper Directory*, 20

17. *Inverness Courier*, 25 May 1847.

18. A. Andrews, *The History of British Journalism* (London, 1859), 347.

19. This estimate is based on my survey of the papers, the proportion of how much material I actually kept and how much I ignored being outside my direct field of interest.

20. As for example by T.M. Devine, *The Great Highland Famine* (Edinburgh, 1988).

21. Donald E. Meek, *Tuath is Tighearna / Tenants and Landlords* (Edinburgh, 1995).

22. Meek, *Tuath is . . .*, 13.

23. In Devine, *Famine*, and in Prebble, *Highland Clearances* (London, 1969).

24. Devine, *Famine*, 130.

25. James Hunter, *The Making of the Crofting Community* (Edinburgh, 1976), 79.

PART ONE

Contempt

CHAPTER ONE

Background

I. Eighteenth-century roots

In 1852 Robert Carruthers, the editor of the prestigious *Inverness Courier*, published a new edition of Boswell's *Journal of a Tour to the Hebrides*. In his own notes Carruthers devoted much space to mark 'the differences and resemblances in Highland affairs between Johnson's days'[1] and his own. Almost eighty years after Johnson's and Boswell's visit, many of the Highland questions were still the same, and mid-nineteenth century newspaper editors were apt to use the parallels in order to stress the hopelessness of the Highland situation. The *Scotsman* in its review of Carruthers' edition put it bluntly:

> What we learn from this book – as indeed from all the very few accounts of eye-witnesses, such as that of Captain Burt, written about forty years before Johnson's visit – is, that 'Highland destitution' is a very old, and long, and unbroken story.[2]

What were the views, then, eighty years earlier which mid-nineteenth century newspaper editors found so similar to their own? And were they indeed all so similar or were they twisted to suit the ideology of the mid-Victorian age? At first glance, much of the perception of the Highland Gaels was indeed very similar.

'Savage', 'ignorant', 'uncivilised' were the words Samuel Johnson found the most suitable to describe the Highlanders when he reached the Highlands in 1773. 'Barbarous', 'indolent', 'ignorant', and 'habitually lazy' were the most common terms that many improvers, government officials and newspapers used seventy years later in the mid-nineteenth century in referring to the Highlanders. Had nothing changed? Similar words, indeed, yet their roots and real meaning were fundamentally different. The nineteenth century, which was often glorified as the 'age of progress', went backwards in certain respects rather than forward, from the mere contempt of the 'civilised' man for the 'uncivilised' to a sense of racial superiority.

For Samuel Johnson, as a classic eighteenth-century mind, the main criterion upon which he judged people and countries was how far they progressed on the scale of civilisation. He did regard those who were less 'advanced' on this ladder of civilisation as inferior, 'primitive' or 'savage', but these judgements came from an essentially cultural point of view and not from a racist one.

By the mid-nineteenth century the *Scotsman* could openly pronounce the Highlanders a barbarous and an inferior race, and even suggest 'racial intermixture' to improve them. Letters to the Editor expressed similar racialist views. Where did it all start? Back in the early 1770s, Johnson did not pronounce the Highlanders as irredeemably inferior, despite his apparent and often rampant prejudices. Johnson did not believe that the 'barbarians' were such because of their race, but rather that the 'primitive' state they were in stemmed from social differences. '. . . For the manners of the mountaineers are commonly savage, but they are rather *produced by their situation than derived from their ancestors*,'[3] he wrote in his *Journey to the Western Islands of Scotland.* He saw their backwardness as a result of their condition and not as a consequence of their nature or race.

However, by the last decade of the eighteenth century, racialist views made their firm appearance, and during the nineteenth century they became fully fledged. On continental Europe, there was a parallel process in the general development of racist thoughts, so Scotland was no exception. In fact, the cultural clashes that occurred between the 'two Scotlands' provided additional fuel for the growth of racist attitudes.

In 1773 Johnson set off on his journey with numerous prejudices against the Scots. He regarded them as backward and uncivilised, not yet as advanced on the scale of civilisation as the English were. To him, the Scots were 'a nation just arising from barbarity',[4] and this positive development Johnson attributed to their increasing contacts with the civilised English. 'Till the Union made them acquainted with English manners, the culture of their lands was unskillful, and their domestick life unformed; their tables were coarse as the feasts of the Eskimeaux, and their houses filthy as the cottages of the Hottentots',[5] he wrote in his *Journey.*

Once under the influence of English civilisation, however, Johnson regarded the Scots as being very capable of advancing fast. In this progress, though, he saw the Highlanders as more backward than the Lowlanders.[6] In fact, the main purpose of his visit was to observe those different manners of the Highlanders which made them a 'people of peculiar appearance' living a 'system of antiquated life'.[7] He found, though, that he was too late: the ancient manners were already disappearing.

At the time of Johnson's visit the Highlands were already in a state of transition. The face of the Highlands and the fate of their inhabitants were being rapidly transformed. The self-sustaining economy based on clanship was breaking up and was becoming increasingly commercialised. Rents were raised as never before. Many clan chiefs started to regard themselves as commercial landlords and were integrating themselves into the British landed classes. They needed more money to subsidise their new social role, and they were also catching the general 'improvement mania'. Some landlords were genuinely concerned about how the rising population could be cared for. Land improvement plans were drawn up on many Highland estates.

The great improvement experiment of large-scale sheep farming began in the 1760s and led to the depopulation of the interior lands, either through direct population relocation to the coastal areas or through the 'voluntary' emigration of those who recognised before the sheep farming reached their lands that they had better go elsewhere. A social distancing between former 'protector-chiefs' and 'clan member-tenants' began, and resulted in severe social disorientation. The inevitable conflict between 'landlord omnipotence and unyielding peasant values'[8] replaced the former customary relationships.

Thousands emigrated to America and Canada in the 1750s and 1760s. During this time some 60% of all Scottish emigrants were Highlanders,[9] who constituted only about one third of the total Scottish population. In some cases whole townships left, sometimes not out of desperation but in search of a better life, of widening opportunities.[10] However, most people who left did so in 'alarm and general anxiety' which the 'relentless march of the big sheep-farmers'[11] caused. 'Preparation for emigration was often a prudent precaution to avoid the expected future catastrophe of complete dispossession.'[12]

The changes that commenced in the previous century and gained impetus after 1707 were to lead eventually to the depopulation of the interior of the Highlands and the disappearance of a whole way of life with its culture, while the improvement plans usually ended in failure. The end result was social displacement in various forms: in large-scale emigration, evictions, relocations, and direct clearances.

What Samuel Johnson in 1773 could observe was a transition, the changes in values and manners. His mind was sufficiently open and broad to enable him to discern the changes, and his initial prejudices against the 'savage' and 'ignorant' people 'on the verge of European life' were fast wearing away.

When he reached the Highlands in the early autumn of 1773 his first reaction was one of dismay. 'We began to leave fertility and culture behind us,' he wrote indignantly. As he looked around the barren rugged hills, his civilised eye was 'astonished and repelled by this wide extent of hopeless sterility'. He saw in them but a 'naked desert', with no trees and 'unimproved life'. To him, the Highlands were no romantic wilderness. He never came to like the land and scenery of the Highlands, but he did grow to like the inhabitants. When asked towards the end of his journey how he liked the Highlands, he replied: 'Who can like the Highlands? – I like the inhabitants very well'.[13] This view was the reverse of the Ossianic and later heavily romanticised perception of the Highlands when the scenery was elevated to mythic heights and the inhabitants were 'improved' into imaginary romantic heroes while their actual state was largely ignored by their romanticisers.

Throughout his journey Johnson continued to despair of the bare, dreary and uncultivated land but whenever he saw signs of civilisation he was ready to praise. He was most impressed by the 'civility' and 'hospitality' not only of the lairds but also, though to a lesser extent, of the ordinary people.

His observations on those positive traits, however, were often tinged with a tone of surprise at finding such civilised manners in a supposedly barbarous people. 'You find', he wrote in a letter to Mrs Thrale, 'that all the islanders, even in these recesses of life are not barbarous.'[14] In another letter a few days earlier the tone of surprise is even more palpable: 'the Highland girl made tea and looked and talked not inelegantly, her father was by no means an ignorant and a weak man; there were books in the cottage'.[15]

Although he often described the Highlanders as bearing some aspects of savages when he saw them *en masse*, when he encountered them personally, he tended to praise them: 'We had two Highlanders to run by us, who were active, officious, civil and hardy'.[16] Adjectives such as 'active' and 'civil' were the exact opposites of what Johnson usually defined as barbarous. In his *Dictionary* the definitions of 'civil' include 'civilized not barbarous'. In his *Journey* he went so far against his own initial prejudices as to pronounce 'civility' 'part of the national character of the Highlanders . . .', which was 'diffused from the laird through the whole clan'. And he defined 'civility' as 'freedom from barbarity, the state of being civilised', and as 'politeness, elegance of behaviour . . . and rule of decency'.

Samuel Johnson, like most great minds, was a complex character, though. Having acknowledged the civility of the Highlanders, he again called them a barbarous people when it came to the issue of the Scottish Gaelic language, or the 'Erse language', as Johnson and his contemporaries called it. Although he himself admitted that he knew almost nothing about their language, he still passed strongly penned judgement on it: '. . . it is the rude speech of a barbarous people, who had few thoughts to express, and were content, as they conceived grossly, to be grossly understood'. Yet, at the same time he compared listening to a song in Erse to listening to an Italian opera, 'delighted with the sound of words' he did not understand. And, again in seeming contradiction of his judgement on the 'rude' Erse language, after his return from the Highlands it was mainly owing to his influence[17] that the New Testament was allowed to be translated into the 'Erse language'.

Where is the real Johnson, then? One possible explanation for the apparent contradiction may lie in his passion for argument, often just for the argument's sake. One example of this is his dispute with the philosopher Lord Monboddo on savages and shopkeepers. When Monboddo was making a case for savages, Johnson made his for the shopkeeper. His letters to Mrs Thrale revealed his real motives: 'Monboddo declared boldly for the savage, and I, perhaps for that reason, sided with the citizen'. Or, in Boswell's *Life*: '. . . I might have taken the side of the savage equally, had anybody else taken the side of the shopkeeper'.

The same love of argument and challenge lies also behind his frequent teasing of Boswell over his Scotch sensitivity. Johnson never made such extreme remarks on the Scots as when he made them to Boswell. For Johnson, it was another form of challenge to seek out the other party's weak points.

At the time of his journey one of Johnson's favourite intellectual challenges was Macpherson's *Ossian*, which Johnson was determined to prove a fake. Later in his discourse on the 'Erse language' it becomes clear that the criticism was primarily written as an attack on Macpherson and the 'Ossian believers': 'After what has been lately talked of Highland bards and Highland genius, many will startle when they are told that the Erse language never was a written language . . .' Therefore, the argument goes, Ossian can only be a fake.' The 'Erse language' or Scottish Gaelic *had* been a written language long before Johnson made his comment but he was unaware of it and never really made serious inquiries about it, as he himself admitted elsewhere. The point was, however, to discredit Macpherson mainly for two reasons: Johnson was passionately against any form of romanticisation and was especially against it if it concerned 'less civilised' people.

Johnson was one of the notable exceptions who never romanticised the 'old Highland way of life', which was to move so many romantics in the following two centuries. For his part, he regarded it as totally barbarous and undesirable. His objection to romanticisation is powerful throughout his *Journey* and his *Letters*, and comes through in a number of dialogues with Boswell.

Being a true mind of the European Enlightenment, in which 'Raison' or Reason was the primary ruler of human life, he had no time for such philosophers as Rousseau who, despite belonging to the French Enlightenment, is also considered the father of Romanticism with his 'back-to-nature' ideal. In a letter complaining about the 'naked desert' of Skye, Johnson clearly refers to Rousseau: '. . . [there] a being with all those powers which education expands, and all those sensations which culture refines is condemned to shelter itself from the wind and rain. Philosophers there are who try to make themselves believe that this life is happy . . .'[18] In Boswell's account the same argument is recorded at the time of their visit to Coll. When seeing a smoky hut there Johnson remarks: 'And this is what the philosophers call happy. Boswell: 'the philosophers, when they placed happiness in a cottage, supposed cleanliness and no smoke'. Johnson: 'Sir, they did not think about either'.

To Johnson, romanticising was an act of deliberately ignoring reality, ultimately leading to falsification. It was his main objection to the Ossian cult, which he also saw as a symptom of the Scottish national character. His criticism here is perhaps one of the most challenging ever made of the Scottish psyche:

> The Scots have something to plead for their easy reception of an improbable fiction: they are seduced by their fondness for their supposed ancestors. *A Scotchman must be a very sturdy moralist, who does not love Scotland better than truth:* he will always love it better than inquiry, and if falsehood flatters his vanity will not be very diligent to detect it. Neither ought the English to be much influenced by Scotch authority, for of the past and present state of the whole Erse nation, the Lowlanders are at least as ignorant as ourselves. To be ignorant is painful, but it is dangerous to quiet our uneasiness by the delusive opiate of hasty persuasion. But this is an age in which those who could not read, have been supposed to write, in which the giants of antiquated romance have been exhibited as realities. If we know little of the ancient highlanders, let us not fill the vacuity with Ossian.[19]

A penetrating criticism undoubtedly. But is it not true for all other nations as well? Is it only specifically Scottish? Or perhaps a characteristically 'small nation' symptom?

Johnson probably did not yet think in terms of small and big nations. This concept was to flourish from the nineteenth century onwards. To his way of thinking, this 'fondness for supposed ancestors' and flattering fairy tales derived from being a 'less civilised' nation, which, like a not yet fully matured person, was more inclined to listen to the voice of fancy and flattering falsehood than to the adult voice of reason.

With no inclination for romance, Johnson was interested in the realities of the Highlands, and above all, of their inhabitants. He was critical of many changes: of the large-scale emigration, especially that of the tacks-men, of the ejections of tenants – the Clearances as they later came to be called – and of hasty improvements with little regard to the people themselves. To him, an empty country would not contribute to the general happiness:

> To banish the tacksman is easy, to make a country plentiful by diminishing the people is an expeditious mode of husbandry; but that abundance, which there is nobody to enjoy, contributes little to human happiness.[20]

By the time Johnson travelled around the Highlands and Islands the economic and social changes which led to increasing commercialisation and the break-up of the clan system were widespread and visible. The transformation bringing commercialisation commenced in the early eight-eenth century and was accelerated by the post-Culloden measures abolish-ing the clan chiefs' prerogatives.

Most contemporary commentators and even present-day scholars as well as popular perceptions hold that the break-up of the clan system and of traditional Highland society was due to the post-Culloden measures, and therefore was imposed from outside by the Westminster government. This view normally presents the pre-Culloden Highlanders as a simple and noble people, living in harmony and holding their chiefs in great veneration. They were then bitterly betrayed, and with the sudden break-up of the clans commercial values were forced upon their traditional society, which respected men more than money.

There is certainly truth in this view since the transformation of the Highland society and economy was indeed quite sudden compared to the 'normal' historical process of transformation from an agrarian, self-suffi-cient system into a modern commercial one. The post-Culloden legislation was indeed radical and imposed from outside. To suggest, however, that without the post-1745 measures Highland society would have remained unchanged is mistaken.

As recent studies[21] have pointed out, commercialisation and the ex-pansion of landownership started well before 1746. Already in the century before Culloden absenteeism, accumulation of debts and rent-raising prompted the criticisms of Gaelic poets. Neither is the view tenable that the break-up of traditional clanship was due to the oppressive measures of Westminster. The demise of clanship had been started earlier by the chiefs themselves very much under the influence of the spirit of the age: 'The demise of clanship was . . . accomplished by chiefs and leading gentry . . . wholeheartedly embracing the Whig concept of progress and deliberately supporting, if not throwing over their personal obligations as patrons and protectors'.[22]

Contemporary travellers well before 1746 observed that the idea of improvement was not at all foreign or alien to the Highlanders. As one English observer in the 1720s remarked: 'Nothing is more common than to hear the Highlanders boast how much their country might be improved, and that it would produce double what it did at present, if better husbandry were introduced among them'.[23]

As the Highlands came into closer contact with the Lowlands, England, and with the continental countries, and as the world as a whole became 'smaller' through the development of trade and its infrastructure, the changes were inevitable. The Highlands could not have remained a reserve of a previous historical era of clans, heroes and happy simple people, or for that matter, barbarous savages. Eventually, changes in the core or central countries do reach the peripheries; the question is how these changes take place or are implemented. One of the most enduring criticisms of the way the transformation of the Highlands occurred is that too little regard was paid to the people and too much to the new social status of the chiefs and to the improvement of the land and rents. In other words, that the social costs were far more severe than was necessary.

Samuel Johnson was one of the very few early commentators who voiced this criticism strongly, and also argued against hasty ejections of tenants as the simplest way of making more profit. 'It is necessary in these countries, where the ejection of a tenant is a greater evil than in more populous places, to consider not merely what the land will produce, but with what ability the inhabitants can cultivate it', he wrote in his *Journey*, adding an ominous prediction: 'An island once depopulated will remain a desert.'[24]

While Johnson himself viewed 1746 as a turning point and seemed to identify the changes in the Highlands as arising from the effects of the post-Culloden measures ('the chiefs divested of their prerogatives, necessarily turned their thoughts to improvement of their revenues'[25]), he saw the seeds of change earlier in the increasing contacts with the 'civilised' world. He primarily attributed the general 'improvement' of the Highlands to the Union which brought Scotland within the compass of English civilisation and generally opened it up to the world. The lure of civilisation, a better way of life, money and commerce would prove stronger, Johnson believed, than the ancient veneration of the chiefs:

This gloomy tranquillity, which some may call fortitude, and others wisdom, was, I believe, for a long time to be frequently found in these glens of poverty: every man was content to live like his neighbours and never wandering from home, saw no mode of life preferable to his own, except at the house of his laird or the laird's nearest relatives, whom he considered as a superior order of beings, to whose luxuries or honours he had no pretensions. But the end of his reverence and submission seems now approaching, the Highlanders have learnt that there are countries less bleak and barren than their own, where, instead of working for the laird, every man may till his own ground, and eat the produce of his own labour. Great numbers have been induced by this discovery to go every year for some time past to America.[26]

This was far from the view which saw the Highlanders as essentially victims of the chiefs' betrayal. Johnson regarded the Highlanders as capable and independent human beings who, once under the lure of 'civilisation', would take their chance of a better life.

This reinforces the argument that Johnson was not racialist. When he talked about barbarians and savages he did not see them as permanently so. To him, the savages were capable of becoming civilised beings once under the influence of civilisation. In other words, they were not 'inherently' barbarous and uncivilised. It was not in their 'nature' but derived from their circumstances. This is one of the fundamental aspects of the perception of the Highlander which was to change during the nineteenth century into an essentially racialist view, which regarded the conditions of the Highlanders as stemming from their 'inherent' traits, from their 'nature'.

While Johnson often called them savage or barbarous – especially in their former state before they came in contact with English civilisation – he was nevertheless tolerant and understanding in seeing why the Highlanders were 'backward'. He looked at the Highlanders as an example of the less civilised peoples, and classified them as 'mountaineers' deriving their characteristics from their terrain:

Mountaineers are warlike, *because* [in] their feuds and competitions they consider themselves as surrounded with enemies . . . Mountaineers are thievish, *because* they are poor, and having neither manufacture nor commerce, can grow richer only by robbery.[27]

In other words, they were not warlike and thievish because they were by nature inclined to these vices but because of their circumstances. The same applied to their much quoted 'idleness', Johnson believed: 'Having little work to do, they are not willing, nor perhaps able to endure a long continuance of manual labour, and therefore considered as habitually idle'.[28] That is, they were not really habitually idle; if more work, more opportunities were given to them they would become hard working, Johnson suggested: 'The possibility of gain will by degrees make them industrious'.[29]

Johnson trusted the abilities of the Highlanders so much that he did not suggest *forcing* them to improve. He thought them capable of doing it themselves.

There were not many other contemporary commentators who shared Johnson's view of the Highlanders' abilities. Edward Burt was one of them. Author of the *Letters from a Gentleman in the North of Scotland*, he was an Englishman who held relatively unprejudiced views on the Highlanders. Little is known of him today, but he appears to have served with General Wade in Scotland during the 1720s.[30] Although he was writing some forty years earlier than Johnson's *Journey*, his account was not published until 1754.

He was one of those few who would not attribute the Highlanders' poor conditions to their 'natural' laziness and 'inherent' barbarity. Although he also considered them lazy and at length described in horror the wretched state of the inhabitants, he emphasised repeatedly that those conditions had not derived from their 'nature', that the Highlanders were not 'inherently' indolent and barbarous. He explained their circumstances as due to the lack of opportunities and proper treatment:

> Let those who deride the dirtiness and idleness of these poor creatures, which my countrymen are so apt to do, . . ., let them, I say, consider, what inclination they can have to recommend themselves? Cleanliness is too expensive for their wages; and what inducement can they have, in such a station, to be diligent and obliging to those who use them more like negroes than natives of Britain? Besides, *it is not anything in nature that renders them more idle* and uncleanly than others, as some would inconsiderably suggest . . .
>
> The working tradesmen, for most part, are indolent, and no wonder, since they have so little incitement to industry and profitable employment to encourage them to do it.[31]

Incentives, opportunities and proper treatment were the remedies he suggested for the Highlanders' poor conditions. Like Johnson, he had no romantic delusions about the Highland scenery. When he did comment on the landscape he found it 'horrible'.[32] He and Johnson were probably the last travellers who did not find Highland scenery beautiful and romantic. From the end of the eighteenth century up to the present it would simply be taken for granted that the chief characteristic of the Highlands is their wild romantic beauty, a reserve for poets, tourists and 'back-to-nature' romantics.

The shift in others' views of the Highlanders from those of Burt and Johnson seems to have begun towards the 1770s with Thomas Pennant and Sir John Sinclair. Both men were well known at the time and exerted considerable influence on contemporaries. The travels of Thomas Pennant, a respected naturalist, excited great interest and the account of his tour in the Highlands was 'so favourable that it has ever since been *inondée* with southern visitors'.[33] Sir John Sinclair, statistician and agrarian reformer, was best known as the compiler of the 29-volume *Statistical Account of Scotland* of 1799. Although he did not publish any travel accounts, he made his views clear on the Highlanders in a series of letters in the press and in his introduction to the *Statistical Account.*

Pennant's opinions form a link from the unromantic, critical and not yet racially based views, to the more racial nineteenth-century attitude of contempt. Sinclair's views are already closer to those of the nineteenth century. Both Johnson and Sinclair were highly influential minds of their age, but it was Sinclair's views that were to persist to a greater degree.

Thomas Pennant travelled in the Highlands in 1769 but his *Tour in Scotland* was not published until 1771. It was a direct influence on Johnson, especially in his lament that the ancient peculiar customs worth observing were fast wearing away. Unlike Johnson, however, Pennant displayed romantic tendencies and praised the Highland scenery. He found the 'naked' mountains 'awefully magnificent', and 'the rocks of Braemar' to be 'exceedingly romantic'.[34] In Pennant's writing two qualities had appeared which later became essential in the romantic perceptions of Highland scenery: wildness and strangeness:

> The scenery of this valley is far the most picturesque of any in the Highlands, being so wild and uncommon as never fails to attract the eye of every stranger of the least degree of taste and sensitivity.[35]

Pennant did not romanticise the inhabitants, though. Like Johnson after him, he was very critical of landowner policies and of emigration. He thought emigration was 'detrimental to the public' and regarded it as a result of bad management, which drove people to despair. He primarily blamed the landowners:

> The rage of raising rents has reached this distant country: in England there may be reason for it (in a certain degree) where the value of lands is increased by accesion [accession] of commerce and by the rise of provisions: but here (contrary to all policy) the great men *begin at the wrong end, with squeezing the bag, before they have helped the poor tenant to fill it*, by the introduction of manufactures. In many of the isles this already shews its unhappy effect, and begins to depopulate the country . . .[36]

While being critical of landlord management, Pennant had a fair amount of contempt for the ordinary Gaels as well. He was horrified at the conditions they lived in, and described at length their 'miserable' houses 'shocking to humanity'. Although he acknowledged a few positive traits such as politeness, quick apprehension, generosity and hospitality, he mainly regarded the Highlanders as indolent and idle. It is his belief in their indolence that links him to the nineteenth century. While Burt and Johnson saw the Gaels' 'laziness' as a result of circumstances, Pennant regarded it as something deriving from their nature and talked about '*native* indolence'.[37] Like children, he said, they were indolent 'unless roused to animating amusement', they were content with little and would not 'bestir themselves' till they faced famine. This point of view would often be repeated in various forms in the mid-nineteenth century, and even served as justification for minimal famine relief or for no relief at all.

In the same year, in 1769, when Pennant toured the Highlands, Sir John Sinclair, himself a native of the Highlands, voiced similar contempt for the lazy Gaels in much stronger language. In a series of letters to the *Caledonian Mercury*,[38] which he reprinted in the introduction to his *Statistical Account*, he called the worst of the Highlanders 'savage' and 'indolent', and considered these characteristics inherent. He did allow, though, that there were 'sober and diligent' ones as well. His contempt and condemnation were stronger and more passionate than the English Pennant's, perhaps because he felt embarrassed by the 'unworthy' among his countrymen. The following lines foreshadowed much of the contempt of coming decades:

> . . . I have travelled every corner of the Highlands of Scotland, it is the place of my birth, and the country of my heart, yet with all my partiality and prejudice for it, I have seen too many of its inhabitants who were pictures of indolence and sloth. Contented to live in inactivity and idleness, without

even the necessaries of life, they would rather starve in the midst of profusion than apply themselves to industry and labour, they would rather mount up with the utmost difficulty to the top of a bleak and barren mountain from whence nothing can be seen but the clouds of Heaven, and the Albion snows, than to strive to attain to independency and freedom, with the sweat of their brow and labour of their hands. They would rather cringe to their landlord and their laird to obtain the crumbs that fall from his table than attempt to get a decent and comfortable livelihood, by cultivating the lands entrusted to their care, or applying themselves to any *trade, (which, though it would perhaps disgrace the blood and the race from whence they sprang)* yet it would in time make them richer even than the chief of their clan.[39]

While the seeds of racist views were just emerging here, twenty years later the historian John Pinkerton was openly spelling out theories on the racial inferiority of the Highlanders. He not only went much further than any eighteenth-century commentator but also clearly echoed general trends in the development of racist thought.

A well-known Edinburgh antiquary, historian, and literary forger, he first put forward his hypothesis on the inveterate inferiority of the Celtic race as opposed to the Scythian or Gothic race in 1787, in his *Dissertation on the Origin and Progress of the Scythians or Goths*. According to his theory, the Celts were the aborigines of Europe, incapable of arts and civilisation, while the Scythians were the 'civilisers' from Asia, where 'rude and cultivated arts' originated. The Celts were what the 'indigenes of America [today] are to the European settlers'. When the superior Scythae had come into Europe, according to Pinkerton, 'the Celtic indigenes soon finding their inferiority seem generally to have fled to the extremities, and Britain and Gaul appear to have been the final receptables of almost all the Celts'.[40]

The racial differences had persisted ever since and were 'radical', Pinkerton contended in tones of annoyance, and added that such differences were such 'as no climate or chance could produce'.[41] He concluded that the Celts were 'savages since the world began, and will be forever savages while a separate people; that is, while themselves, and of unmixt blood'.[42]

Two years later in 1789, in his *An Enquiry into the History of Scotland, preceding the reign of Malcolm III*, Pinkerton expanded his theory, adding specific characterisations of the inferiority of the Highland Celts. For him, the Highlanders were not only savages and inherently indolent but were also a 'weaker' race and had inferior physical and moral characteristics deriving from their race:

> Everyone, who has been in North Britain knows that the Lowlanders of the
> country are as different as the English are from the Welch. The race is so
> extremely distinct as to strike all at first sight. In person the Lowlanders are
> tall and large, with fair complexions, and often with flaxen, yellow, and red
> hair, and blue eyes; the grand features of the Goths, in all ancient writers.
> The lower classes of the Highlanders are generally diminutive, if we except
> some of the Norwegian descent, with brown complexions and almost always
> with black curled hair and dark eyes. In mind and manners the distinction is
> as marked. The Lowlanders are acute, industrious, sensible, erect and free.
> The Highlanders indolent, slavish, strangers to industry.[43]

Pinkerton then proceeded to elaborate on how Celtic poetry was 'almost
wholly melancholic in a supreme degree', which, he said, could only be
expected from a 'weak and dispirited people'. In contrast, Pinkerton
contended, 'Gothic poetry', including that of the Lowlanders, was 'replete
with that warm alacrity of mind, cheerful courage, and quick wisdom,
which attend superior talents'.

What makes Pinkerton's view of the Highlanders and Lowlanders
especially remarkable is that it strangely corresponded to contemporary
anthropologists' descriptions of inferior and superior races. Anthropology,
the preoccupation with description and classification of races, was new, and
was a product of the European Enlightenment and increasing contact with
other peoples of other continents. The second half of the eighteenth
century saw the emergence of anthropology, phrenology and physiognomy:
all concerned with the classification of races and peoples in order to
determine man's exact place in nature and find the 'missing link' in the
great chain of being.

Most anthropologists in the last two decades of the eighteenth century
equated small stature with racial inferiority[44] – just as Pinkerton described
the Lowlanders as tall and the Highlanders as 'diminutive'. More importantly, the ideal type of beauty which was to characterise the superior
race was equated with the classical laws of ancient Greek beauty, that is, a
well-proportioned body and face, fair complexion, blue eyes, fair hair. This
stereotype was indeed later to become the all-too familiar Aryan or Teuton
type of superior race. Pinkerton's description of the Lowlanders as tall, large
with fair hair and complexion, and blue eyes rings strange bells indeed.
Moreover, the way he described the Highlanders presented an even
stranger picture: they have dark complexions, dark eyes and their hair
is not only black but curly. Pinkerton also used the word 'slavish', at the
time when slavery was still widespread and accepted. Any similarity to the

Blacks perhaps, whose features and 'slavish' nature were so widely discussed at the time?

In Pinkerton's description it was not only the outward features that corresponded to current views on inferior and superior races but the 'inner' qualities as well. The Highlanders in Pinkerton's view were essentially and inherently 'lazy', 'indolent' and 'a race incapable of labour'.[45] The Lowlanders by contrast were industrious, sensible, acute and free – very much like good middle-class people. These two sets of traits corresponded to certain contemporary views in anthropology and natural science. The Swedish naturalist Carl von Linné, who was one of the most influential pioneers of racial classification,[46] characterised the white race as inventive, full of ingenuity, orderly and governed by laws: on the whole reflecting middle-class values. By contrast he attributed to the Blacks all the opposite, negative qualities: they were regarded as lazy, devious and unable to govern themselves. Pinkerton's description of the Celtic Highlanders clearly echoed current notions on the Blacks and other supposedly 'inferior' races, a fact that was perhaps unique at the time among other 'white' European theorists, who 'only' classified non-whites as inferior.

Most late eighteenth-century racial classification theories were not yet fully-fledged racist theories as they lacked the notion of inherence. In other words, the inferior races were not such for ever; if their conditions changed, they would change with their environment. This notion derived from the Enlightenment era which regarded man as a product of the environment. Christian Meiners, in his influential *Outline of the History of Mankind* (1785), regards the different racial characteristics as a result of climate and not yet as inherent qualities. In fact, this stage in the general development of racial thinking can be compared to the early stage which Samuel Johnson represented in the evolution of racial attitudes towards the Highlanders, where he derived their usually 'inferior' characteristics not from their race but from their circumstances. Johnson's views were firmly those of the classic Enlightenment, and the changes in perception after him also reflect changes in the general trends in European thinking.

The end of the eighteenth century brought about a growing national consciousness, and 'all but buried the cosmopolitanism of the Enlightenment'.[47] Wide-ranging views on the white race would soon be narrowed down: superior qualities would be attributed not to the whole of the European white race but to certain individual nations. 'The *Homo Europeus* about which the eighteenth century anthropologists wrote would become the German, Slavic or French race.'[48] Anglo-Saxonism, too, and a more rampant anti-Celt racism would become prevalent only in the nineteenth century, but its forerunners, such as Pinkerton, had already appeared.

II. 'Zeitgeist'

By the mid-nineteenth century racialist theories and concepts had become an easily discernible part of the ruling spirit of the age, or 'Zeitgeist' in Europe. It is in this wider climate of opinion that the Lowland contempt for the Highland Gael should be seen. In this context, contemptuous Lowland views, which today would seem shocking and unacceptable, at the time were quite 'natural', fitting into the general pattern of current thought. This wider spirit of the age was essential to the formation of Lowland Saxon contempt for the Highland Gael.

For most mid-Victorians, their age was filled with optimism, even euphoria, and a firm belief that the world was rapidly advancing to unseen heights of civilisation. Innovation, discovery, expansion, and improvement seemed to take place 'daily, if not hourly',[49] as one contemporary chronicler put it. It was an age of self–confidence and strength. It was an age when the boundaries of human achievement seemed limitless. 'We remove mountains, and make seas smooth highways, nothing can resist us. We war with rude Nature, and by our restless engines, come off always victorious . . .',[50] wrote Thomas Carlyle in 'Signs of the Times'.

'Progress' was a key concept of the age. It was so much part and parcel of everyday thinking that even when a Glasgow merchant wrote an advertisement for gentlemen's clothing, he began it by penning an ode to the present age:

> If our grandfathers could come
> From their dark and narrow home
> They would open wide their eyes
>   With incredulous surprise,
>   And would quite bewildered be
> With the sights that they would see.
>   Like a meteor of the night
> Would appear the steam-car's flight,
>   Blinding almost with its rays.
> In their eyes the gas would blaze;
>   Everywhere in every street
> Something startling they would meet; . . .[51]

And indeed, there was much to admire. When one looked at the world map, British supremacy was obvious. The British Empire covered a quarter of the globe. Britain itself had become the 'workshop' of the world, and the model country of development. Both the pace and quantity of achievements were unparalleled. The period between the 1840s and the 1870s witnessed an 'extraordinary economic transformation and expansion'.[52]

In the first half of the nineteenth century the population of Britain had doubled, its imports had increased more than threefold, and both exports and production had increased more than tenfold.[53] It was the 'golden age of high farming' in agriculture, producing greater yields than ever before. The supply of power and number of machines had been increasing, and the progress of industry was indisputable.[54] Developments in transport made the world shrink, with communication rapidly transforming the pace of life. A triumphant celebration of this progress was embodied in the Great Exhibition in 1851, which had set out 'to present a true test and a living picture of the point of development at which the whole of mankind has arrived'.[55] The Crystal Palace had 13,000 exhibitors and six million visitors, and was both a 'fairy tale and a success story'.[56]

The comforts of everyday life and the standard of living increased for many, especially for those whose voice would represent public opinion: the middle classes. They saw no need to be dissatisfied with the rate of progress or the position they had achieved. They were content and confident. Increasingly, the past seemed barbarous and inferior, and the present appeared the only true state of civilisation.

When at the middle of the century *The Economist* paused to reflect on what had so far been achieved in 'The Age of Progress and Race',[57] the author listed with dismay the details of the previous standard of living. This horrifying list included bad roads, poorly-lit streets, 'neglected sanitary matters', 'pestilential prisons', bull and bear-baiting as favourite amusements, slow locomotion, tedious and costly transmission of letters, inferior food, heavy taxes on both the necessaries and luxuries of life, and too few newspapers. He then went on to say that 'the worst part of the descent into barbarism' was a Draconian criminal law, no freedom of discussion, trampled religious rights, an unreformed parliament, drunk gentlemen, no steamboats, and an eight-week voyage to America instead of one of ten days. By contrast, the present age was 'rich beyond nearly all others'; it had witnessed political events of 'thrilling interest and mighty moment', and unparalleled moral and social improvements. *The Economist*'s final characterisation of the age was euphoric:

[The age] has witnessed a leap forward in all elements of material well-being such as neither scientific vision nor poetic fancy ever pictured. It is not too much to say that in wealth, in arts of life, in the discoveries of science and their application to the comfort, health, the safety, and the capabilities of man, in public and in private morality, in the diffusion if not in the advancement of knowledge, in the sense of social charity and justice, in religious freedom, and political wisdom, – the period of the last fifty years has carried us forward faster and further than any other half-century in modern times.[58]

And the future? *The Economist* confidently hoped for 'the realisation of all those dreams, almost of perfectibility, which a comparison of the past with the present entitles us to indulge in'.[59] Expectations were high, and the belief in progress and improvement was so firm that it gave the Victorians a strong sense of self-righteousness.

How was this enormous progress explained at the time? What were the underlying factors which gave rise to such industrial power, and to such a vast 'leap forward'? One of these factors was certainly the Victorian 'work ethic'. 'Industry', 'hard work' and 'perseverance' were some of the most frequently repeated terms of the Victorian period. Diligence and work were not only useful values but absolute duties, without which no success in business or any other area of life was possible. It was hard work and self-reliance which made the nation great, and which was indispensable to any progress. This particular work ethic, embodied in a 'continually repeated, often almost passionate preaching of hard, continuous bodily and mental labour',[60] was not a Victorian invention, nor was it a new idea. It was essentially the old Protestant work ethic, born sometime around the mid-eighteenth century, which was fundamental to the development of the capitalist system. As Max Weber described it in his seminal *The Protestant Ethic and the Spirit of Capitalism*:

> . . . the peculiarity of this philosophy of avarice appears to be the ideal of the honest man of recognised conduct, and above all the idea of duty of the individual toward the increase of his capital, which is almost an end in itself. Truly what is here preached is not simply a means of making one's way in the world, but a peculiar ethic. The infraction of its rules is treated not as foolishness but as forgetfulness of duty. That is the essence of the matter. It is not mere business astuteness, that sort of thing is common enough, it is an ethos.[61]

Work had come to be considered in itself the ultimate purpose of life, and unwillingness to work was now considered one of the gravest sins. St Paul's

'He who will not work shall not eat' was binding for everyone, and was often repeated in the press and in the private correspondence of government officials dealing with the poor and the destitute. The old Protestant work ethic had attained complete ascendancy by the mid-nineteenth century.

One of the most telling indicators of the popularity of this 'work ethos' is the sheer number of editions of the Scots-born Samuel Smiles' *Self-Help*. This book became virtually the gospel of work and a manual for thousands intent on 'improving' themselves in the mid-nineteenth century. First published in November 1859, it went into four more editions in the same month, then another thirteen editions between 1860 and 1870, and another twenty-five by the end of the century.[62] The number of copies sold was remarkable: in the first year 20,000 were sold, 55,000 in the first five years and over a quarter of a million by the end of the century.[63] These sales were bigger than any of the great nineteenth-century novels. It was also translated into several languages, including Japanese and Arabic, and was followed by a number of sequels, whose titles themselves were telling: *Character, Thrift, Duty,* and *Life and Labour.*

Although published in 1859, the book originated in the mid-1840s when Smiles gave a lecture series before an evening class of Leeds working men who had set up their own school 'to improve themselves'. Smiles remarked later in his introduction, that seeing these men he 'could not fail to be touched by the admirable self-helping spirit which they had displayed'.[64] Samuel Smiles did not invent the idea of hard work, he simply gave voice to the prevalent ethos of work, echoed everywhere in the press, in literature and in government policies.

His main tenets were self-reliance, perseverance, self-discipline, self-control, honesty and 'upright performance of individual duty'. The book was primarily a collection of individual examples from the lives of great men, using each as a lesson in self-help, and was interspersed with short philosophical discussions. The men selected by Smiles would be '. . . always at work, always in advance, always accumulating', and would earn their distinction with 'strenuous individual application', for, Smiles concluded, 'it is diligent hand and head alone that maketh rich – in self-culture, growth in wisdom and in business'.[65]

This sense of work ethic was indeed so prevalent in mid-nineteenth century Victorian society that it even permeated popular culture. *The People's Journal* was an early popular newspaper published in London, and in 1846 it ran this poem by Charles Mackay, 'one of the most popular poets of the day',[66] from his volume entitled *Voices from the Crowd*.[67]

DAILY WORK

Who lags for dread of daily work
And his appointed task would shirk,
    Commits a folly and a crime:
        A soulless slave –
        A paltry knave –,
    A dog upon the wheels of Time,
With work to do, and store of health,
The man's unworthy to be free,
        Who will not give
        That may live
    His daily toil for daily fee.

No! Let us work! We only ask
Reward proportioned to our task.
We have no quarrel with the great;
        No feud with rank –
        With Mill or bank –
No envy of a Lord's estate.
If we can earn sufficient store
To satisfy our daily need;
        And can retain
        For age and pain
    A fraction, we are rich indeed.

No dread of toil have we or ours;
We know our worth, and weigh our powers;
    The more we work, the more we win:
        Success to Trade!
        Success to Spade!
    And to the Corn that's coming in!
    And joy to him, who o'er his task
    Remembers toil is nature's plan,
        And, working, thinks –
        And never sinks
    His independence as a man.

Who only asks for humblest wealth,
    Enough for competence and health;
And leisure, when his work is done,

To read his book,

> By chimney-nook,
>
> > Or stroll at the setting of the Sun.

Who toils as every man should toil

> For fair reward, erect and free;
>
> > These are the men –
> >
> > The best of men –

These are the men we mean to be!

This 'urban Kailyard' piece with its strong didactic flavour well represented the same self-improving movement given expression by Samuel Smiles and others. Expressions such as 'Let us work!' and 'toil is nature's plan' pointed to the sense of duty which Victorians had towards work, not only the middle class but the lower classes as well.

This sense of duty, however, also bred a sense of self-righteousness, which regarded those who did not work with abhorrence and pronounced 'indolence' a grave sin. As Mackay put it in the poem above: 'Who lags for dread of daily work/ And his appointed task would shirk,/ Commits a folly and a crime'. And just as success was considered the result of self-help, hard work and individual achievement, so poverty was seen as personal failure.

This powerful work ethic thus created a new attitude both to the poor, and to the 'traditional way of life'. The very nature of this work ethic was in sharp contrast to traditional values and ways of thinking. One of the main differences between the two ways of thinking was that for the traditional mind, earning more was not more attractive than working less: the important thing was to be able to take care of the traditional needs. So if a worker was offered a higher wage for more work, he would rather choose the same wage for the same or less work. As Max Weber put it: 'A man does not "by nature" wish to earn more and more money, but simply to live as he is accustomed to live and earn as much as is necessary for that purpose'.[68]

The new Victorian society was now split into the 'diligent' and the 'indolent'. Poverty was often linked to indolence, and was regarded with utter contempt. As a lady writer expressed it in the *Inverness Courier* in 1845:

IDLENESS – The idler, like the idiot, stands in the lower scale of humanity, morally considered; even lower, for indolence wastes what imbecility wants; the one who abandons himself, the other has been abandoned. The stream of life is fraught with golden sands, but it flings to the idler nothing but froth, and he falls like the dank weed on Lethe's stream, without ever having flourished.[69]

The 'idler' was considered not only morally and socially inferior but often even as a social liability best got rid of for the sake of the well-being of society. The most celebrated mid-Victorian philosopher Herbert Spencer argued in 1851 in his *Social Statistics* that the 'purifying process' by which animals kill off the sickly, the malformed and the aged, was equally at work in human society:

> The poverty of the incapable, the distresses that come upon the imprudent, the starvation of the idle, and those shoulderings aside of the weak by the strong, which leave so many in shallows and miseries are the decrees of a large, far-seeing benevolence, . . ., [sick labourers, widows and orphans] when regarded not separately, but in connection with the universal interest of humanity, these harsh fatalities are seen to be full of the highest beneficence – the same beneficence which brings to early graves the children of diseased parents, and singles out the low-spirited, the intemperate, and the debilitated as the victims of an epidemic.[70]

In Spencer's view society was an organism similar to the human body, functionally organised, and if a disease attacked the body it was best to operate and remove the sick part. Eventually, increasingly efficient societies would be created by this struggle for survival. Spencer was one of the great influences on Charles Darwin, and the 'survival of the fittest' was actually his term.[71] He applied evolutionary ideas to human society, and has often been termed *the* 'social Darwinist' with his 'sanctioning of a ruthlessly competitive social order'.[72]

While this competitive social order led to new attitudes towards the weak and the poor, the expanding British Empire had increasingly come into contact with other, very different peoples around the world, 'the natives'. Colonisation was linked to the civilising mission. Firstly the natives had to be pronounced backward and inferior in order to justify their subjugation. Then they had to be taught, like children, how to become civilised. They were regarded as belonging to a previous stage of civilisation, the stage of barbarians mostly, and were judged by the criteria of 'western' culture. Attitudes towards them were often similar to those towards the poor and the weak. They were regarded as 'inherently' indolent, unruly and doomed to extinction in the march of progress.

The white races, especially the Anglo-Saxons, were increasingly seen as *the* civilised race, 'inherently' possessing that 'energy', 'industry' and 'character' which distinguishes the superior and 'civilised' people from the 'lazy natives'. The *Economist* argued in 1850 that 'the Anglo-Saxon race' was distinguished by 'energy . . . in whatever climate it may take up its abode'.[73] Samuel Smiles believed that the 'spirit of self-help, as exhibited in the energetic action of individuals has in all times been a marked feature in the English character, and furnished the true measure of our power as a nation'.[74]

Civilisation and progress were increasingly linked to race. As the British Empire expanded, and as Britain became the most developed nation, the 'workshop' of the world, the concept of English or Anglo-Saxon superiority over Indians, Africans, or even just the Celts became commonplace, the accepted norm. The notion was 'in the air', it was taken for granted, and was one of the main elements of the climate of opinion. The historian of the age, T.B. Macaulay, expressed it clearly: 'The English have become the greatest and most highly civilised people that ever the world saw, have spread their dominion over every quarter of the globe'.[75] In a sense, the very fact that English dominion was so extensive and English power so great was regarded as empirical 'proof' of the innate racial superiority of the Anglo-Saxons.

The idea of Anglo-Saxon racial superiority was not entirely new. Its seeds had been sown in the eighteenth century by such historians, antiquarians and scientists as Thomas Percy, John Pinkerton, and Sharon Turner. In the nineteenth century the growth and expansion of British supremacy coincided with the general growth of interest in the 'races of men'. From the first half of the nineteenth century ethnology, phrenology, and anthropology had flourished, and all pointed towards the Anglo-Saxons as 'the final product of a long line of superior beings'.[76]

By the 1840s, the importance of Race was almost undisputed. As the prestigious *Edinburgh Review* commented in 1844: 'of the great influence of Race in the production of National Character no reasonable inquirer can now doubt'.[77] And the often-quoted phrase from Benjamin Disraeli's *Tancred* in 1847 echoed the same notion: 'All is race; there is no other truth'. As one of the few historians who paid attention to this 'vital ingredient in English . . . thought in the nineteenth century'[78] pointed out:

> The 1840s were a watershed in the surging growth of Anglo-Saxonism. Those ideas of Anglo-Saxon freedom that had persisted in English thought since the sixteenth century were now melded, on the one hand, with the ideas of Teutonic greatness and destiny developed by the comparative philologists and German nationalists, and on the other, with the ideas of inherent Caucasian superiority developed by those interested in the science of man. Many of course resisted the surge of racist doctrines but an increasing number were swept away in an emotional tide of racial theory.[79]

One of the most extreme waves of this tide was undoubtedly represented in the mid-nineteenth century by the famous Scottish anatomist Robert Knox. His best-known work *The Races of Men*, published in 1850, is regarded today as 'one of the most articulate and lucid statements of racism ever to appear'.[80] It contained all the main ingredients of modern racism: race war, race extermination, racial segregation and racial biology. The book was published with a series of illustrations of the different races, showing either the classical beauty of the 'fair' race or the animal-like ugliness of the 'dark races'. Some of these pictures, like the sequence of profiles from an Oran Outan through a Black to a white man, would become widely used by twentieth-century racists. *The Races of Men* makes daunting reading.

Knox's popularity was not to be underestimated; he was 'an influential Fellow of the Edinburgh College of Surgeons, where by the session of 1828/29 he had over 500 students and lectured for three hours a day'.[81] He also spread his ideas in lectures in England between 1844 and 1847 and his book was based on these lectures.

Knox's main thesis was that all human affairs were absolutely dependent on race, and could only be understood through race. In a very similar statement to Disraeli's *Tancred*, he declared in the introduction of his book that 'Race is everything: literature, science, art – in a word, civilisation, depends on it'.[82]

Knox defined the main racial division between the 'dark' and the 'fair' races, with the Saxons as the only truly fair race, and the Africans as the worst dark race, who were hardly more than animals. The Saxon was superior to other races in industry, was 'a lover of labour', 'order', 'punctuality in business, of neatness and cleanliness'.[83] The Saxon was also the only truly democratic race, and would eventually subdue or exterminate other races.

The world's destiny would ultimately be decided in a 'war of the races', in the 'approaching struggle of race against race', Knox predicted.[84] In this war, which he saw already starting with the revolutions on the Continent and in the colonial fights around the world, 'the weaker race must in time be obliterated'.

The race war, 'the destruction of one race by another', was nothing to get emotional about, Knox emphasised, it was simply 'a fact' which regulated men's existence on the globe. This 'war of extermination' was 'natural', and would eventually produce the domination by the Saxon race of the 'dark races', in which Knox included the Jews and Gypsies as well. In a truly remarkable passage, he actually suggested shooting

natives randomly in order to speed up the process of racial extermination:

> A ready way too of *extinguishing* them [natives of Australia] has been
> discovered; the Anglo-Saxon has already *cleared out* Tasmania. It was a cruel,
> cold-blooded, heartless deed. Australia is too large to attempt the same plan
> there; but *by shooting the natives as freely as we do crows in other countries, the
> population must become thin and scarce in time.*[85]

It was not only the 'dark races', in Knox's view, who were best to become
extinct, or at least, to use a modern term, 'cleansed' from the world of the
superior fair race. Closer to home, in his own country, he found another
greatly inferior race: the Celt:

> To me the Caledonian Celt of Scotland appears a race as distinct from the
> Lowland Saxon of the same country, as any two races can possibly be: as
> Negro from American; Hottentot from Caffre; Esquimaux from
> Saxon . . .[86]

The Caledonian Celtic race, like the Gypsies, Knox said, were lazy in the
extreme: 'rather than labour, they would willingly starve', as they had
'discovered the grand secret, that they can live by the labour of others'. Like
the Gypsies and other lower races, the Caledonian Celts too were doomed
to extinction, which had already begun at Culloden, Knox believed, when
the 'Lowland Saxon Scotch took part against them, . . . the Celtic race
cannot too soon escape from under Saxon rule'.

Eventually, the Caledonian Celts would have to be forced off and cleared
from their soil, as there was no hope of converting them into good Saxons,
and, according to Knox, they were also in the way of the English nation and
its interests:

> The really momentous question for England, as a *nation*, is the presence of
> three sections of the Celtic race still on her soil: the Caledonian or Gael; the
> Cymbri, or Welsh; and the Irish, or Erse; and how to dispose of them. The
> Caledonian Celt touches the end of his career: they are reduced to about one
> hundred and fifty thousand . . . The race must be forced from the soil; by
> fair means, if possible; still they must leave. England's safety requires it.[87]

In a clear reference to the Clearances, Knox suggested that this process had
in fact started, and was all for the better; a consequence of the inevitable
struggle of race: 'The dreamy Celt . . . exclaims, at his parting moment
from the horrid land of his birth, 'We'll maybe return to Lochaber no
more':

And why should you return, miserable and wretched man, to the dark and filthy hovel you never sought to purify? to the scanty patch of ground on which you vegetated? Is this civilisation? Was it for this that man was created? Chroniclers of events blame your religion: it is your race.[88]

Knox's views were extreme, but his ruthlessly well-articulated ideas were echoed, albeit only in softened form, in much contemporary Lowland opinion expressed in the press and pamphlets of the mid-nineteenth century. Newspaper editorials, readers' letters and pamphlets increasingly argued for a large-scale and systematic emigration scheme to remove the 'inherently lazy' and 'useless' Celt or Gael to other parts of the world, away from the neighourhood of the 'industrious' and 'superior' Saxon Lowlander.

Not only the Knoxian concepts were echoed in many contemptuous expressions in the press: so were the thoughts of Spencer, Smiles and 'pre-Darwinian' notions of the war of races. From the concept of progress linked to race to the overriding work ethic with its condemnation of the 'lazy', all the main elements of the mid-nineteenth-century 'Zeitgeist' were clearly present in the pages of the contemptuous Lowland newspapers.

Notes

1. 'Boswell's Journal of a Tour to the Hebrides with Samuel Johnson', *Scotsman*, 29 September 1852.
2. *Scotsman*, 29 September 1852.
3. My italics. Samuel Johnson: *A Journey to the Western Islands of Scotland*, 1775, Penguin ed. 1993, 63.
4. *Letters of Samuel Johnson*, L.L.D., ed. by G. Birkbeck Hill (Oxford 1892), 30 September 1773.
5. Johnson, *Journey*, 51.
6. Johnson was also very aware of the deep gap between Lowlanders and High-landers, and attributed it to ignorance and prejudice. 'To the southern inhabitants of Scotland the state of the mountains and islands is equally unknown with that of Borneo or Sumatra', he wrote of the Lowlanders, and elsewhere he remarked that the Highlanders would not be willingly taught by the Lowlanders 'for they have long considered them as a mean and degenerate race'.
7. *Journey*, 73.
8. T.M. Devine, 'The Highland Clearances', 42. in: *New directions in economic and social history*, eds. Digby, Feinstein, 1989.
9. M. Anderson, D.J. Morse, 'The People', in: *People and Society in Scotland, Vol. 2, 1830–1914*, Edinburgh, 1990.
10. See J.M. Bumsted, *The People's Clearance: Highland Emigration to British North America, 1770–1815* (Edinburgh, 1982).

11. Devine, 'Landlordism and Highland Emigration', 92–93, in: Dickson, *Scottish Capitalism*, London, 1980.
12. Devine, 'Landlordism and Highland Emigration', 93.
13. James Boswell: *The Journal of a Tour to the Hebrides with Samuel Johnson*, 1785, Penguin ed. 1993, 394.
14. *Letters*, 30 September 1773.
15. *Letters*, 21 September, 1773.
16. *Letters*, 6 September 1773.
17. Boswell, *The Journal*, 389.
18. *Letters*, 30 September 1773.
19. My italics, Johnson, *Journey*, 119.
20. Johnson, *Journey*, 96.
21. See A.I. Macinnes, 'Scottish Gaeldom: The First Phase of Clearance', in *People and Society, Vol.* 1, 1760–1830, eds. Devine, Mitchison, 1988. Somewhat less recently, W. Ferguson argued in his *Scotland 1689 to the Present* that improvement gained impetus after 1707, and does not see 1746 as a particular watershed in the transformation of Highland society and economy.
22. Macinnes, 'Scottish Gaeldom', 72.
23. Edward Burt *Letters from a gentleman in the north of Scotland*, first published in 1754, quoted in AJ. Youngson, *Beyond the Highland Line*, 109.
24. Johnson, *Journey*, 101–2.
25. Johnson, *Journey*, 101.
26. *Letters*, 30 September 1773.
27. Johnson, *Journey*, 64., my italics.
28. Johnson, *Journey*, 93.
29. Johnson, *Journey*, 73.
30. *Dictionary of National Biography*.
31. Burt: *Letters*. In: Youngson, *Beyond the Highland Line*, 54–56, my italics.
32. Like Johnson, Burt, too, commented on the gap between Lowlanders and Highlanders: '. . . notwithstanding the Lowland Scots complain of the English for ridiculing other nations, yet they themselves have a great number of standing jokes upon the Highlanders.' – Burt, 124.
33. *Dictionary of National Biography*.
34. Pennant, *Tour in Scotland*, qouted in Youngson, *Beyond the Highland Line*, 128 and 139.
35. Pennant, *Tour in Scotland*.
36. Pennant, *Tour in Scotland*, 156, my italics.
37. Pennant, *Tour in Scotland*, 131, my italics.
38. According to the *Waterloo Directory of Scottish Newspapers and Periodicals*, the *Caledonian Mercury*, published in Edinburgh, was said to have been the 'most ancient general newspaper in Scotland', and was a 'favourite family paper with the better class of shopkeepers'. It was an 'essentially political newspaper', a Whig then a Liberal Party supporter.
39. *Statistical Account*, Vol. I, 36–37, reprinted from letter to the *Caledonian Mercury*, 5 October 1769. My italics.
40. Pinkerton, 'Dissertation . . .', in: *An Enquiry into the History of Scotland preceding*

the reign of Malcolm III, or the year 1056, *including the authentic history of that period.*, 2 vols. (Edinburgh, 1790, 1814), 55.

41. Pinkerton, *An Enquiry into the History of Scotland,* 36.
42. Pinkerton, *An Enquiry into the History of Scotland,* 36.
43. Pinkerton, *An Enquiry into the History of Scotland,* 339.
44. George L. Mosse *Toward the Final Solution: A History of European Racism* (London, 1978), Chapter, 'Eighteenth Century Foundations'.
45. Pinkerton, *An Enquiry into the History of Scotland,* 406.
46. As described in Mosse, *Toward the Final Solution.*
47. Mosse, *Toward the Final Solution.*, 34.
48. Mosse, *Toward the Final Solution.*, 34.
49. W.A. Mackinnon: *History of Civilisation* (London 1846), 361.
50. Quoted in Walter E. Houghton, *The Victorian Frame of Mind* (Yale Univ. Press 1957), 40.
51. 'The Present Age', advertisement for Hyam's National Clothier, *Glasgow Herald,* 29 March 1850.
52. E. Hobsbawm, *Industry and Empire.*
53. These figures are given in *The Economist,* 1851, reprinted in the *Glasgow Herald,* 27 January 1851.
54. See Asa Briggs, *The Age of Improvement,* Chapter 8.
55. Quoted in Briggs, *The Age of Improvement,* 398.
56. Briggs, *The Age of Improvement,* 398.
57. Reprinted in the *Glasgow Herald,* 27 January 1851.
58. *Glasgow Herald,* 27 January 1851.
59. *Glasgow Herald,* 27 January 1851.
60. Max Weber's phrase in *The Protestant Ethic and the Spirit of Capitalism,* 1930, ed. quoted here is London, 1976.
61. Weber, *The Protestant Ethic,* 51.
62. These figures are given in the 1906 edition.
63. These sales figures are quoted in Asa Briggs, *Victorian People,* 125–126.
64. Samuel Smiles, *Self-Help,* 1906 ed., x.
65. Smiles, *Self-Help,* 121.
66. James Grant Wilson, *Poets and Poetry of Scotland* (London, 1877), 381.
67. The poem from *The People's Journal* was reprinted in the *Perth Constitutional,* 10 June 1846.
68. Weber, *The Protestant Ethic,* 60.
69. *Inverness Courier,* 5 March 1845, signed as Mary Leman Grimstone.
70. Herbert Spencer, *Social Statistics, or the Conditions Essential to Human Happiness,* 1851, ed. 1868. 354.
71. R.N. Stromberg, *European Intellectual History Since 1789* (New Jersey, 1986),126.
72. Stromberg, *European Intellectual History,* 128.
73. The *Economist,* reprinted in the *Glasgow Herald,* 27 January 1851.
74. Smiles, *Self-Help,* 6.
75. T.B. Macaulay, *Critical, Historical and Miscellaneous Essays,* 1878, quoted in Houghton, *The Victorian Frame of Mind,* 39.

76. Reginald Horsman, 'Origins of Racial Anglo-Saxonism in Great Britain before 1850', in *Journal of the History of Ideas*, XXXVII, July-September 1976.

77. *Edinburgh Review*, January, 1844, quoted in Horsman, 'Origins of Racial Anglo-Saxonism', 99.

78. Horsman, 'Origins of Racial Anglo-Saxonism', 387.

79. Horsman, 'Origins of Racial Anglo-Saxonism', 387.

80. Banton, *Race Relations*, quoted in James Lachlan Macleod, 'Race Theory in Nineteenth Century Scotland', paper presented to the annual conference of the Association of Scottish Historical Studies, in April 1994.

81. Macleod, loc.cit.

82. Robert Knox, *The Races of Men, A Fragment*, London, 1850, v.

83. Knox, *The Races of Men*, 54.

84. Knox, *The Races of Men*, 22.

85. Knox, *The Races of Men*, 145.

86. Knox, *The Races of Men*, 14.

87. Knox, *The Races of Men*, 378–379.

88. Knox, *The Races of Men*, 378–379.

CHAPTER TWO

Contempt

1. 'Lazy but improvable'

The voices of contempt were by far the loudest and most prevalent in the mid-nineteenth-century Scottish press. The two largest and most influential papers, the *Scotsman* and the *Glasgow Herald*, had fundamentally contemptuous views of the Highland Gaels, as did 'the newspaper of the Highlands', the *Inverness Courier*, although to a lesser degree. The total circulation of these three papers was double that of the three main sympathetic papers: the *Witness*, the *Inverness Advertiser* and the *North British Daily Mail*.[1] Many of the smaller papers, such as the *Perth Constitutional* and the *Fifeshire Journal*, whose editor became the *Scotsman*'s special 'commissioner' or reporter in 1847, expressed very strong views not only of contempt but of sheer hatred with openly racialist tones. These more extreme views expressed in smaller papers would be reprinted in larger papers such as the *Glasgow Herald* or the *Scotch Reformers' Gazette*, giving them greater impact.

Newspaper attention in Scotland, as well as in England, had become increasingly focused on the plight of the Highlanders from the mid-1840s.[2] Between 1845 and 1847 the three main papers, the *Scotsman*, the *Glasgow Herald* and the *Inverness Courier*, were regularly dealing with the state of the Highlands, publishing reports on the 'condition of the people', giving space to many 'letters to the Editor' on the subject, writing passionately worded editorials, sending up their 'own' or 'special' commissioners to investigate the 'causes of destitution', and generating heated public debate on 'what to do' with the Highlands and the Highlanders.

The peak of newspaper attention came in 1847, one of the worst years of the Famine. Both the *Scotsman* and the *Inverness Courier* published something on the Highland question in every issue, the *Inverness Courier*, a weekly, often carrying several long articles each week. In addition, many smaller papers joined in the debate, sending their own reporters, as the *Fifeshire Journal* did in 1847, and copiously reprinting articles both from the bigger English papers, such as *The Times* and the *Morning Chronicle*, and from the *Scotsman* and the *Inverness Courier*. From 1848, and especially from 1850 this extensive newspaper attention declined, and would only occasionally revive in the first half of the 1850s. There were many reasons for this fluctuation, one being the nature of events, such as the alarming spread of the Famine in the Highlands from the autumn of 1846, and its climax in 1847.

However, before the famine fully hit the Highlands, press attention had already been directed northwards. During May and June 1845 the press suddenly resounded with the 'Glencalvie case', the ejection of tenants there creating quite a scandal, which even reached the House of Commons. The issue of the 'Clearances' was back on the agenda of public debate, this time with greater force than in previous decades. Due to the growth of the press, public opinion now carried much weight, as the *Scottish Herald* put it at the time: 'Times are changed since the extirpation of the Highland people was first attempted, public opinion is a sharper, keener, and more powerful weapon'.[3] Indeed, the Glencalvie case became quite a weapon in the hands of newspaper men and some MPs, who used it either to crusade against the 'exterminating policy',[4] or to approve the clearances and denounce the Highlanders.

Glencalvie was a small township in Ross-shire near Tain, where a number of tenants were served with 'summonses of removal' in May 1845. They were first issued with the summonses in 1843, but in an act of resistance the people, mostly women, set fire to them, and the factor extended the deadline. The people were now awaiting ejection. In May 1845 the Glencalvie people placed an appeal in *The Times*, at which point the editor decided to send up his 'Own Commissioner', one of the first of his kind. The 'Commissioner' sent a series of sympathetic reports of some thirteen lengthy letters throughout May, June and July, which created quite a sensation, being reprinted in many Scottish papers[5] and prompting passionate reactions. The 'Commissioner' strongly condemned the Clearances, warmly defended the people, blamed the landlords, especially the infamous Duke of Sutherland, and proposed employment as a remedy for destitution.

Although Glencalvie generated more sympathy than contempt, some of the most hostile papers were already grasping the opportunity to express their condemnation of the Highlanders.

The *Glasgow Herald*, while stating in an editorial that it formed no opinion of its own relating to the Clearances, was quick to pick up the *Spectator*'s tirade in early June, which was one of the first strongly worded articles to blame their destitution on the Highlanders themselves. This article was also reprinted in the *Edinburgh Evening Courant*, which had a circulation around 1,800, and together with the *Herald*, with over 3,500 copies, the original *Spectator* article, with an estimated 2,000 copies, more than doubled its audience. What it said was to become one of the typical arguments of the hostile press. The core of the argument was that the reason why the people in the Highlands still 'vegetated in semi-savage condition' lay in themselves. Some landlords tried to remedy the poverty and held out inducements but:

> . . . the apathy which through poverty-stricken generations had become part of their character rendered these efforts unavailing. They preferred their habitual mode of life – their few days of desultory labour intermingled with weeks of lounging gossip – their half-clad half-fed condition – to regular well repaid toil.[6]

The argument that the Highlanders themselves actually preferred to remain in miserable conditions rather than work hard was often to be repeated over the coming years of the Famine.

Meanwhile, one of the most extreme apologists for the Clearances, the *Perth Constitutional*, had already launched its long campaign against the 'lazy' Highlanders. Although it had a relatively small circulation of just over 600, some of its articles were reprinted in larger papers such as the *Inverness Courier* and the *Edinburgh Evening Courant*. In mid-May the *Perth Constitutional* ran its first long editorial on the Glencalvie case, which was also published in the *Inverness Courier* 'at the request' of some of their readers. It endorsed the Clearances by saying that they were the only solution for a people with a 'life of lethargy and indolence':

> They merely vegetate in a state of poverty and inactivity, alike unprofitable to themselves and to their landlords, and in many instances a clearing of this kind has greatly advanced them in the scale of society, and by compelling them to acquire industrious habits, has rendered them happy and independent, instead of continuing to protract their existence in idleness and discomfort.[7]

In defending landlord policies, by a rather absurd twist the editorial went as far as accusing the tenants themselves of oppressing the landlords: 'We hear . . . much of the oppression of the landlord: Is it not possible that landlords themselves may suffer grievous oppression from such refractory tenants, and those who thus goad them on?'[8]

In the *Perth Constitutional*'s view, elaborated in a series of leaders, the Clearances were highly beneficial for the Highlanders – even if they did not realise it at first – because they 'compelled them to improve',[9] and were a form of 'social reformation'.[10] The paper even formulated its own definition of the 'clearings' as: '. . . the removal of a starving population from the scene of their lazy and indolent habits to other parts of the property, where they can and are in some measure obliged to better their circumstances by active industry'.[11]

In a more moderate tone, a very similar stand was taken by the *Inverness Courier* by the end of the summer. Often proudly dubbed the 'newspaper of the Highlands', the *Inverness Courier* was one of the great advocates of Highland 'Improvement' and of the Clearances, at least initially, – better deserving perhaps the title of 'the newspaper of the landowners of the Highlands'. While it was a medium-sized paper, with an approximate circulation of 1,500, its articles on the Highlands were abundantly reprinted in the *Glasgow Herald*, the *Scotsman*, and the *Edinburgh Evening Courant*. Its influential editor was the able and professional journalist, Robert Mackay Carruthers, whose background and values were thoroughly Low-land.[12]

The editorials and reports often proclaimed the paper's sincere concern for the well-being of the Highland Gaels, and a desire to raise them to a more advanced level of civilisation. Passionately promoting the idea of 'moral' improvement, the *Inverness Courier* was like a stern headmaster in reproaching the Gaels' old habits, and intent on teaching them the 'lesson of industry'. Especially before the Famine, it had very little sympathy for the 'habitually indolent' Highlanders.

In the Glencalvie debate the *Courier*'s stance was similar to the views of the *Perth Constitutional*. In its long editorial of August 1845, it claimed that the Clearances were 'grossly misrepresented',[13] and argued that they were beneficial because they gave the Highlanders 'the same chances of improvement as the rest of the civilised world', instead of leaving them 'in the same semi-barbarous state in which they slumbered for ages'.

On those who criticised the Clearances the leader poured some strong vitriol: '. . . it is not a little amusing to follow the sentimental stranger up one lonely glen and down another, bewailing the absence of man, pointing with melancholy finger to each vestige of an old black bothy, or half-effaced trace of the spade, and then triumphantly calling attention to the pitiful increase of population . . .' Instead of 'sentimentalising' about the 'happy' past of the Highlanders, people should adopt a realistic approach and admit that 'the proper amount of inhabitants' ought to be determined by the productive power of the land.

Most of the land of the Highlands, in the *Courier*'s view, was ideally created for sheep, and therefore the paper found the clamour against sheep-farming 'extremely absurd'. The Clearances merely sought 'to restore to order a deranged system of things, to place men and animals, respectively, in their fitting positions'. The landlords simply followed the 'obvious design of nature' by putting sheep on the mountains and men on the coast. The paper's editor was not alone with this theory. Earlier in the summer a reader had already suggested the same idea. In a letter to the Editor, the sober reader signed 'A Water Drinker' declared: 'It has always been an axiom of mine that mountains and hills were made for sheep, and sheep for them'.[14]

The *Courier*'s main argument was that the Clearances had been 'of much good to many', because they improved formerly 'idle' people whose lives were 'useless and comfortless'. The Clearances became the source of much improvement, the paper contended, even if they caused 'a painful shock at first'. In fact, as a criticism of the Clearances, the leader went on to say that the new measures in some cases were 'hurried on too rapidly', without consideration and provision for the people. But such things are inevitable, the editor argued, describing the process of improvement in a manner reminiscent of some technical handbook of social or human experimentation:

> These are blunders which cannot always be avoided in bringing new and untried measures into operation. The working of new machinery is ever somewhat uncertain, and perfection can only result from the experience derived from repeated failures. No change of system can be unattended with loss to those who still pursue the old: but that can never be held as a reason to declare against all change . . . the inconvenience inevitably inflicted on a few [cannot be] a valid cause for preventing or retarding an immense national improvement.[15]

This was in fact the old utilitarian argument. The Benthamite key for social welfare, the sum total of units of individual happiness, was still very much alive in the mid-nineteenth century. In the philosophy of the 'greatest good of the greatest number' an individual's usefulness is judged on the basis of how much he or she contributes to the sum total of happiness. The Highlanders were 'useless' because they were an obstacle to progress, and prevented the greater, national improvement, instead of accepting that they had better suffer for the greater good of society. Although, after its lengthy editorial, the *Inverness Courier* paid less attention for a while to the question of the Clearances, and the topic was fading from the pages of the other Scottish newspapers, it did not die completely. As late as early 1846, the *Perth Constitutional* was still fuming away. In a remarkable editorial invention, it ran its attacks in poems, disguised as Letters to the Editor, but strongly suggesting the same hand (presumably the editor's) behind them. The main message of these poems was that the Glencalvie case was

nothing but a big farce, deceiving the naive public, and that the Highlanders were in no need at all. The first of these poems, apparently written
by 'a Lady', not only stated that the Glencalvie folk deceived the world, but
contained the usual images of the 'lazy' and 'filthy' Highlanders:

> *The Glencalvie Case*
>   Ye fouk o'Fife and other climes
> Who read the *Witness* and the *Times*,
>   And have observ'd, in ample space,
> The great Glencalvie clearings' case, –
>   A case at first designed to be
>   A fairy treasure to the *Free*.
> He of the *National* came north,
>   to raise the cry from Clyde to Forth,
> The Free-kirk clergy walk'd him round
>   To every cot on all the ground;
>   He saw the people black and hearty,
>   But saw no *want* among the party,
>   Except the want of *will* to *toil*,
> To *clean* themselves, or plough the soil.
>   He wonder'd none about the shift
>   The landlord *meant* for raising thrift,
>   And all the *verdict* he could give
> Was – in their *dirt* they wish'd to live.
> The *Times* came north in haste to see
>   And raise the slogan of the *Free*,
>   but he could visit few abodes.
> As gigs don't suit Glencalvie roads.
> But what a mournful tale *he* made it!
> Caus'd London ladies greet who read it
>   A kirk-yard story gilt with care
>   That gull'd the crazy to a hair.
>   The money then came in like stour,
> All meant to help Glencalvie poor.
>
>   . . .
>
>   Now, be it known to those who read
>   Glencalvie folk were in *no* need.[16]

Two weeks later another Glencalvie letter followed, but this time
apparently written by the Glencalvie cottars themselves (signed 'A
present dweller in the glen'), unveiling their deceit and admitting that

they had indeed cheated the people by pretending to be poor and in need:

> But when we knew they money get
> All for us, glen folk, every groat,
> We wearied for its coming north,
> And as we hinted all we knew
> It gave your tale to better view,
> They thought our heads by far too thick
> For finding out some things so quick
> We knew their craft before, so we
> Could act the farce with better glee;
> They knew full well we were not poor
> And in their minds were quite secure,
> No charity we were in need of,–[17]

This self-disclosure is so extraordinary and unparalleled as to suggest that both letters must have been the editor's forgeries, especially since the rhythm of both poems is similarly awkward. That the *Perth Constitutional* had been militant in campaigning against the Highlanders gives further grounds for this suspicion. It also seems highly unlikely that Highland cottars would have read the *Perth Constitutional* in the first place, and that they then would have thanked the paper and wished it well, as the author of this poem did:

> Myself and clansmen all do join
> In wishing *far* your paper *spread*
> To learn folks the tricks o'trade.[18]

The *Perth Constitutional* campaign in 1845 and early 1846 foreshadowed what was yet to come from other larger papers during the famine years. The heightened interest and debate on Highland destitution would only start in earnest in late summer in 1846, and at first it generated enormous public charity. By early 1847, however, the opinion that too much charity had been given to the Highland Gaels became more widespread. What the *Perth Constitutional's* unique poem said in 1846 later turned out to be prophetic:

> For time to come the rich should be
> More careful of their charity.[19]

In August 1846 the first reports of the potato failure were just arriving, creating quite an alarm as people were afraid that it would reach the scale of the Irish Potato Famine, which had broken out in the previous year. In every district of the Highlands and Islands the potato blight appeared and spread rapidly. As the black and yellow spots appeared on the leaves, the shaws began to wither and rot, emitting a most offensive smell. The *Inverness Courier* received 'a mass of communication'[20] on the disease from almost all parts of the Highlands and Islands, describing with alarm the 'fearful' scene of the rotting potatoes. The various correspondents, mostly farmers, gentlemen and clergymen, warned of the 'likelihood of starvation with all its horrors'. Alarm at the spread of the blight and fear of the ensuing famine were great, as one correspondent from Stornoway described it:

> It is truly lamentable to witness the fearful ravages of the potato rot in the island of Lews, and still more melancholy to contemplate the sad consequences to the poor during the next twelve months, many of whom are already representing themselves as in a starving conditions.[21]

The failure was indeed serious. More than sixty-seven per cent of the districts which reported to the Destitution Committee indicated a total failure and only thirteen per cent said the failure was only partial.[22] The epicentre of the disaster was the western mainland, and also the Hebrides, the very heart of crofting society, where people were most dependent on potatoes.

The blight was caused by the fungus *Phytophthora Infestans*, which had afflicted potato crops not only in Ireland the year before but also on the Continent. But in Ireland and in the Scottish Highlands the disease had a more serious effect than in the continental countries because potatoes were the main sustenance of the people, their dependence on them frequently being almost total. As T. M. Devine has pointed out, the Great Highland Famine was more than just a biological disaster, it had 'profound economic origins'. The dependency on the potato was 'one hallmark of the intrinsic poverty of the Highlands, and, however extensive the blight, famine would not have occurred if the population possessed the economic resources to acquire substitute food supplies from elsewhere'.[23]

Estimates varied as to how many people were on the verge of starvation. The first press reports talked about 'thousands'. The Rev. Dr M'Leod at a public meeting of the Destitution Committee in early 1847 put the total figure at 300,000, half of them actually starving. This figure was widely quoted in other papers, but was increasingly doubted, especially by the *Scotsman*, which said that it was grossly exaggerated for propaganda purposes. Modern estimates now put the figure at around 200,000.[24] It is certain, though, that no crofter or cottar in the western Highlands and Islands could escape the effects of the blight, and that the Great Highland Famine was more widespread than any before.

Although the Famine was so severe, no calamity on the Irish scale occurred, and while people remained destitute for many years, there were only a few instances of death from starvation. This was due to the combination of a number of factors: the overall strength of the Scottish economy, the effective mobilisation of relief, the assistance of the land-owners in relief, and emigration – all played their part in preventing more starvation.

Another undoubtedly significant factor was the contemporary press and its role in alerting the public. At the beginning the alarm was especially great because people feared the Irish tragedy would be repeated in the Scottish Highlands too. Together with calls for relief the papers were also urging an investigation into the cause of the condition of the destitute people. The call of the *Scottish Guardian* in September, which the *Glasgow Herald* reprinted, was typical of the early press coverage:

> . . . we press it upon the public attention the more earnestly that no time may be lost in inquiring into the condition and prospects of the population who are thus deprived of their chief, and in the majority of instances, the sole means of subsistence. We have seen some startling indications of the destitution which begins to prevail, and which we have no hesitation in saying, is on the eve of involving thousands of poor islanders in all horrors of starvation.

One of the first papers to send a special commissioner to investigate the causes of famine and destitution was, again, *The Times* of London. The commissioner was sent up to Ross-shire to follow up reports daily arriving from 'the weak extremities of the empire' foreshadowing a 'substantial calamity', as an editorial put it in early September.[25] Its correspondent now, however, was far from sympathetic to the Highlanders as the former reporter had been in the Glencalvie case the year before. What *The Times* correspondent had to say had great impact not only because many of his reports were reprinted in the Scottish papers, in the *Scotsman, Glasgow Herald* and *Perth Constitutional*, but also because his views were so extreme at times that they prompted even the *Inverness Courier* to speak out in defence of the Highland Gaels.

After describing the generally destitute state of the Highlanders, the commissioner in his second letter on the 'Condition of the people in the Highlands of Scotland' presented his remarkable theory as to the root of the evil. How was it possible that while Ireland and Scotland had long been exposed to famines, England had not been affected? What was the difference that explained it? The commissioner's 'investigation' led to quite a revelation. He started off by quoting Adam Smith's *Wealth of Nations*, portraying the English as a nation who continually bettered their own condition, and were wealthy because they were frugal and industrious. People in Ireland and Scotland were poor and starving, and that, according to *The Times*, must have opposite causes, that is, the people there were poor because they were not industrious but lazy. In *The Times*' view, the Irish were simply 'the laziest people on the face of God's earth',[26] and their extreme poverty was 'the natural result of their extreme laziness'. In areas where 'the pure Irish' were to be found, the correspondent informed the readers, one would continually hear phrases such as 'I'll not take the trouble', 'It's not worth the trouble'. The attitude was not much better 'among a kindred Celtic race', the Scottish Highlanders. Here the commissioner found similar attitudes. He could not get herrings, 'swarming in the lake', or grouse from the hills, for dinner. When he asked why, the answer given was: 'they couldna be fashed about it'. His conclusion was thus quickly drawn: 'Like the fear of "trouble" in Ireland, the fear of being "fash'd" in the Highlands stands greatly in the way of comfort and prosperity'.

This attitude was, in fact, rooted in the difference of race, the commissioner was soon to conclude. His observations in different parts of the Highlands pointed to this. He saw a 'diversified population', one belonging to the 'Danish or Norwegian race',[27] one to the 'Highland, Celtic race'. The Norwegian race, living in Caithness, Shetland, and Orkney was a race 'accustomed to work, clearly distinguishable by their complexion and houses and appearance'. They were 'stout, fair haired, ruddy and blue-eyed', their houses were 'stone-built, good dwellings usually with little gardens in front', and despite their bleak and exposed environment their country was 'cultivated and thriving'.

However, the neighbouring county of Sutherland, with a 'Highland, or Celtic race' presented a very different picture to the eyes of *The Times*' commissioner. The houses there were 'turf huts, or bothies, with nondescript chimnies', smoky and filthy, 'of the same pattern as the cottages and huts in Ireland'. The people looked different too. They were 'dark-haired' and spoke only Gaelic. 'There is no mistaking the people, they are a distinct race', the correspondent stressed. And when he added that there was no famine in Caithness and Aberdeen, the counties of a different race, the conclusion clearly was that the Famine was 'race-related', that it was rooted in some inherent qualities of the Celtic race. One such inherent Celtic racial quality was the lack of industry.

The racial difference was also behind the absence of a middle class in Highland society, the commissioner contended. It was a patriarchal state, with only landlords and poor, while in England, 'the commercial spirit, the energy, the persevering vigour, the enterprise, and the industry of the people' gave rise to the middle class. The Highlanders, however, had no 'commercial spirit', no 'innate energy', no 'persevering vigour', they were incapable of enterprise, and rather stuck 'with faithful and dogged prejudice' to the habits and legends of their fathers.

These 'radical differences' were thus to blame, according to the commissioner, for the lack of a middle class, industry and wealth. As a final, powerful conclusion on the roots of the evil, *The Times* came up with the revelation, which fitted well the spirit of the age: 'The difference, in fact, is in the difference of race.'[28] The case for the theory of 'race-related famine' had been made, and was to be echoed and repeated with growing force by several Scottish newspapers over the years of the Famine.

While some of the more hostile papers such as the *Scotsman* and *Fifeshire Journal* were to reinforce these views of 'race-related famine', they upset Robert Carruthers, the editor of the *Inverness Courier*. The series of reports in *The Times* prompted him to write one of his strongest leaders on the issue of Highland destitution.[29] After dismissing the writer as 'not being very witty, very original, or very profound', the leader makes its firm statement against any racist view of the Highlanders:

> We are not disposed to attribute any importance to the circumstances of national descent. It is easy to revive English prejudices, and to repeat the Gothic arguments of Pinkerton;[30] but in fact, no nation is pure or unmixed . . . Races of men, like races of plants or of the inferior animals, are modified by situation and circumstances. It is our duty to improve the latter for the benefit of our fellow-men – not to indulge in dissertations equally fanciful and offensive, which can only deaden the efforts of enterprise and damp the zeal of philanthropy. *We wish to improve the Highlands; and we do not believe, in spite of the Times, that the Celts are unimprovable.*[31] . . . let the people be relieved by labour, not by alms, and future Commissioners will have little to say of the inferiority of the Celtic race.

While the *Courier* often viewed the Highland Gaels with contempt, and scorned their idleness, it believed, for a good while, that it would be possible to 'improve' them, that is, that the Highlanders were indeed inferior and lazy but that theirs was not a hopeless case as their condition stemmed from their circumstances rather than their blood. And it was a duty to raise these poor, but largely the 'deserving poor', to the level of civilised people, instead of 'deadening the efforts of enterprise'.

The chief slogan of the *Courier* was 'to instruct and guide the people', and it constantly advocated land improvement: 'The remedy is – cultivate the waste lands, drain, trench, and improve, and thus create both food and labour'.[32] It advocated improving management and instructing people before it would contemplate 'that harsh and painful alternative, the compulsory emigration'.[33] The *Courier* remained highly enthusiastic about any Highland improvement up until the early '50s, well after other papers had given up completely on the Highlands.

As winter approached, the state of the destitute people deteriorated and alarm over the worsening Famine grew. Reports reached the major papers about 'great distress' and 'considerable activity' in providing relief, chiefly at this time by the landlords, private charity and the Free Church. A 'gentleman travelling in the West Highlands' informed the *Courier* that 'the instances of suffering and want which constantly meet the eye are distressing in the extreme'.[34] An 'agricultural friend', warning that 'the wild days of winter are at hand', told the *Glasgow Herald* that 'generally speaking, much distress already exists, and absolute want will ensue, unless something more than has hitherto been the case be done'.

More was indeed done, and the Famine never reached the scale of the Irish tragedy. Few incidents of death by starvation were reported. The Free Church and the Edinburgh and Glasgow Destitution Committees were very active, calling forth an unprecedented flow of charity. At the end of 1846 and in early 1847 long lists of subscribers to relief were published in the newspapers, often taking up several full pages in small print with several columns.

The committees' appeals fell on fertile soil. Charity and philanthrophy were, by the mid-nineteenth century, firmly established in Victorian society. From the 1840s onwards, charitable societies expanded as never before, and members of the middle class, especially women, were expected to take part in such activities. Charity was almost a fashion, which defined and underlined status. As one historian of philanthrophy put it: 'Standing in the community was in this sense related to the part played in the charitable world . . . Men and women were flattered to be invited to collect subscriptions, to serve on committees, to inspect homes and hospitals'.[35]

In a sense, philanthrophy was part of the 'improvement mentality' of the age, since, unlike charity, it sought more than the temporary relief of distress and was aimed at the permanent improvement of the human condition. Highland destitution well fitted this philanthrophic scenario, presenting a great opportunity for social engineering. While previous charity would simply seek to ease misery, Victorian philanthropy was determined to do more than that: it vowed to 'teach a lesson', 'to improve' both conditions and people. One of the most important elements of this new ideology was the idea that charity should only be given in return for work, in order to avoid 'encouraging laziness'. As the work ethic mentality linked poverty to personal failure stemming from lack of hard work, it was a logical conclusion that only hard work would permanently alleviate distress.

The policy of the destitution and relief committees was part of this broader outlook, but it was also coupled with an added element of Lowland contempt for the Highland Gael. Since Lowlanders believed that the Highlanders were 'inherently', or at least 'habitually', lazy, the determination to teach them the lessons of industry was even more powerful than in the case of the 'ordinary' poor.

From early on, it was a firmly established principle of the relief operations that food should only be given in return for labour. It was an overriding element in the policies of both the destitution committees of the Free Church, and later of the Central Board, which took over in February 1847 and assumed full control. At a meeting of the Edinburgh Destitution Committee in December 1846, one member, Lord Cuninghame, stated this principle, as the papers reported, 'amid applause':

> He was afraid that the sweets of being maintained without working were very contagious, and he trusted, therefore, that in affording relief to the Highlanders, it should be in return for employment, so that they might be trained to habits of activity and industry.[36]

Another member of the Committee, Dr Candlish, agreed, and added that it was 'extremely dangerous to grant relief without work', and proposed that 'a special condition' should be made that 'not even temporary relief should be given to a party who refused to work, either on the spot or at some railway in the neighbourhood'.[37] Accordingly, the Destitution Committee drew up a plan to transport some 3,000 able-bodied men from the Highlands for construction work on the railways in the Lowlands in 1846–47.[38]

By 1847 the Free Church Committee report on Highland Destitution clearly defined the 'relief for labour only' idea as their chief principle: 'The

Local Committee shall hold it as a general rule, that work of some kind should be given in exchange for relief; and shall impress upon the people that food given is not a gratuitous gift, but it is to be paid for in one way or another'.[39]

This principle of 'food for labour' became prevalent not only in the policies of the destitution committees but in most press reports and analyses as well. An editorial in the *Inverness Courier*, aptly entitled 'No Relief Without Employment', reminded its readers that they had repeatedly urged those involved in the distribution of relief to give it only 'in the shape of labour' for meal or money, and added: 'To give assistance to the able-bodied without demanding work in return will be highly injurious to them, and only holding the premium for idleness'.[40] Other papers argued that the previous famine in 1836/37 had already proved that after 'eleemosynary aid' it was difficult to induce people to 'active habits'.[41]

While many papers urged against 'eleemosynary aid', a virtual campaign arose, from the rumoured refusal of the Highlanders to work, in the pages of the *Scotsman*, the *Scotch Reformers' Gazette,* the *Perth Courier* and the *Fifeshire Journal* in February 1847. This campaign was intended to illustrate the idleness of the Highlanders and to reinforce the principle of demanding work for relief.

The *Perth Courier* reported that an overseer of one of the railways had offered permanent employment to five hundred men but could not get them to accept it because they told him that they were going to receive meal from the government without any equivalent.[42] In another story the *Scotch Reformers' Gazette* (which had the second largest circulation after the *Glasgow Herald* with around 3,000) reported that it understood a certain gentleman in Glasgow was ready to employ three hundred Highlanders from Tiree, but only seventy came, and even those, after a few days of work, insisted on a rise of four shillings, and as the gentleman did not comply at once, 'they set a piper amongst them and marched away'.[43] This story was also printed in the *Scotsman*, which in the same issue ran an editorial on it, which warned that the Highland Destitution Committee should 'exercise a very strict vigilance' and be 'firm to sterness' in order to prevent the money for relief from being 'converted into an encouragement to idleness and dishonesty'.[44] The editor cited further examples of Highlanders avoiding work, either by returning home or by not taking it up at all. The reason given, stated the *Scotsman*, was that 'they would get "plenty of porridge" at home for nothing'.

II. 'Vicious dirty race'

Meanwhile, perhaps the most concentrated campaign ever was being waged against the Highland Gaels in the pages of the *Scotsman* and the *Fifeshire Journal*. Both papers sent their 'special commissioner' and 'correspondent' on a tour to investigate the real state of Highland destitution. The two men knew each other well. The *Scotsman*'s commissioner was a former editor of the *Fifeshire Journal*, whose present editor was now his companion, as becomes clear from their almost identical itinerary.[45] The views expressed in the two series of letters are extreme, often verging on racism, and, within the hostile press, make some of the most incredible reading of the period.

The *Scotsman*'s commissioner was James Bruce, a well-known journalist, who first took up journalism in his native city of Aberdeen. He was editor of the *Fifeshire Journal* from 1840 to 1847 then, after his appointment to investigate the state of Highland destitution, the *Scotsman* commissioned him to report on the moral and sanitary conditions of Edinburgh. Afterwards he edited a number papers including the *Madras Atheneaum*, and the *Northern Whig*. According to his obituary in the *Scotsman*, he was 'one of the most remarkable men . . . both in intellect and scholarship . . . that the newspaper ever [employed]'. And as a man, he 'had a heart utterly free of guile and hatred'.[46] Perhaps this was true of Bruce generally, but not when it came to the Highland Gaels. In his famous series of letters in 1847 as the *Scotsman*'s commissioner, later published in pamphlet form, he exhibited a prejudice and hatred towards the Highlanders.

Between the end of January and beginning of March James Bruce sent fifteen long letters from his tour around the western isles of Mull and Skye, and from Ross-shire on the mainland.[47] His appointed task was to make personal observations and inquiries as to the condition of the people in the Highlands and Islands and the extent of destitution there. At first he was relatively restrained. He interviewed various people, described the extent of the Famine and concluded that the distress was indeed great. He also talked to the local people, who effectively blamed the Clearances and landowner-ship for their problems, telling him that 'the ruin of the people in Skye is that there are whole miles of the country with nothing but sheep and gentlemen upon them, and no room for any to work at home'.[48] Bruce was 'as much pleased as surprised' that some people expressed a willingness to work and that such opinions were being given expression. Two days later, however, in his second letter, the tone changed considerably, and Bruce no longer had anything positive to say about the Celtic inhabitants. Perhaps, stranded as he was on Mull due to the 'boisterous state of the weather', he had become irritated by 'the ugly and offensive language of Ossian'. While waiting for better weather, he visited a few 'miserable huts' and his horror began to rise. He was lost for words in recounting what he saw: 'an indescribable piece of furniture which served as a bed', and 'a creature' who turned out to be a nephew. The more he saw, the more convinced he became that 'there *is* idleness in the distressed districts'. By the end of his second letter he lost his restraint and expressed his distaste in a long denunciation:

> I have seen stout men crying about destitution, and at the same time refusing to do a piece of work at anything like a working Lowlander would consider a fair remuneration. I have seen men able to work going about the whole with their hands in their pockets, and *only relieving the monotomy of their idleness by resorting to cunning* and low imposition on strangers. . . .
>
> I know that all this evidence is quite in the teeth of all that Highlanders tell us of themselves – of their noble pride, their manly independence, and so on – but I know also, that what is considered respectable in the Highlands would be called meanness in the Lowlands. I know that what is called working in the Highlands would be called play in the Lowlands. That the Highlanders have pride, he would be a bold man to dispute; but there may be a fair difference of opinion on the question whether the pride of the Highlanders has yet taken a proper direction – a direction by which society is benefited . . . His pride, it may be submitted, would be more noble itself, more to his credit, and much more for the good of the society, if it would make him too proud to remain the starving indolent serf of a mighty chief, with centuries of ancestors of unpronouncable names – if it would make him *proud enough to remove with his family* to a locality where a comfortable livelihood is to be had for hard labour . . .

The climax of the whole tirade was remarkable:

> I know that by praising Highlandmen a reward may be obtained, and that for telling the truth, and for attempting to do them good, a man will incur their mortal enmity. Yet *it is a fact that morally and intellectually they are an inferior race to the Lowland Saxon* – and that before they can in a civilised age be put in a condition to provide for themselves and not to be throwing themselves on the charity of the hard-working Lowlander, *the race must be improved by a Lowland intermixture*, their habits, which did well enough in a former stage of society, must be broken up by the force of Lowland example . . .[49]

If 'racialism' or 'racism' had been nineteenth-century terms, Bruce would have earned all claims to them. To a twentieth-century ear phrases like 'racial improvement by intermixture', and 'morally and intellectually inferior race' sound shocking or at least ominous. In Bruce's time their use was commonplace for Blacks, Indians, and similar 'natives'. Bruce simply lumped the Highland Gaels together with the much despised lower races of the time. They were racially inferior, in Bruce's eyes, with sins such as idleness inherent in their nature; therefore, they were useless in a developed and 'civilised' Britain. The solution the *Scotsman*'s commissioner suggested in the above passage was therefore either to change the character of the Celts (possibly by 'racial intermixture'), or to persuade them to move elsewhere. This was just the beginning of Bruce's tour, but his first two letters sum up his whole stance.

As Bruce continued his *Inquiry*, he made some remarkable observations about the physical appearance of the islanders. He found that idleness was 'marked in the very personal appearance of the most indigent of the male sex in the Highlands'.[50] While the industrious Lowlanders, 'even in the prime of their life', had bent backs and rounded shoulders, 'the effects of laborious and earnest employment', Bruce explained, in the Highlands he met no one like that, only men who walked 'as erect as an idle nobleman'. Bruce drew his conclusion: '. . . the real cause of their destitution is the idleness that is rooted in their very nature'. Therefore, he repeated, the remedy could only be that the 'Celtic nature' must be changed 'in great measure' if Highland destitution was ever to have an end. One way of achieving this change in the Celt's character was, Bruce suggested, to break up 'entirely, with a firm hand' the whole cottar system, which, according to Bruce, had 'fostered and cherished all the indolence of the Celtic character, and all the vices which follow in the train of indolence'.[51] Another possible way he suggested to change the Celtic character was education, though at the same time he was highly sceptical about the intellectual abilities of the Gaels.

As the commissioner proceeded on his tour, the words he chose to describe the Highlanders became increasingly gross and aggressive. On the third week of his journey he spoke of their wretchedness as being 'the fruit of no temporary calamity, but of the degradation, the deep ignorance, and the *real barbarism* of the people'.[52] He repeated several times how incredible it was to him to see so much 'degradation' and 'barbarism', which he had so far encountered only in travel books about uncivilised countries and savage tribes. A few passages later he said that 'stealing is far from uncommon'. A certain amount of vitriol began to creep into his statements: he said that the Highlanders' 'furniture is filth', their 'idea of happiness is inaction' and their 'antipathies are mainly directed against light and air'. And eventually he spelled it out all too clearly: 'the real truth [is] that the people of Skye are an indolent, ignorant, and *dirty race*, steeped in such wretchedness as never yet fell on a whole people'.[53]

The *Scotsman* commissioner's public abuse of the Gaels was only exceeded by one man: his colleague and travelling companion from the *Fifeshire Journal.* Compared with the *Fifeshire Journal*'s 'Notes of a Winter Tour', Bruce's letters were restrained and balanced. Being a much smaller and more marginal paper[54] than the *Scotsman,* it perhaps could afford to advocate more extreme views. However, the fact that the *Scotsman* chose the *Journal*'s editor as its special commissioner, and that other papers sometimes reprinted its articles, suggests that its influence was not as small as its circulation. Together with the *Perth Constitutional,* the *Fifeshire Journal* took the most extremist line in its contempt of the Highlanders.[55]

Soon after the *Scotsman* dispatched James Bruce on his Inquiry, the editor[56] of the *Fifeshire Journal* set off as well. He sent back six long letters during his two-week tour. At first he filled his correspondence mainly with descriptions of the scenery, which he found romantic. Soon, however, he started to visit 'wretched huts', like Bruce, an experience which brought him to similar conclusions to those of the *Scotsman* on the Gaels. He visited some of the very same huts as the *Scotsman*'s commissioner at Roag, near Dunvegan. They may well have visited them together, but while Bruce only briefly referred to the Gaels' 'antipathies . . . against light and air', he dwelt on them at great length, expressing much disgust:

> The most vivid description would not do justice to the extraordinary and disgusting filthiness of Roag . . . The people barricade themselves up behind their cows in the farthest and smallest end of the hut, and there the whole family sit in dirt, and smoke, and darkness, and stare from morning to night into a peat fire, and appear quite contented. The only things that they wish to protect, and defend themselves against, are the free air and the free light of Heaven, and the contact of clean water; and they constructed their horrid dens so as very effectually to keep off these blessings from coming near them.[57]

The most frequent adjectives which the *Journal*'s editor found appropriate for the Highlanders throughout his letters were 'degraded', 'perverse', 'vicious', and 'filthy'. And the fact that they seemed to him 'quite contented' in their 'degraded' state reinforced his belief in the Gaels' infamous laziness.

As the *Scotsman* blamed Celtic indolence for the plight of the High-landers, so did the *Fifeshire Journal*: 'The great cause of destitution is – not the failure of the potato crop last year, but – the intense and abominable idleness of the inhabitants'.[58]

> It is impossible for any working man . . . not to be filled with disgust and indignation at hearing what the men in these places have been accustomed to consider working . . . they sit in the other six months at the fire side literally doing nothing . . . Year after year they have submitted to the annual visitation of famine, and have folded their arms, and prayed for better times, but to put shoulders to wheel, to know that Providence helps those who help themselves, is a lesson which they have yet to be taught . . . they have no notion of praying to God to be delivered from the dreadful calamity of sloth – the curse that has fallen on their tribe.[59]

The expression of 'the curse' fallen on 'their tribe' not only suggested that the Highlanders were a barbarous people, but also implied that they must have committed some sin for which a 'curse' had been their punishment. This view sat well with other extreme views that the destitution was really a 'fruit' of the Highlanders' 'vices'.

The *Journal*'s editor also expressed one of the most recurrent themes in Lowland complaints against the Highlanders: their irregular work. Again, a clash of two worlds and cultures lay at the heart of this contention. The Highland work cycle was fundamentally different from the Victorian 'capitalist' work pattern, which was based on constant hard work, almost to a manic degree. The Highland work pattern was basically subsistence agriculture, a pastoral economy, which involved more work in the spring, summer and early autumn, but less in late autumn and the winter, when there was simply not much to do apart from feeding the animals. The hard-working Lowlanders found this 'sitting around' in the winter deeply offensive to their own principle of 'sustained' and regular work. Not everyone, however, drew such conclusions from this different work pattern as did the *Journal*'s writer. He took it as an obvious symptom of their inherent indolence, which also meant that it was their own fault that they could not 'get over' the Famine, and that they were 'hopeless' about ever coming out of their destitution:

> The consequences of the late failure in the potato crop a virtuous people would have got over; but here the calamity fell on a degraded and indolent race, and it crushed them to the ground . . . let no man imagine that all the subscriptions that can be raised will do more than give a very brief relief to

this people, or that the next winter will not be worse than this winter, whether the potato crop be good or bad. The whole wealth of the Lowlands, if it were now poured into the Highlands, would wither away, as if under a judgement from Heaven, amongst the idle hands of this people. No man has here the least intention of ever working more than six months a year. Under all their destitution, they are determined that for six months they will sit and look at the fire in their filthy huts.

To the topical 'what to do with the Highlanders' question, the *Journal*'s answer was a form of strict moral reformation. They had to be taught, the editor wrote in his last letter, that depending on one's neighbour's charity was as bad as theft, that he who did not 'strain every nerve and labour from sunrise to sunset' was 'worse than an infidel', and perhaps even more importantly, that 'all the talk' of their virtues, morals and religion was 'just as much nonsense and falsehood'. In other words, the *Journal*'s message to the Gaels was that they should admit that they were a horrible, dirty, lazy inferior race, and then quickly reform themselves for the benefit of Lowland society.

The effect of this tour by the correspondents of the *Scotsman* and the *Fifeshire Journal* was considerable. It was now becoming a firmly established notion in the hostile press that, as one of the *Journal*'s editorials put it, 'the causes of destitution really lie in the character and habits of the people', and consequently that charity was misdirected and, instead, a strict moral, if not even racial, improvement was needed.

The immediate effect of the *Scotsman*'s series was a flood of readers' reactions, mostly saying that they had been deluded and deceived, and now realised how unworthy the Highlanders were of Lowland assistance. One *Scotsman* reader from St Andrews, who signed himself 'A Lover of Justice and a Friend of the Distressed', wrote:

> The days of poetry and romance in the Highlands are gone. Love and innocence in a Highland glen are all very well; but the picture of your Commissioner of hulking dirty fellows, snuffing and smoking all day in a cottage, staring at a cow, with a dirty wife and eight children, reduces the Highlanders to a mere state of mortal men.[60]

The commissioner's views were not wholly palatable to everyone, though. As during *The Times* reports in 1846, too much racism was unacceptable even for the *Inverness Courier*. Although the *Courier* agreed that the Gaels were 'lazy', 'filthy' and 'degraded', it believed that these traits were not 'inherent' but due to their circumstances, therefore the Celts were 'improvable' and should be given encouragement. While agreeing with the *Scotsman* on the general condition of the Highlanders, the *Courier* consistently differed as to its cause:

> The 'Commissioner' complains that there is idleness in the distressed districts . . . We know that indolence is the bane of the poor Highlander; but what pains have been taken to make him better? He has never known the value of time or the effects of steady labour. Let him be instructed.[61]

The idea that general improvement of land and people was a possible remedy for the destitution was steadily held by the *Courier* throughout the decade. Other papers, however, were becoming increasingly impatient with the problem of Highland destitution, which showed no sign of improvement but was rapidly deteriorating in 1847.

That year saw perhaps the heaviest concentration of newspaper attention on Highland destitution. The sheer number of articles was twice that of the previous famine year and over three times more than the following years. From the *Scotsman*, the *Glasgow Herald*, and the *Inverness Courier*, down to the smaller papers like the *Perth Constitutional*, almost every issue contained articles on the Highland Famine, accompanied by extensive readers' correspondence. The attention was general and continuous, and left a lasting mark on Lowland public opinion.

The *Scotsman*'s and the *Fifeshire Journal*'s series of reports at the beginning of the year well represented the tone of the whole year, with a growing sense of impatience and hatred coupled with radical language. During this watershed year of a virtual flood of articles the main themes were the same. The 'indolence' of the Gaels was repeated again and again, the argument that their plight was exaggerated and the charitable public had therefore been deceived was growing into a virtual campaign, the principle of 'no relief without work' had become firmly established, and the idea that large-scale emigration was the best solution was gradually gaining credence. All these old arguments were now made with greater force and harsher language than ever before. But the new element was that most of them were now centred on the activities of the Central Board of Management for Highland Relief.

The Central Board was set up in February 1847 in order to co-ordinate and carry out the aims of the existing relief committees. It acted as a supervisory body over the committees, and was led by top government officials, such as Sir Charles Trevelyan, Assistant secretary to the Treasury. Relief operations were to be defined and supervised by the Central Board officials and implemented by the local committees. Responsibility for different regions was delegated to the two main committees in Glasgow and Edinburgh. The Glasgow 'Section' dealt with relief operations in the Outer and Inner Hebrides, except Skye, Argyll and western Inverness. The Edinburgh Section had Skye, Wester Ross and the eastern Highlands.

During 1846/47 the Central Board was able to dispose of an unusually large amount of public charity. By the end of 1847 the Board had over £200,000, which was 'probably the greatest single cash sum raised voluntarily in nineteenth century Scotland for the relief of distress'.[62] Meal was distributed through channels other than the Board and government depots, primarily by the landlords. The fact that no great mass of people died from starvation was largely due to the efforts of the committees, the Free Church, charities and landlords.

Meal purchased with the charity funds, however, was not to be distributed free; it was doled out as a form of payment for compulsory labour. Only as a last resort was meal ever given free. Such principles of relief were largely shaped by leading members of the Central Board and the Sections. One such person was the Glasgow Section secretary, Charles Baird, who had already been involved in the provision of relief during the famine of 1836–37. A pamphlet he co-authored in 1838 showed clearly not only the seeds of the main principles of relief during the Great Famine but also the different shades of opinion of the Highlanders a decade earlier. Baird in 1838 firmly believed that the Highlanders were indolent not because of some inherent vice or consequence of blood but because of the circumstances in which they had been placed. It was in the universal nature of man, Baird contended, that human beings would not exert themselves until 'stimulated by want, or by the effects of enlightened education and good example'.[63] The Highlanders ought to be given encouragement and inducement and they would not sink into 'cheerless apathy'.

This stance was similar to that taken by the *Inverness Courier*, and by the relief committees during the Great Famine. The difference was, however, that in 1836–37 encouragement and inducement were seen as gradual progress, mainly by education, example, and incentives, but by the period of the Great Famine relief officials as well as public opinion were urging more drastic methods. In addition, while in 1836–37 there was no talk at all about any apparent racial or cultural inferiority of the Gaels (neither Baird nor the 1830s press reports mentioned anything like 'inherent laziness' among the 'evils'), in the late 1840s it was a powerful recurring theme, not only in the press but among relief officials as well.

The three most influential government officials on the Central Board and main Sections – Sir Charles Trevelyan, William Skene and Sir John M'Neill – were far from immune to the prevaling ideas of the age, and their private correspondence reflected views similar to those expressed in the contemporary hostile press. Although Trevelyan regarded the Highlanders as originally well-disposed and 'very improvable', he still thought them indolent. Charity, therefore, would have been 'dangerous and degrading'. This firm conviction of the need for moral reform of the lazy Gaels served as justification for the implementation of harsher relief measures, in the form of compulsory labour.

On the principle of 'no food without labour' the contemporary hostile press fully agreed, since they had been advocating it ever since the Famine had broken out. Yet the Central Board was almost constantly under fire, especially from the *Scotsman*, and from papers such as the *Fifeshire Journal*, *Glasgow Citizen* and *Aberdeen Herald*. There were essentially two bones of contention between a large section of the press and the Board. One was the constant press criticism that the Board was not strict enough in implementing the 'work for food' principle, that it was too liberal with the Highlanders. Of all papers the *Scotsman* was the most persistent critic of the Board's activities, and played the role of a champion of truth throughout the year. It ran editorials on almost every single Board report or meeting, reminding its readers that its special commissioner had already said it all about Highland sloth, and that the Board should be very careful in administering relief. One consequence of the *Scotsman*'s constant criticism was that in early summer the Central Board appointed Captain Robert Elliot to inspect the Local Committees' relief administration. His report seemed to confirm the newspaper's allegations; he had found regulations being broken, maladministration, and too liberal provision of relief. A lengthy leader in the *Scotsman* reacted to these results with self-congratulation:

> Last winter, when we gave currency to statements from our 'Commissioner' and from other quarters, asserting that the distress was to a considerable extent *chronic*, and in great part attributable to the sloth of the population, and that therefore the committees should exercise great caution in their proceedings, a number of well-meaning people laughed at or condemned such a mode of viewing the subject.[64]

Now, however, the writer continued with glee, the findings of the Board seemed to make the same points, indicating the 'ignorance and sloth of the people as the main source of distress . . . these are the very points on which our 'Commissioner' and others mainly insisted'. By this time the *Scotsman* was using nearly every opportunity to repeat its principal theme; the racial inferiority of the Highland Gaels. The editorial continued:

> . . . the contrast which in almost every case you find existing between the habits and condition of the men of two races thus living side by side, point[s] pretty clearly to the main cause of destitution . . . The evil is in the character and the inveterate habits of the race.

During 1847, the *Scotsman* and some other papers reiterated this theme so frequently that the inferiority of the Highlanders had become almost a cliché. Soon, however, emotions surrounding the Highland question were to be fomented again.

The controversy broke out in early September when the Central Board announced the suspension of its operations, and from its new Report it became clear that it had a considerable surplus left from the accumulated relief funds. The surplus amounted to £114,000, which was some two thirds of the total collection. The Board's plan was to keep it in the bank and decide how it could best be used for the permanent improvement of the Highlands. It was also feared that, despite the apparent abatement, the Famine was likely to recommence the following year.

The *Inverness Courier*, whose basic stance on the Highlanders was similar to that of the Board, supported the plan, and actually welcomed the surplus, saying that it was better to do that than apply the full amount to 'injurious' charity. In an editorial the *Courier* argued that the surplus could be used to 'originate a better system' of permanent improvement:

> The money is safe in the bank, and we trust great care will be taken in its disposal. To accustom the people to charity, instead of depending on their own exertion, will be fatal to their character and habits; but public works might be instituted, with the co-operation and support of the proprietors, furnishing profitable employment for the people and conferring permanent advantages on the country. The chief object, at this crisis, should be to elevate the condition of the poorer classes, and prevent them, if possible, from being forever on the brink of famine.[65]

The *Courier's* stance on the use of the surplus was a direct consequence of its conviction that the Highlanders were improvable and should be given incentives instead of being dismissed as hopelessly inferior. In fact, as the campaign against the 'Highland sloth' grew increasingly spiteful, the *Inverness Courier* was becoming more and more sympathetic, though still largely patronising, towards the Gaels. This gradual and subtle change of attitude and tone of voice, which climaxed in the 1850s, started around the autumn of 1847 when this leader appeared:

> Let us endeavour to rescue that large portion of our countrymen – suffering and complaining – from their hapless condition, for ever on the brink of famine. We admit their want of energy and steady industry, but let us try to give them something to work for. Let them be instructed, assisted, and encouraged.

What was it that prompted this more sympathetic, almost patriarchal, sentiment in the editors of the *Courier*? It may well have been the sheer extent of the abuse that had erupted on the pages of other papers around the destitution fund surplus. Editorials and readers' letters on the pages of *Scotsman*, the *Fifeshire Journal*, the *Aberdeen Herald* and the *Glasgow Citizen* were crying deceit and urging that the funds be given back to the subscribers or used for the benefit of the Lowland poor.

Among the first papers to express strong indignation at the surplus was the *Aberdeen Herald*, which had a relatively large circulation of over 2,000:

> What a patient, long-suffering, forgiving animal the charitable public is! . . . No matter to what extent its goodness may have been abused – no matter how often and grossly it may have been deceived – its ear is still open to every tale of distress, fictitious or real, its hand ever ready to dole out charity, provided the appeal to its benevolence be sufficiently clamorous. Never has the amiable weakness of the charitable public been better exemplified than in the recent subscription for the relief of Highland destitution.[66]

The same fury at the deception of the Lowland public inspired the *Glasgow Citizen* to almost unparalleled sarcasm on the issue of Highland destitution. The *Citizen*, too, had a circulation of over 2,000, and was a supposedly 'progressive, tolerant, liberal'[67] newspaper:

> The fact of L.114,000 simmering savourily in Lowland coffers, and only awaiting the call of Highland want to irrigate with golden streams the misty valleys of the north and the breezy uplands of the west, will be borne along many a craggy shore as on the wings of the sea-gull, and up many a rugged path as in the footsteps of the red-deer. In the fishy wherry, in the reeky clachan, and on the boggy heath, it will be talked of in sputtering gutturals when ways are wintry and nights are drear. Celtic lads will sing of it to their mistresses. It will be the El Dorado of their sleeping and their waking dreams . . . With a large accumulated treasure set apart for their use, proclaimed as their own, and ready for their necessities, who can wonder if destitute

Highlanders should spring up, not here and there, or at decent intervals of time, but in multitudes and at once, like Roderick Dhu's men, when his whistle sounded, and the mountain side became a living mass?[68]

After this inspired poetic introduction, the *Citizen*'s editorial switched to a sterner tone and demanded that the money collected 'on false pretences' be returned to the pockets from which it had been 'wrongfully abstracted'. The surplus money, the editorial explained, no more belonged to the Highlanders than to 'the Hill Collies', or the subjects of 'Queen Pomare'; in other words, the Scottish Gaels were just as alien or foreign a people to the Scottish Lowlanders as some Asian or other far away, and presumably inferior, people.

Lowland indignation became so widespread after the Central Board decided to keep the surplus for the next year and use it for improvement schemes in the Highlands, that the *Scotsman* was able to reprint two articles from different papers in each issue during October. From the *Caledonian Mercury* to the *Elgin Courier*, and from the *Edinburgh Courant* to the *Dumfries Courier*, a host of papers were protesting against the surplus and demanding its refund to the Lowland population.

The *Scotsman* itself ran an editorial in almost every single issue during the autumn, variously denouncing the Central Board operations as 'pampering Highland laziness', a 'farce' or simply as 'humbug'. By this stage the *Scotsman* relentlessly called for an end to any relief for the Highlands, saying that it was time the Highlanders helped themselves: 'There always has been distress in the Highlands, and always will be, till the Highlands, freed from the cruel kindness of Destitution Committees, learn to help themselves'.[69]

As before, it was the *Fifeshire Journal* which expressed the most ruthless Lowland sentiments. A long editorial, which was also picked up by the *Perth Constitutional*, produced one of the fiercest tirades ever written on the Highlands.[70] It started off by referring to the *Scotsman*'s series of articles on the surplus, which had opened the eyes of the 'deluded public' to the 'gigantic . . . imposition' of the Central Board. One sin of the Board was, according to the *Journal*, that it deceived the public into giving charity to a people who 'neither deserved nor needed relief', and for whom charity 'proved a real curse by encouraging them in their vicious and beggarly habits'.

The leader then launched a remarkable diatribe:

. . . charity, like all former charities given to the Highlandmen, and like all alms bestowed on the undeserving, has just served to plunge them more and more into demoralisation and wretchedness, to make their wants greater and their clamours louder and more impudent. It is not more notorious that the sons of Ethiopia are black, than it is to all who know them, that High-landmen will not work if they can get their meat by any other means . . . It is an utter misapprehension of their true character to think that they do not like to live on charity. They like, and have always liked to get alms since the time they found it inconvenient to live on plunder . . .

The destitution of the Highlanders . . . is the natural and legitimate fruit of their national vices . . . there is abundant proof that laziness is the darling sin which the Highlandman cherishes amidst all his imagined piety and morality.[71]

After quoting from several letters from relief officials and clergymen on the idleness of the Highlanders, as further proof of the *Journal*'s point, the leader made perhaps the single most harsh statement ever on Highland destitution:

This wholesale robbery for the purpose of maintaining vicious idleness must be put an end to – the large sum of money on hand must be kept for some really benevolent purpose; and let it be known throughout all the lands and islands, from Oban to Lewes, that the industry and means of the Lowlands are no longer to be taxed to support the laziness of the Highlands. *Let those who will not work starve – their doom is just and righteous, and for the benefit of society.*

No other paper went as far as the *Journal* in saying 'let the Highlanders perish'. Hatred, abuse, anger and contempt would run high during this time, but no other correspondence or editorial would openly express such extreme views.

The flood of editorials was accompanied by a similar flood of readers' letters. During September and October the *Scotsman* sometimes published two or three letters per issue. These readers invariably demanded the Lowland money back and expressed their anger at having been deceived. Again, the idea that people in the Lowlands had nothing more to do with the Highlanders than with some other far away natives of the world was clearly present in some of these letters. As a *Scotsman* reader, signed 'One of the Deluded', put it:

At all events, we protest against the application of our money to any such purpose as the Committee seem to contemplate. The destitution of the Highlands having been relieved, they have no more right to employ the surplus funds in carrying out their crotchets for the prospective improve-ment of Kamschatka or Tahiti.[72]

Other readers, such as the one signed 'Warm to the Tartan', protested that the subscribers had not been consulted on what to do with the money.[73] There were also people writing in who, in their anger, went as far as suggesting that the Highlanders were actually 'better fed and cared for during this year of famine than during years of plenty', and warned that, after this deceit, the public would 'never again be duped'.[74] Most readers agreed that the money refunded should be used to relieve the poor at their own doorstep, and given, for instance, to the local infirmaries.

The fury and controversy around the Destitution Surplus were not confined to the respectable broadsheets alone. They grew to such an extent that they reached down to the largest popular miscellany, the *Chambers Edinburgh Journal.* Compared with the broadsheets, the *Chambers Journal* had an enormous weekly circulation of 55,000, and it was one of the most successful Scottish literary and useful knowledge miscellanies of the decade. Although it was primarily an educational magazine touching few current topics, the case of the Destitution Fund surplus was picked up by this paper as well. Its views were midway between those of the *Inverness Courier* and the *Scotsman.*

The *Chambers Journal* shared the *Scotsman*'s conviction that charity was injurious, and that the Highland destitution was exaggerated, and it talked about the 'strange manoeuvres of the supposedly destitute Highlanders'. But at the same time it took the *Inverness Courier* line in blaming circumstances rather than the Highlanders' character or 'inherent nature' for their destitution: 'We are not disposed to speak severely of a people who have many claims on our sympathy, and who may be said to have been demoralised by a train of circumstances over which they could exert no proper control'.[75]

While a large part of the controversy arose from Lowland anger that the Highland destitution had been exaggerated and that the Highlanders were 'undeserving' anyway, a significant part of the intense criticism was the allegation that the Board intended to use the surplus for the improvement of Highland estates rather than the alleviation of distress. Critics pointed to plans for road building and drainage on Highland estates out of Lowland charity funds. In this sense, part of the controversy was directed more against the Highland landowners than against the Highland poor. The radical *Glasgow Argus* put this clearly in an editorial:

> . . . the industrious professional man, or the prudent merchant, who has parted with his money, will be asking where it goes, and who is to profit by it; and a more unpleasant inquiry for the Highland proprietors, who, it

seems, are in some shape or other to get the greater part of the money, could not be instituted. It will then be found that after paying our own poor-rates – poor-rates aggravated in amount by the number of the Highlanders sent among us from the cleared estates – we subscribe to make roads and fences for men who derive large incomes from their property, and pay their paupers a maximum allowance of ten shillings a year.[76]

The *Argus* was not alone in pointing out this extraordinary use of the relief funds. While the Central Board would justify such use by arguing that giving employment to the people was part of the programme for their moral reformation, much of the press would not swallow this argument. The *Scotsman* was a constant critic, but so were smaller papers such as the *Elgin Courier*:

> That a body of intelligent gentlemen, appointed to administer funds for the destitute inhabitants of the Highlands and Islands should attempt to assume the management of Highland property, simply because they happen to have the command of a large sum of money raised for charitable purposes, seems to us, eventful as the times are, the most extraordinary occurrence of the day.[77]

By early 1848 Lowland hostility towards Highland destitution and the Relief Board was significant. In many papers the general consensus of editors and readers appeared to be that no more charity should be given to the Highlands. It was a 'cry wolf' message that the *Scotsman* and several other papers sent from their pages to the Central Board, reminding them that the Lowland public was not going to credit any longer their 'stories' about destitution, and that they were not willing to finance Highland estate improvement under pretence of relieving distress.

The Central Board did not appear to be much affected by the ongoing campaign of criticism when in January 1848 it resumed its relief operations. Ambitious schemes for the strict moral improvement of the Highlanders – on Lowland charity funds – were continued with increased determination to an even more stringent programme. The two central factors were the 'destitution test' and 'co-operation' between landlords and the Board.

The new 'Destitution Test' was effectively a nineteenth-century equivalent of forced labour: starving people were only given food if they worked for it on some road construction on the estate. A pound of meal, 'a bare subsistence', was given in exchange for a whole day's work. That amount of meal was half of the prison fare, as critics had pointed out. And not even this whole amount of food was given if the Board's inspectors decided that the labourers did not give 'sufficient work', in which case those people 'persisting in indolent habits' could be struck off the roll of recipients.[78] The meal could also be stopped if the inspectors were not satisfied with the improvement on the part of the recipients, if, for instance, they did not find their houses clean enough, as Rule 8th stated in the instructions to sub-inspectors: 'the house must be clean, and the pool of water and dirt removed from before the door, or else their meal will be stopped'.[79] At the worst periods of the Famine the majority of the destitute were fed by the Board according to this system. In the spring of 1849, for instance, almost four fifths of the people of Barra, two thirds of the inhabitants of Skye and half of the people of Wester Ross were receiving the Central Board's 'meagre pittances'.[80]

Roads built by these people in North Uist and Harris came to be called 'the destitution road' or 'committee road'. Although these roads were not useless, there were instances of forced labour in the service purely of an idea. In North Uist near Scolpach, for example, a round tower, dubbed by locals 'the folly', in the middle of a small loch, was built in this way by the destitute islanders.

The theory behind the severe Destitution Test was that only those truly in a condition of severe destitution would accept relief on these terms, and that the destitute had to pay 'their debt to the society by work'.[81] The officials of the Board, who were the main ideologists behind these schemes, were driven by missionary zeal. As William Skene, the Secretary of the Edinburgh Section, put it in a private letter to Trevelyan: '. . . the stringent nature of the test may appear harsh and unfeeling . . . yet we are consulting the best interests of the people in enforcing it and they will in time find their permanent advantage in what we are now doing'.[82]

The Destitution Test was of course a direct consequence of the contemporary assessment of the Highlanders as inherently lazy and inferior beings who needed a lesson in industry. Their 'indolence' was considered a 'moral disease', which was best cured by a strict regimen of 'the task of at least eight hours' hard work'.[83] Compulsory labour for food was part of an extraordinary scheme of social engineering.

Part of this scheme was cooperation between landlords and the Board. Landlords shared the costs of relief, but the work done by the destitute in return for their meal was devoted to estate improvement in the form of road building, trenching and drainage. This practice, even before it was officially named the 'co-operative system', had been strongly criticised in the press, and now, the outcry was equally great.

The Board defended the system by arguing that the public works, such as roads and fishery piers, were 'beneficial to the whole community' and that the proprietors did not derive an 'exclusively private advantage'.[84] But the papers would not accept it. The *Aberdeen Herald* took to capital letters (an unusual practice at the time) to express its indignation: '. . . this is what has been accomplished: "THE VALUE OF LAND HAS BEEN RAISED IN ALL THESE QUARTERS"!'[85] Ironically, this was actually quoted from a self-congratulatory report of the Board.

The Central Board was by and large satisfied with the effects of the new system. The immediate result was a decline in the numbers on the relief lists, which the inspectors took as proof of the efficiency of the system. They were also well satisfied with what they saw as the true long-term aim: the reformation of the Highlanders themselves.

The initial reports were especially enthusiastic. After a tour of inspection in March 1848 Captain Elliot told the meeting of the Edinburgh Section that he had witnessed a change for the better, and the Highlanders had now entered a 'transition state'. 'They were now seeing the necessity of throwing off their former habits; . . . and were also turning their attention more to hard labour'.[86] By the end of the year the report of the committee of management of the Board expressed a great deal of satisfaction with the results: 'The strict enforcement of the labour test has . . . done much to make those under its influence better workers, and to break down, in some degree, their idle habits and indolence of disposition'.[87]

The moral reformation of the Gaels seemed to have begun. However, the distress did not go away, but persisted year after year. At the same time, when the Board's reports spoke of the success of the moral improvement scheme, they had to admit that 'the present condition and the future prospects of the people [were] gloomy indeed'.[88] Destitution still existed, the potato crop was still failing, and despite all the improvement schemes of trenching, drainage and road building, the state of the Highland poor only deteriorated.

The bubble burst. The time arrived when many simply gave up on the Highlands. From 1849 a sense of frustration at the failure of so many repeated efforts came to the fore among relief officials, landlords and the public. There was less and less talk about improvement, and more and more about emigration, as the only real solution for the Highlands.

This giving up on Highland improvement was linked to more radical attitudes towards the Gaels. While at the beginning of the period they were regarded as inferior but 'improvable', a few years later, after the often racist campaigns of the *Scotsman* and other papers, the Highland Gaels were

CONTEMPT

increasingly seen as a 'vicious dirty race', inherently inferior and therefore beyond improvement. The only solution suggested from the early 1850s onward was to get rid of these 'burdensome' and 'useless' people. Emigration as the only permanent remedy was the new magic formula.

III. Removing the 'diseased part'

> Collective emigration is, therefore, the removal of a diseased and damaged part of our population. It is a relief to the rest of the population to be rid of this part.[89]

Quote in Scotsman

This harsh contention came from a pamphlet by a certain Mr. Burton in 1851 and gained a wider audience through the pages of the *Scotsman*, with the paper's full endorsement.[90] By the 1850s it was far from a marginal view.

The *Scotsman* and Burton were not alone in their belief that the Highland Gaels formed some sick and rotten part of the 'superior' and 'healthier' population of Britain. Many other newspapers and their readers, as well as landlords and relief officials, shared the same view. The Highland Gaels were increasingly pronounced a 'surplus' and 'useless' population best got rid of.

Those who in the 1840s campaigned for the moral and social reformation of the Highland Celts now gave up and dismissed any further attempts as futile and hopeless. Even the former relief officials of the Central Board now decided that emigration was the only remaining option and they began planning grandiose schemes of population transportation to Australia. The Chairman of the Highland Emigration Society, Sir Charles Trevelyan, Assistant Secretary to the Treasury, reckoned that at least 30,000 people constituted 'surplus' population and spoke of the need for a 'national effort' which would 'rid our operatives of the swarming Irish and Scotch Celts'.[91]

Trevelyan's prejudices, typical of the age, were reflected widely in the pages of many contemporary newspapers. The *Scotsman* editorial quoted at length from Burton's pamphlet, which argued strongly in favour of getting 'rid of' the useless Highland Gaels. The 'uselessness' of the Highlanders here was directly linked to their race, just as previously their destitution was also seen as race related:

> It would be invidious to say what it is that makes a part of the population thus a burden. Some people say that it is the effect of race; and they point to the Celts of Kerry and of Barra, distant some four hundred miles from each

other, yet precisely in the same condition of hopeless, listless, actionless, useless penury . . . It is enough for the present purpose to keep in view that there *are* classes of this kind, and to consider how far their removal from the country is the proper remedy for the evil . . . It becomes clear at once that it is the interest of the productive members of society to get rid of all these classes.[92]

The *Scotsman*'s editorial reiterated the same point, impressing upon its readers that the root of the evil was in the difference of race: 'On one side of the Firth of Clyde, you find the county of Ayr, teeming with industry and plenty, and on the other, the county of Argyle, rotting in idleness and famine'. Again, the image of rotting and disease, originally applied to the potatoes during the famine, was now extended to the people themselves. And while racialist overtones had been equally present from the mid-1840s, race was now becoming the basis for deciding who was 'useless' and best 'got rid' of in the interest of the 'useful', 'productive' section of society.

One consequence of these extreme views was a new wave of clearances: a 'fantastically dynamic brutalist expulsion'.[93] Clearances were now directly linked to forced emigration, and people were cleared in order to be pushed onto ships to Canada or Australia.

The first widely known case in this period was the Sollas or North Uist evictions in August 1849. The Sollas case signalled a new era of forced removals, leading to some of the worst clearances in Knoydart and Greenyards in the early 1850s. It was a widely publicised clearance, mainly because it involved considerable resistance and violence. The *Inverness Courier* dispatched its own reporter and wrote several long editorials on it; the *Glasgow Herald* reprinted in full the *Courier*'s long despatches and even the *Scotsman* took much of the reporting, although not the editorial comments from the *Courier*.

Sollas was a district of North Uist, a long sandy bay studded with crofts, with a population of about 600 people. It belonged to the estate of Lord Macdonald but was, like many other Hebridean estates, under trust, administered by the agents of trustees for the creditors of the landowner.

Macdonald and the agents planned to remove 400–500 people from the estate and send them off to Canada, but the people refused to go. They threatened 'instant death' to any officer who should attempt to evict them. After the first attempt some officers stayed overnight in order to try again the following day, but the people surrounded the place where they slept, threw stones and eventually compelled them to flee. The *Inverness Courier* reported from the scene that 'a spirit of determination possessed the people' and that their numbers had swelled to several hundreds.[94] Its correspondent then went on to suggest that some external political 'demagogue' must have been at work behind the scene:

> Their conduct altogether was very unlike what Highlanders might be expected to exhibit, and some mischievous demagogue must have been amongst them. *One man said that before they would be turned out, they would do as the Hungarians did with the Austrians!*[95]

It seems extraordinary that on this remote Hebridean island crofters would evoke a war of independence raging in the heart of central Europe. However, 'the springtime of peoples', the series of revolutions in 1848, did hold the attention of the whole of Europe, including Britain, which traditionally managed to avoid any revolutionary convulsion. All Scottish papers devoted large sections to reports of events on the Continent. By July 1849 only Hungary held out in the struggle for a modern civic state and political independence.

The Scottish papers, especially the *Inverness Courier*, were fascinated by the 'Hungarian struggle' and drew romantic parallels between past Scottish rebellions and the struggle for independence. Oddly, therefore, the Hebrides and Hungary were not as far apart in the mind of the Scottish public as they would have appeared on the map. Determination to fight against 'oppression' linked the North Uist crofters and the Hungarian freedom fighters in 1849, at least in the crofters' minds.

The following day resistance grew further in North Uist. Macdonald's commissioner, Mr Cooper, returned with thirty-six constables from Inverness and 'expressed his intention to proceed with the ejectment of the whole population of the district of Sollas, unless the offers previously made by him to the people as to emigration were agreed to'.[96] However, the crofters 'resolutely persisted in refusing to leave the island' despite Cooper's 'renewed attempts to obtain the consent of the people to emigrate'.[97] They at least wanted to stay until the next season, saying that it would be too late to start in a new country. But Cooper would not consent to this.

The following day Cooper returned with the police force and 'the work of ejectment then began'.[98] The all-too-common scenes took place: furniture thrown out, bothies left roofless, weeping mothers with infants in their arms evicted, and old, infirm people not spared either. However, as the evictions proceeded a hostile crowd gathered at a distance and started to shout and throw stones at the police force. The crowd soon grew into a 'band of from fifty to one hundred women, with a few boys and men', and armed with large stones they compelled the removal men to run for shelter.

The police then charged and took several people prisoners. The evictions were then resumed but the women kept up their resistance and they were forcibly removed.

The resistance and violence eventually persuaded Cooper to allow the people to stay until the following spring on condition that they committed themselves to emigrate afterwards. In several instances people refused to give a written promise to emigrate 'until steps had been taken [regarding] the destruction of the unwilling party's house'.[99]

The Sollas evictions once again focused press attention on the general condition of the Highlands and on the old debate of whether or not the Clearances and emigration were economic and social necessities.

The *Scotsman* was adamant that the Clearances and emigration were the only solution, and were beneficial for all. It had long maintained that the Highlands were not viable economically and that a social reformation was necessary for the 'lazy' Highlanders by removing them from their 'scene of idleness'. An editorial on the Sollas evictions firmly repeated the *Scotsman*'s basic stance on the Clearances by saying: 'That the removal of the cottars in the Western Highlands will generally be a benefit to the land, and through that to the country at large, is, we fear, *indisputable*'.[100]

The *Inverness Courier*'s stance was not so extreme. In fact, it was around this time that the paper began to exhibit the first signs of a shift from contempt towards sympathy. The paper, which previously fully supported the Highland landowners, now warned in an editorial that 'the extra-ordinary power possessed by one individual' was 'anomalous' and should be 'exercised with great moderation and humanity'.[101] Then it went on to call for 'some new system of management', arguing that under the present system of southern trustees there was no sympathy for the Highlanders:

> When the lands are heavily mortgaged, the obvious, though *harsh* resource, is *dispossessing* the smaller tenants, to make room for a better class able to pay rent, and this task generally devolves on south-country managers or trustees, *who look only to money returns, and cannot sympathise with* the peculiar situation and *feelings* of the Highland population.[102]

There was a slight shift here not only in opinion but also in language, suggesting a more sympathetic tone than before. The highlighted words in the above passage were typical of the language of the sympathetic papers. From the end of 1849 the *Courier* developed a growing sense of sympathy towards the Highland Gaels, and by 1853 its stance was much closer to that of the generally sympathetic papers than to the hostile ones such as the *Scotsman*. While the *Scotsman* and other papers campaigned heavily for a forced emigration scheme, the *Courier* raised its voice against 'an extensive and systematic expatriation of the people'.[103] While maintaining that emigration in certain cases was indeed inevitable, the paper's Skye Correspondent in 1849 warned against any harsh methods:

> . . . emigration and colonisation in particular, are not to be discouraged, but should be carried out for the benefit of the part of the people themselves who emigrate, and also for the future advantage of the nation at large. There is, however, a right and a wrong way of doing even what may be proper in itself; and I maintain that *it is not the right way to conduct such important matters, to neglect, and harass, and grind down, and then forcibly, in a manner, to expatriate the people* who are thus sent forth.[104]

The *Courier* also continued to argue for improvement at home rather than immediate emigration. It increasingly advocated granting leases with a 'fixity of tenure', a demand which featured so largely during the crofters' war in the 1880s. An editorial in early 1850 pointed out that its Skye Correspondent's 'persevering advocacy of leases' won the support and sympathy of the Relief Board. It quoted the Board's report, in which Captain Elliott stressed the need for fixity of tenure by saying: '. . . there is one keystone to every exertion on the part of the crofter – open to all – and that is, granting security of tenure by leases'.[105] The *Courier's* editorial then characteristically summed up the paper's basic stance on the core problem of Highland destitution:

> The great argument for the granting of leases is, that as it legally secures to the tenant the fruit of his own and his family's industry, it supplies the most powerful of all motives for exertion, that of self-interest. The Highland race has been branded as indolent beyond belief; and at first sight a stranger might reasonably suppose that good cause existed for the charge. Neglected and depressed in spirit and means, they have not always done as much for themselves as they might have done; but experience has shown that under direction, and with a palpable reward before them, they prove apt, active, and persevering workmen.[106]

This was the *Courier's* old paternalistic line but with growing sympathy in its tone.

Soon, however, the debate over whether improvement with leases or large-scale emigration was the answer to the Highland problem became overshadowed by yet another outbreak of severe destitution. The potato crop failed again in the summer of 1850. Reports by August were unanimous that the disease had struck once more:

The existence of the potato blight is no longer matter of doubt. Blackened tops, shrivelled leaves, a putrid smell, and even diseased tubers, are the too sure indications of the re-appearance of this mysterious spoiler of the poor man's food . . . A poor cottar or crofter walks of an evening with pride and hope through his little patch of blooming and healthy potatoes, and rises next morning to have his hope dispelled, and his honest pride supplanted by soreness of heart, when he sees the midnight doings of the unsparing visitant.[107]

The severity of the situation was coupled with the fact that the Destitution Fund was exhausted and the Relief Board had announced that its operations would cease entirely at the end of 1850.

By this time the Board was determined that the Highlanders should not receive any more aid but be finally left to their own 'exertions'. At a meeting in Edinburgh members of the Board expressed their satisfaction that the Highlanders had been given a 'lesson' by 'the late destitution', and that the improvements would have beneficial results.[108] The Board members were also adamant that the termination of relief by the end of the year should be made very clear to the people. Instead of relying on relief they were to help themselves, now armed with the useful 'lessons' they had received. As the Board's Chairman put it at the meeting:

. . . it was absolutely necessary that the people should know that there was to be no further relief given; the board could not do so without another appeal for a national subscription, and that would not be so easily raised. The Highlanders must be taught to aid themselves, not only by their own individual exertions, but by the instructions they have of late received.[109]

Further relief would only 'depress the condition of the population and perpetuate their dependence on other means of subsistence', the Board's report concluded at the end of year.

The *Scotsman* was triumphant at the Board's report. 'We predicted it four years ago', its editorials kept trumpeting, referring to their many calls to stop relief and leave people to themselves. Despite all the public expenditure the situation was worse than before, the paper insisted: '. . . the money is done and the people are as bad as ever as to destitution and worse than ever as to demoralisation'.[110] Aid, philanthropy, relief societies, attempts at improvement would all be in vain, the *Scotsman*'s editor asserted later. 'In the end, the cure will come only through the wholesome processes of nature', he concluded.[111] The idea that the 'wholesome processes of nature' would cure social evils, bringing solutions which human intervention could not manage, was *laisser-faire* liberalism in the extreme, with an added element of social Darwinism.[112]

Meanwhile, 'the processes of nature' were at work in the Highlands in the form of growing starvation and destitution. By spring 1851 the destitution was widespread and newspaper reports became increasingly alarming. The *Glasgow Citizen* reported several cases of death by starvation and described an 'appalling calamity', with 'emaciated countenances' and 'wide-spread and utter want'.[113]

The *Glasgow Herald*, previously unsympathetic to the Highlanders, now ran heartrending reports in order to 'effectually plead the cause of these suffering Islanders with the humane'.[114] A letter from Skye described the state of the inhabitants in a highly emotional passage: 'I could not help shedding tears . . . while listening to their woeful statement, cries of famishing children, dreadful are the cries of the poor people'.

The prospect of yet another year of severe destitution loomed large while pressure from the press and public opinion were increasingly of the view that only emigration could relieve the problem of the Highlands. The final, official verdict came with Sir John M'Neill's *Report to the Board of Supervision in Scotland* in July 1851. The *Report* dismissed charitable relief and declared that assisted emigration was the only remaining solution.

Sir John M'Neill, Chairman of the Board of Supervision of the Scottish Poor Law, set out on his special inquiry into the distressed western Highland districts in February 1851 and spent three months investigating the condition of twenty-seven parishes. The subject of the inquiry was the extent of the distress and the possible means to avert it.

The first conclusion M'Neill made was that there were too many people and too little employment for them. The second was the old argument that charity and 'eleemosyonary aid' had an injurious effect on the character of the people because it made them dependent on external assistance rather than relying on their own efforts. Aid had a 'demoralising effect', and now people would actually exaggerate their poverty in order to get relief, the *Report* suggested:

> . . . Men of all classes and denominations concur almost unanimously in the opinion that the relief thus administered had a prejudicial effect on the character and habits of the people; that it induced them to misrepresent their circumstances, with a view to participate in it; and caused them to relax their exertions for their own maintenance. The extent to which they had become demoralised frequently extorted from the older inhabitants expressions of bitter lamentation . . . the fact is unquestionable, that a people who

some years ago carefully concealed their poverty, have learned to parade, and, of course, to exaggerate it.[115]

The final and most important conclusion was that the population could not be made self-sustaining unless a 'portion' was removed. Even the people themselves saw this necessity, M'Neill asserted: 'The working classes in many parishes are convinced that the emigration of a part of their number affords the only prospect of escape from a position otherwise hopeless'.[116] Systematic and assisted emigration was the only possible solution, the *Report* concluded, and it urged the government to act immediately:

> If emigration is necessary to the well-being of the population, and to their extrication from their present difficulties, there can be no doubt that the sooner that measure is put in operation the better for all parties.[117]

M'Neill estimated that in some parishes more than half the inhabitants would want or need to emigrate, but left 'the nature and amount of interference' to the government's discretion. Removal of some portion of the population was absolutely necessary to avert 'some fearful calamity', he concluded.

What M'Neill said in his *Report* was nothing new. Leading newspapers like the *Scotsman* had been pressing the same argument for years, but the *Report* now firmly established an official policy. It led to the passage of the Emigration Advances Act which gave cheap loans to landowners to assist emigration from their estates.[118] The *Report* and M'Neill himself also played an important part in the formation of the Highland and Island Emigration Society.

Emigration was the new magic formula. Improvement or alternative employment was almost entirely abandoned. The Highlands were declared hopeless. M'Neill's *Report* reinforced the stance of many newspapers, which were now even more eager to urge extensive schemes for the 'removal of the surplus population'. At the very same time as the M'Neill *Report* was published, a powerful article in the respected London *Athenaeum* was reprinted in several Scottish newspapers: in the *Scotsman, Glasgow Herald* and *Fifeshire Journal.* It conveyed well the prevailing sense of despair and the urgently felt need to get rid of this burdensome 'surplus' population:

> *But nothing will work well in these remote districts, every report has to make known the failure of all attempts to meet a growing evil, we begin to fear that these benevolent efforts tend only to prolong the action of a disease which requires sharper and more effective remedies.* Statesmen should go to the heart of the

question: will the soil support the increased number of inhabitants or will it not? If it will, the causes which at present prevent its doing so might be discovered and removed. If it will not, *the Government should carry away at once all the surplus population* to some of the healthy and productive islands and continents which constitute our colonial empire.[119]

The major Scottish papers now launched a campaign for extensive emigration. The *Scotsman* felt its day had finally arrived: the M'Neill *Report* justified its old arguments. Now the paper could go further and make it clear that extensive emigration should also serve to drive out the 'inferior' Celtic race. In a series of articles throughout the summer it reiterated assertions about the inferiority, barbarity, and habitual idleness of the Celts, and rejoiced that 'the public had made up its mind no longer to support the idle Highlander, and that *he must go or starve*'.[120] The editor was jubilant that a 'turning point' had been reached and that 'people talk of emigration as inevitable'.[121] The editorial saw emigration as the fulfilment of a natural process in which the idle race of Celts was finally driven out by the industrious Saxon. In one of the most remarkable passages, the paper painted a picture of the racial decay of the Celts as a consequence of modern political economy:

> In fact, *the utilitarian march of Lowland enterprise must inevitably settle this question by the imperious laws of political economy,* and the function of the philanthropist will not be in attempting to prevent the conversion of the paddocks into sheep-walks – for that must take place – but in the modification of the process by mercy and kindness to the poor Celt. Gradually he was driven from the flat country to the mountain because an active energetic people could apply the plain to use. The same people now find in sheep-farming a use for the mountain, and, *by the gradual industrial pressure which drives the idle out of the heritage of industry, the Celt must give up the mountain to the sheep-farmer. He must be 'improved out',* as the Americans call it . . .[122]

The *Fifeshire Journal,* as so often, went even further. Only a few days after the *Scotsman's* article, the *Journal's* editorial echoed the same idea of the inferior Celt being driven out by the superior Saxon. As in the 1840s, it was again the *Fifeshire Journal* which took the most hostile line:

> Ethnologically the Celtic race is an inferior one, and attempt to disguise it as we may, there is naturally and rationally no getting rid of *the great cosmical fact that it is destined to give way – slowly and painfully it may be, but still most certainly – before the higher capabilities of the Anglo-Saxon.* In the meantime,

and apparently *as a part of the natural law which had already pushed the Celt from continental Europe westward, emigration to America is the only available remedy for the miseries of the race,* whether squatting listlessly in filth and rags in Ireland, or dreaming in idleness and poverty in the Highlands and Islands of Scotland.[123]

This amounted to nothing less than the theory of race decay. For the *Journal*'s editor and many others, emigration was part of a 'natural' and 'cosmical' law by which the inferior Celtic race was inevitably doomed to extinction. Facilitating it, therefore, was merely acting out a universal fate. It was now in the name of the 'natural law' that the 'unhealthy' Celtic inhabitants of the Highlands had to be cleared off to other parts of the world.

Practice soon followed theory. Extensive emigration schemes and unprecedentedly brutal evictions ensued, becoming the predominant features until the mid-1850s.

The most ambitious scheme came from Sir Charles Trevelyan, formerly one of the main figures behind the Central Board. By 1852 he was Chairman of the London Committee of the Highland and Island Emigration Society, and soon became 'the fundamental influence on the whole Society's future development'.[124] Trevelyan aimed at nothing less than providing 'a final settlement' of the Highland problem by transporting a 'surplus' of 30–40,000 people to Australia at a cost of £100,000.[125]

Although Trevelyan, like many others involved in Highland emigration schemes, often emphasised that large-scale emigration was also beneficial for the people themselves and was an economic necessity, one of his letters reveals a clearly racist motivation behind his scheme. In this letter in 1852 he 'contemplated with satisfaction'

. . . the prospects of flights of Germans settling here in increasing number – an orderly, moral, industrious and frugal people, *less foreign to us than the Irish or Scotch Celt,* a congenial element which will readily assimilate with our body politic.[126]

Trevelyan planned to settle the industrious, superior Germans in place of the lazy, inferior Celts. This flew in the face of the 'overpopulated Highlands' argument. For Trevelyan, the Highlands were not actually overpopulated but populated by the *wrong kind of people.* The Celts were 'foreign' to the rest of Scotland and should therefore go somewhere else. Trevelyan wanted to see a 'less foreign' race of people in the Highlands, superior Saxons rather than inferior Celts.

Trevelyan was not only one of the most powerful members of the Highland and Island Emigration Society but was primarily a prominent government servant in the Treasury. This 'intimate connection' between the Emigration Society and officers of the State effectively made the Society more than just a private, philanthropic agency.[127] It was actually a 'quasi-government organisation carrying out a substantial programme of emigration which the government of the day was unwilling to undertake officially and directly because of constraints of both ideology and costs', as one of the foremost authorities of the period points out.[128]

The Society operated in partnership with Highland landowners and the Colonial Land and Emigration Commission. Landowners paid one third of the costs and money was also raised through public subscriptions. The landlords were directly involved in the entire process, including the selection of emigrants.

This selection of emigrants often led to forced removals when people were cleared directly onto emigration ships. Not only landlord critics but even officials involved in the emigration schemes, like Sir Edward Coffin and Sheriff Fraser, saw a connection between organised emigration and large-scale clearances.[129] Although the relationship of destitution, clearances, and emigration was complex, and some major clearances would have occurred anyway, the link was certainly there between the new wave of clearances and the emigration schemes. As in the case of the Sollas evictions earlier, many people were now not only forced off their lands but forced directly onto ships to Australia. It was during this time that the most brutal evictions in the history of the Highland clearances occurred in Knoydart and Greenyards.

The Knoydart evictions in 1853 were the last major clearance to attract widespread newspaper attention and loud public outcry. The evictions and the subsequent hunting down of those refusing to board the emigration ship were so brutal that even the *Scotsman* strongly condemned them as 'gross inhumanity'.[130] Both the *Inverness Courier* and the *Scotsman* sent up their own correspondents to the scene, and the fate of the people occupied long newspaper columns for several months.

Knoydart, in the parish of Glenelg, was the last remaining part of the Glengarry estate where the crofters and cotters had yet to be replaced by sheep after several emigrations. In June 1852 the estate came under trustee management by Mrs M'Donell, and soon after notices to quit were served to the crofters. They were told they must leave the estate or be shipped to Australia. The destination was shortly changed to Canada and people were told that 'the most determined measures would be adopted for their removal'.[131]

A ship capable of carrying away the entire population of the five townships was chartered with money borrowed from the government, and the removal began on 2 August. Mrs M'Donell sought no consent from the people; the choice was between boarding the ship or being expelled from the estate. Four days later all who would go were on board – some 300 people – but about twenty families refused to leave. It was against these people that 'the most determined measures' were deployed.

These measures amounted to the destruction of houses and a hunting down of the 'refugees', who were hiding in makeshift shelters. The first removals lasted for three days with sixteen families evicted mostly by the use of force. Old women clung to their huts and fought the officers. By the end of the clearance all the houses were destroyed and the inhabitants left exposed to the open air, where they spent several weeks from August until late October in cold and wet weather. Whatever shelter they put together was regularly destroyed by the local managers.

Even the *Scotsman*, which had been one of the least sympathetic papers, reported on the state of these people with a tone of shock:

> This family I found under the shelter of a turf-wall in a little structure into which I crept, and where a child of eight years old could scarcely stand upright . . . This frail fabric had been *five times* pulled down by the agents of the estate, and as often re-erected after they were gone. The last occasion was late on a wild stormy night, just as darkness came on . . . At the time of my visit, a sharp squall of northerly wind came on, accompanied by a penetrating rain, and a sprinkling of snow covered the tops of the hills. I need not attempt to paint the scene; anything more wretched, excepting in gypsy life, I never saw.[132]

The correspondent chronicled many other cases of shelters pulled down several times over the heads of frail old folk, of sick people treated harshly, and of violent scenes of eviction.

The brutality of these Knoydart scenes must have been great if even the *Scotsman*'s reporter, while acknowledging that he had 'conscientiously sided with the evicting landlords', now strongly condemned the trustee at the end of his report: 'I grant that she had a perfect right to do so, and further, that she behaved most liberally to those who left the estate; but I am also compelled to think that she has been guilty of gross inhumanity in her treatment of the miserable and helpless remnant of the people who remain'.[133]

The *Courier* devoted much space to the Knoydart case throughout the autumn, and many of its readers reacted strongly to the cruelty of the

'Old times and new times' - a print of the Highland cottar and his surroundings 'before and after' improvement. From a handbook for improvers, entitled *Hints for the Use of Highland Tenants and Cottagers* by Mackenzie, F. of Gairloch, 1838.

'Ewen MacPhee the Outlaw'. Romanticised image of a Jacobite outlaw. From a picture book depicting the 'antiquated' life and customs of the 'ancient' and 'picturesque' Celtic people. McIan, R.R. - Logan, James, *Gaelic Gatherings, or the Highlanders at home, on the heath, the river and the loch*, 1848.

'Gathering dulse' - 'a wholesome article of food' - from the sea rocks, habitually done by women and children. From *Gaelic Gatherings, or the Highlanders at home, on the heath, the river and the loch*.

'Gille Calum', or the 'Sword Dance', of martial origin. An idyllic image of dancing of 'simple people' in their home. From *Gaelic Gatherings, or the Highlanders at home, on the heath, the river and the loch*.

'The Highland Shepherd' - a sketch made by Duncan MacNiven, in the service of Campbell of Monzie. Lone and lamenting the 'unhappy change' to sheep farming, which brought 'desolation' and 'ruin' to the land. From *Gaelic Gatherings, or the highlanders at home, on the heath, the river and the loch.*

The Last of the Clan by Thomas Faed (Glasgow Art Gallery and Museum) - one of the most widely known representations of the Clearances.

Passenger ship advertisements on the front page of the *Glasgow Herald*, March 21st 1853, covering the whole page, indicative of the rise in emigration. (The Mitchell Library, Glasgow)

eviction procedure. One 'gentleman' wrote to them 'deprecating the harsh measures of turning out old and infirm people upon the roads and the hill-sides', saying:

> It is all very well to insist upon the young and able accepting terms of emigration; but it is a totally different case with the aged, whom I hold it to be cruel and monstrous to banish at a time of life when they cannot hope to be able to establish themselves, even if they live to reach Australia or Canada.[134]

While in the case of the Knoydart evictions, people were pushed onto emigration ships or forcibly turned out of their houses and then hunted down like dogs to drive them away from the land, they were at least not yet beaten severely. The use of force, however, increased steeply a year later in Greenyards, in possibly the cruellest case recorded. Like the Sollas case in 1849, it was resistance to removals which sparked off great violence.

At the end of March 1854 summonses of removals were served to tenants on the property of Major Robertson of Kindeace in Greenyards near Bonar Bridge. The people refused to leave. The following morning the Sheriff of Tain was sent with a police force of thirty men to enforce the law. According to the *Inverness Courier*, the opposition was formidable.[135] About three hundred people, two thirds of them women, had assembled armed with stones and sticks. After the Sheriff failed 'to reason' with the crowd, a small battle broke out. The chief sufferers were the women. More than fifteen were reported seriously hurt, especially in the head and face, and in their 'other parts'. The policemen themselves escaped almost unhurt, after they had used their batons 'with great force'.

Interestingly, little more was told about the Greenyards evictions and the ensuing fate of the people. Although violence was much greater in Greenyards than at Knoydart or Sollas, the extent of newspaper coverage and public outcry was much smaller than before in the leading papers.

This apparently sudden silence in the press was part of the prevailing sense of giving up on the Highlands. In addition, by this time removals and large-scale emigrations were seen as the only possible solution in the majority of the Scottish press, and therefore they were less and less of a sensation.

Another reason may have been that by 1854 both the tide of clearances and that of emigration seemed to recede, and therefore the Greenyards evictions could perhaps be seen as an isolated case. The outbreak of the Crimean War also put a halt to the exodus as men could now be channelled into the army. By 1856 the recovery of the potato crop and a new vigour within Scottish industry also reduced the number of those who emigrated as a last resort.

In 1857 the Highland and Island Emigration Society terminated its operations. In the final count 'only' 5,000 people had emigrated through the Society. Trevelyan's grand plan to transport 30–40,000 people was never realised. That many of the emigrants went of their own free will did not, however, mean that in the minds of many contemporaries such as Trevelyan, emigration officials, newspapers editors, and common readers, basic attitudes towards the Highland Gaels had changed. Many saw them leave with a sense of relief, believing that the Highlands would thus have fewer of those 'burdensome', 'useless' and 'inferior' people.

Some of the large-scale Highland emigration in the early 1850s was voluntary. However, much of this willingness arose from the realisation that it was impossible to remain because the pressure of poverty was too great. It is debatable to what extent that destitution was a result of earlier clearances or of deliberate policies to make the Gaels' living conditions on their native land impossible.

By the 1850s conditions in much of the Highlands were indeed desperate for many. As emigrants themselves said, they felt 'that they yielded to an inflexible and hard necessity which they neither could control nor evade'.[136] By that time many agreed that it was too late to save the Highlands' entire original population because the land, as it was, could no longer support all of the people. And at the time, there was no realistic hope of any land reform or change of landlord policies. Many felt they simply had better go because of economic pressure and went willingly though not happily. The point here, however, is not whether or not emigration was an economic necessity but that part of it was forced and was coloured by racial considerations.

The racist attitudes of the 1840s had reached a stage by the first half of the 1850s where emigration could be viewed as a form of 'racial purification' or even as a nineteenth-century version of 'ethnic cleansing' in the name of social and economic progress. In its underlying ideology, – as demonstrated in the press at the time – it was indeed a form of 'ethnic cleansing', although there were no mass deportations or bloody pogroms, and the extent of Highland clearance was much smaller than in other instances. Nevertheless, the attitudes, the ideology, the motives and, to some extent, the practice did amount to what we today call 'ethnic cleansing'.

Such 'clearances' or 'cleansing' were of course far from unique to the Scottish Highlands. In fact, it is the Highland Clearances which are normally left out of the long list of historical 'ethnic cleansings'. Although the term 'ethnic cleansing' is a recently coined term, first used in 1991, what it describes is as old as history.[137] In varying degrees of brutality, it has been around since ancient times.

The long list of 'ethnic cleansings' includes: forced resettlements by Assyrian rulers in the eighth century BC, the recurring expulsions of the Jews in the Middle Ages, the expulsion of the Irish by the English in the seventeenth century, the removals and massacres of the American Indians, nineteenth-century Turkish atrocities against Greeks and Armenians, the Armenian holocaust in 1915, and the Holocaust itself – a culmination of all ethnic cleansings – and, after the Second World War, the mass expulsion of Germans from eastern Europe. The list is long. However, the term defies easy definition, as the author of 'A brief history of ethnic cleansing' points out:

At one end it is virtually indistinguishable from forced emigration and population exchange while at the other it merges with deportation and genocide. At the most general level, however, ethnic cleansing can be understood as the expulsion of an 'undesirable' population from a given territory due to religious or ethnic discrimination, political, strategic or ideological considerations, or a combination of these.[138]

Other definitions include 'removal or eradication of a portion of the indigenous population of an area',[139] and 'euphemism for the practice of kicking out minority populations'.[140] Whatever definition we may apply, the fact that when the phrase 'ethnic cleansing' became widely used most people understood what it meant, shows that the idea had been around for a long time, under other names. As Neal Ascherson aptly put it: 'It amounts to this proposition: that a majority can live more "healthily" by casting out a minority that is in some way alien'.[141]

The idea of health and purity opposed by disease and dirt, is at the core of any kind of 'ethnic cleansing'. They all include the idea that 'alien' groups have to be purged from the 'body' of the ethnically or racially pure nations. In its most extreme form in our century of modern nationalism and fascism, ethnic cleansing was built on 'a false analogy between sociology and medicine: the collective body of the nation had to be purified of infections . . .'.[142] This 'false analogy' between sociology and medicine was already there, at least in embryo, in mid-nineteenth century prejudices against the Gaels. It was there when the *Fifeshire Journal* talked about the 'cosmical fact' that the more energetic and hard-working Saxons would push out the 'weaker', 'inferior' Celts, or when Sir Charles

Trevelyan preferred the more congenial Germans to the 'alien' Celts. When the *Scotsman* talked about the 'removal of a diseased and damaged part' of the population, the underlying idea was the same. Such concepts, as we have seen, were acceptable, if not even commonplace, by the 1850s in the larger, hostile section of the Scottish press.

Notes

1. For circulation figures see *The Waterloo Directory of Scottish Newspapers*, Jack, *Newspaper Directory*, and Mitchell, *Newspaper Press*.
2. The following survey is based on a systematic search of the *Scotsman, Glasgow Herald,* and *Inverness Courier* between 1845–1855, and on a selected search of some 25 other Scottish newspapers.
3. 'Highland Clearings', *Scottish Herald*, May 1845, reprinted in *The Times*, 26 May 1845.
4. 'Highland Clearings', *Scottish Herald*, May 1845, reprinted in *The Times*, 26 May 1845.
5. Papers reprinting *The Times* reports included *The Scotsman*, and the *Edinburgh Evening Courant*.
6. 'Scotland, The Far North', reprinted in the *Edinburgh Evening Courant*, 5 June 1845 and the *Glasgow Herald*, 9 June 1845.
7. *Perth Constitutional*, 14 May 1845.
8. *Perth Constitutional*, 14 May 1845.
9. *Perth Constitutional*, editorial, 11 June 1845.
10. 'Sutherland As It Was', *Perth Constitutional*, 9 July 1845.
11. *Perth Constitutional*, 9 July 1845.
12. He was born and brought up in Dumfries.
13. 'Scottish Poor-Rural Improvement', editorial, *Inverness Courier*, 20 August 1845, reprinted in the *Scotsman* in abridged form 23 August 1845.
14. *Inverness Courier*, 16 June 1845.
15. *Inverness Courier*, 16 June 1845.
16. *Perth Constitutional*, 21 January 1846.
17. 'The Glencalvie Cottars', *Perth Constitutional*, 11 February 1846.
18. 'The Glencalvie Cottars', *Perth Constitutional*, 11 February 1846.
19. 'The Glencalvie Cottars', *Perth Constitutional*, 11 February 1846.
20. 'Failure of the Potato Crop', *Inverness Courier*, 26 August 1846.
21. 'Failure of the Potato Crop', *Inverness Courier*, 26 August 1846.
22. T.M. Devine, *The Great Highland Famine*, 35.
23. T.M. Devine, *Clanship to Crofters' War*, 147.
24. T.M. Devine, in an interview with the author, in December 1993.
25. *The Times*, 8 September 1846.
26. *The Times*, 1 October 1846.
27. *The Times*, 1 October 1846.
28. *The Times*, 7 October 1846.

29. '*The Times*' Commissioner has closed his labours . . .', leader, *Inverness Courier*, 21 October 1846.

30. A well-known Edinburgh antiquary, historian, and literary forger, he was one of the first theorists to put forward a hypothesis on the inveterate inferiority of the Celtic race as opposed to the Scythian or Gothic race in 1787, in his *Dissertation on the Origin and Progress of the Scythians or Goths*. Pinkerton in fact is one of the major forerunners of the mid-nineteenth century racially based views on the Highland Gaels. See Chapter One, Background.

31. My italics.

32. 'The Highlands before the era of potatoes', *Inverness Courier*, 25 November 1846.

33. 'The West Highlands', *Inverness Courier*, 18 November 1846.

34. 'The West Highlands', *Inverness Courier*, 18 November 1846.

35. Olive Checkland, *Philanthropy in Victorian Scotland.*

36. 'The Destitution in the Highlands, Meeting of the Edinburgh Committee', *Inverness Courier*, 30 December 1846.

37. 'The Destitution of the Highlands, Meeting of the Committee', *Scotsman*, 26 December 1846.

38. T.M. Devine, *The Great Highland Famine*, 165.

39. Reports of the General Assembly of the Free Church of Scotland regarding the Highland Destitution, Edinburgh, 1847, Second Statement of the Free Church, quoted in Devine, *The Great Highland Famine*, 157.

40. *Inverness Courier*, 10 February 1847.

41. *Perth Courier*, February 1847, quoted in the *Inverness Courier*, 10 February 1847 and in the *Fifeshire Journal*, 4 February 1847.

42. 'Destitution in the Highlands and Refusal of Labourers to take employment', *Perth Courier*, reprinted in the *Scotch Reformers' Gazette*, 6 February 1847.

43. 'Destitution in the Highlands and Refusal of Labourers to take employment', *Scotch Reformers' Gazette*, 6 February 1847.

44. 'Return of Highland Labourers', *Scotsman*, 10 February 1847.

45. Their itinerary was identical in place and time from Tobermory January 22 as far as Kyleakin February 5; they even visited the same huts and cottages. The *Fifeshire Journal* also printed four letters from the *Scotsman*, with the editorial comment that they 'have the pleasure of being intimately acquainted with the gentlemen selected by the *Scotsman*'. While the *Scotsman*'s reports are fairly well known today, the fact that the editor of the *Fifeshire Journal* was travelling with the *Scotsman* and sending a separate series of letters has not so far been uncovered.

46. *Scotsman*, 22 August 1861.

47. The series of letters ran under the title 'Inquiry into the Distress in the Highlands and Islands', from 30 January 1847 to 10 March 1847.

48. *Scotsman*, 30 January 1847.

49. All italics are mine in the three passages quoted.

50. *Scotsman*, 3 February 1847.

51. *Scotsman*, 3 February 1847.

52. *Scotsman*, 10 February 1847.

53. *Scotsman*, 10 February 1847; italics are mine.

54. Its circulation was only between 500–600, and limited to Cupar, St Andrews, Kirkcaldy and Dunfermline. Source: *Waterloo Directory.*

55. Since so far the *Fifeshire Journal* has never been used as a source on the Highlands, and consequently its extreme views have not yet been explored and uncovered, the following extracts are quoted in greater length for their new source value.

56. It is not clear who he was as there is no indication of editor between 1847 and 1853 in any of the consulted directories. The conclusion that it was the editor who went on the tour comes from the fact that in a Letter to the Editor shortly after the tour, one reader said: 'I daresay it is not the best time to address you on this subject, having so recently experienced such filth and abomination in *your* tour through the Highlands, . . .'

57. 'Notes of a Winter Tour', *Fifeshire Journal*, 11 February 1847.

58. 'Notes of a Winter Tour', *Fifeshire Journal*, 11 February 1847.

59. 'Notes of a Winter Tour', *Fifeshire Journal*, 11 February 1847.

60. *Scotsman*, 10 February 1847.

61. 'The West Highlands', *Inverness Courier*, 3 February 1847.

62. T.M. Devine, *The Great Highland Famine*, 153.

63. A. Fullarton and C.R. Baird, *Remarks on the Evils at Present Affecting the Highlands and Islands of Scotland*, Glasgow 1838.

64. 'Highland Destitution – Skye', *Scotsman*, 21 July 1847.

65. Leader, *Inverness Courier*, 14 September 1847.

66. 'The Destitute Board's Funds', *Aberdeen Herald*, reprinted in the *Scotsman*, 8 September 1847.

67. According to Cowan, *Newspapers in Scotland.*

68. 'The Destitution Surplus', *Glasgow Citizen*, reprinted in the *Scotsman*, 13 October 1847.

69. Leader, *Scotsman*, 6 October 1847.

70. Editorial entitled 'Highland Destitution', *Fifeshire Journal*, 23 September 1847, reprinted in the *Perth Constitutional*, 29 September 1847.

71. Editorial entitled 'Highland Destitution', *Fifeshire Journal*, 23 September 1847, reprinted in the *Perth Constitutional*, 29 September 1847.

72. 'Highland Destitution Fund', letter to the Editor, *Scotsman*, 25 September 1847.

73. 'The Destitution Question', letter to the Editor, *Scotsman*, 18 September 1847.

74. 'The Highland Destitution Surplus', letter to the Editor, *Scotsman*, 16 October 1847.

75. 'The 1846 Potato Calamity', *Chambers Edinburgh Journal*, 12 October 1847.

76. 'The Destitution Surplus', *Glasgow Argus*, October 1847, reprinted in the *Scotsman*, 20 October 1847.

77. 'The Destitution Surplus', *Elgin Courier*, October 1847, reprinted in the *Scotsman*, 20 October 1847.

78. Report of the meeting of the Edinburgh Section of the Highland Destitution Board, 'Highland Destitution Board', *Scotsman*, 18 March 1848.

79. Instructions given by Captain Fishbourne, inspector for Skye, under the Central Relief Board, to the sub-inspectors of Skye, reprinted in the *Inverness Courier*, 7 March 1848.

80. T.M. Devine, 'Highland Landowners and the Potato Famine', in: *Perspectives in Scottish Social History*, 1988, 147.

81. Instructions given by Captain Fishbourne, inspector for Skye, under the Central Relief Board, to the sub-inspectors of Skye, reprinted in the *Inverness Courier*, 7 March 1848. Rule 8th.

82. Skene to Trevelyan, 21 February 1848, HD7/47.

83. Sir Charles Trevelyan in a letter to James Loch, 15 January 1848, HD7/46.

84. 'Highland Destitution Board,' Meeting of the Edinburgh Section, *Scotsman*, 6 December 1848.

85. 'Highland Destitution', *Aberdeen Herald*, reprinted in the *Scotsman*, 2 December 1848.

86. 'Highland Destitution Board', *Scotsman*, 18 March 1848.

87. 'Highland Destitution Board, Edinburgh Section', *Scotsman*, 6 December 1848.

88. 'Highland Relief Board', *Inverness Courier*, 30 November 1848.

89. Quoted in the *Scotsman*, editorial, 26 July 1851.

90. The pamphlet was entitled 'Emigration in its Practical Application to Individuals and Communities'.

91. Quoted in Devine, *The Great Highland Famine*, 251.

92. Quoted in *Scotsman*, 26 July 1851.

93. The expression comes from Prof. Tom Devine, in an interview with the author in December 1993.

94. *Inverness Courier*, 'Disturbances in North Uist', 26 July 1849.

95. *Inverness Courier*, 'Disturbances in North Uist', 26 July 1849.

96. 'The North Uist removals', *Scotsman*, 11 August 1849.

97. 'The North Uist removals', *Scotsman*, 11 August 1849.

98. 'The North Uist removals', *Scotsman*, 11 August 1849.

99. 'The North Uist removals', *Scotsman*, 11 August 1849.

100. *Scotsman*, editorial, 18 August 1849; my italics.

101. 'State of the West Highlands', *Inverness Courier*, reprinted in the *Scotsman*, 25 August 1849.

102. In *Scotsman*, 25 August 1849. My italics.

103. 'From Our Skye Correspondent', *Inverness Courier*, 1 November 1849.

104. 'From Our Skye Correspondent', *Inverness Courier*, 1 November 1849. Italics are mine.

105. 'The Highlands – Prospects of the future', *Inverness Courier*, 24 January 1850.

106. *Inverness Courier*, 24 January 1850.

107. 'North Uist', *Inverness Courier*, 22 August 1850.

108. 'Highland Destitution Board', *Scotsman*, 17 July 1850.

109. 'Highland Destitution Board', *Scotsman*, 17 July 1850.

110. *Scotsman*, editorial, 9 November 1850.

111. *Scotsman*, editorial, 1 January 1851.

112. Although Darwin was yet to publish his theories in 1859, and the 1860s, the core ideas of social Darwinism was already present in the 'spirit of the age' through Spencer and others. See Chapter One on 'Zeitgeist'.

113. 'Destitution in Skye', *Glasgow Citizen*, reprinted in the *Glasgow Herald*, 26 May 1851.

114. 'Destitution in Skye', *Glasgow Herald*, 6 June 1851.

115. 'The Report of Sir John M'Neill on Highland Destitution', *Scotsman*, 26 July 1851.

116. 'The Report of Sir John M'Neill on Highland Destitution', *Scotsman*, 26 July 1851.

117. 'The Report of Sir John M'Neill on Highland Destitution', *Scotsman*, 26 July 1851.

118. Devine, *The Great Highland Famine*, 125.

119. 'Destitution in the Highlands', *Atheneaum*, reprinted in the *Scotsman*, 12 July 1851. Italics are mine.

120. *Scotsman*, editorial, 30 July 1851.

121. *Scotsman*, editorial, 3 September 1851.

122. *Scotsman*, editorial, 3 September 1851.

123. 'New light on the Highlands', *Fifeshire Journal*, 11 September 1851.

124. Devine, *The Great Highland Famine*, 248.

125. Devine, *The Great Highland Famine*, 251.

126. Devine, *The Great Highland Famine*, quoted from SRO HD4/2 Letterbook of H.I.E.S. (2), Trevelyan to Commissary-General Miller, 30 June 1852.

127. Devine, *The Great Highland Famine*, 251.

128. Devine, *The Great Highland Famine*, 251.

129. Devine, *The Great Highland Famine*, 261.

130. 'Late evictions in Knoydart', *Scotsman*, 26 October 1853.

131. 'Late evictions in Knoydart – State of the people', *Scotsman*, 22 October 1853.

132. 'Late evictions in Knoydart', *Scotsman*, 26 October 1853.

133. 'Late evictions in Knoydart', *Scotsman*, 26 October 1853.

134. 'Evictions in Knoydart', *Inverness Courier*, 15 September 1853.

135. Report of the Greenyards case here taken from the *Inverness Courier*, 'Removal of Tenants – Riotous proceedings', 6 April 1854.

136. 'Highland Emigration', *Glasgow Herald*, 6 June 1851.

137. The origin of the term 'ethnic cleansing' is somewhat uncertain. According to the American writer Bill Bryson it was coined by Russian observers and first used in *The Times*, July 1991. Louise Branson, a reporter of *The Times*, says it was coined by Vojislav Seselj, the notorious nationalist Serb politician. Other experts say it was first used in connection with the pogroms and concentration camps in Bosnia.

138. Bell-Fialkoff, Andrew, 'A brief history of ethnic cleansing', *Foreign Affairs*, Summer 1993, v72n3, 110–112.

139. Bill Bryson, *Made in America*, London, 1995.

140. Andrew Marshall in *The Independent*, 29 July 1992.

141. Ascherson, N. 'The tragically easy path to ethnic cleansing', *The Independent on Sunday*, 2 August 1992.

142. Ascherson, N., 'The tragically easy path to ethnic cleansing'.

PART TWO

Sympathy and Romance

CHAPTER THREE

Sympathy

I. The Critics of the 1840s

The liberal *Glasgow Argus* was one of the first newspapers to react fiercely to the outburst of attacks in the press in 1846/47 against the alleged inferiority of the Celts. It was also among the first papers to demand land reform with the redistribution of the soil and the abolition of the 'antiquated, absurd and most mischievous' feudal laws.[1] The *Argus* saw the Highland Gaels as no worse and no better than anyone else, and strongly refuted charges that the Celts were an inferior race. The *Glasgow Argus* was a thoroughly anti-landlord paper set up in 1833 to campaign for burgh reform, direct taxation, free trade and the abolition of patronage in the established church.[2] It spoke for the 'educated Radicals' and produced a high level of journalism.[3] It began as a medium-size twice-weekly paper with around 1,000 copies per issue, but by 1845 its circulation had fallen below 700.[4]

The editors of the *Argus* believed that they had a mission to fulfill, to fight 'on the side of justice and truth' and combat 'the evils' of their time.[5] By 1846 they saw one such 'evil' manifested in Highland landlord policies and the alarming spread of the potato famine.

The famine brought the 'social mismanagement' of the Highlands to a crisis, the paper argued in 1846. It put the bulk of the blame on the landlords, who had neglected their duties as proprietors and could not now provide for the starving people on their estates:

> The landlords cannot do their duty; and for all we know of them, it is but too well-founded an assertion to say, that they would not if they could. All experience is against any belief in them. (. . .) they are not equal generally (in consequence of their own bad management and reckless extravagance in former years) to any such emergency as this.[6]

But the paper's criticism went beyond anti-landlord rhetoric. The landlords were negligent and impoverished because they were paralysed by the Law of Entail and the absence of a proper Poor Law, said the *Argus*. And the people, who the paper simply denoted as 'serfs', were degraded because of the 'unequal distribution of the soil'. The system itself allowed this 'unequal distribution of soil', whereby, said the paper, masses of people had to exist on inferior land after having been cleared from better areas. In short, the evil was rooted in land ownership, in the 'oppressive feudal system of management of the soil'. As one *Argus* reader put it:

> It is the feudal system that presses like a black nightmare on the energies of the Highlands.[7]

The only true solution was new land laws, the *Argus* contended. It did not use the phrase 'land reform', but what it demanded was not very far removed from that. Its basic principle was that 'land is by right the land of the people' and individual property should only be allowed while it was 'conducive to the public interest'.[8] What the *Argus* demanded was essentially the abolition of the feudalistic land laws in the Highlands as well as in Ireland:

> The land and property of Ireland must be made to maintain the people of Ireland. The land of the Highlands and Islands of Scotland must be made to maintain the maligned and oppressed people who were once its boast. . . .
> We must give the poor man the right to live – we must have a thorough and just Poor Law – we must abolish the antiquated, absurd, and most mischievous laws which regulate the possession and transmission of landlord property.[9]

The abolition of entail was seen as crucial to any land reform not only by the *Argus* but by many other contemporary critics. In the ensuing years both Robert Somers and Hugh Miller were adamant that the Law of Entail should be abolished entirely. By the mid-nineteenth century more than half of the land in Scotland was estimated to be strictly entailed, and the issue of entail was a subject of great controversy.[10] Even after the Rutherford Act in 1848, which considerably eased the strict regulations by making it possible to disentail land, critics such as the *Witness* continued to argue for complete abolition. It was not until 1914 that entails were eventually entirely forbidden.

Arguing for new land laws was just one aspect of the *Argus*'s campaign for the Highlands. It fought even more fiercely against the widespread accusations that the Celts were habitually lazy and racially inferior, and therefore had brought the famine on themselves.

In an editorial in January 1847, the *Argus* rebuked other papers for not questioning prevalent statements that the famine was race-related, affecting only the 'inferior' Celts. It quoted an article from the *Daily News* of London, which blamed the indolence of the Gaels for the famine. Calling the *Daily News* writer 'well-meaning but mistaken', the editorial argued that the writer was 'ignorant of the causes which have reduced the once high-minded, and active Celts to this state of degradation'.[11] Not many papers at the time would ever call the Celts active and high-minded. The *Argus* blamed the landlords and not the indolence of the Gaels for the calamity. As this editorial put it:

> . . . the unhappy landlordism by which Celtic Ireland and Celtic Scotland have been afflicted has deteriorated the condition of the people, *naturally as laborious and intelligent, and independent as any other people on the globe.*[12]

The *Argus* refused to have anything to do with the belief that the Celts were in any way racially different, they were like 'any other people on the globe'. With this conviction, the *Argus* stood quite alone among the Scottish press at the time.

It even argued that the campaign of accusations was in fact a clever way of disguising the ill-treatment of the Gaels, a shrewd excuse. As another editorial expressed it:

> As to the charge against the Highlanders which is just now going round the papers (. . .): the guilt of their inferiority lies at the door of those who caused it; and it is no excuse for either past or present ill treatment of them on our parts, to allege that the people are idle, and prefer ease and the coarsest sustenance to hard labour and the physical comforts it would procure them.[13]

The *Argus*, however, could not long continue its defense of the Gaels. After fifteen years of existence the paper shut down in November 1847. The Highland cause was not among its professed campaign when it set out in 1833 to promote burgh reform and free trade. In its 'Farewell Address' the editors said that they felt they had achieved the original targets and would leave the ground for others. Why the paper really closed down remains uncertain. Its circulation certainly fell low enough, to around 600, for any newspaper editor to think hard about survival. For the time being, the Scottish newspaper scene had lost a radical campaigner for Highland land reform and a fervent defender of the Gaels. But there were others to follow and take up the missionary task. As the *Argus* said in its farewell, there was much to battle for yet:

> . . . we believe that there is a fair field of labour in the department of human amelioration.[14]

Hugh Miller was perhaps the best known and the most respected among _witness_

Miller

the critics of the treatment of the Highland Gaels. His forum, the *Witness*, had the highest circulation of any paper sympathetic to the Highlanders. In his stance over Highland issues, Hugh Miller is usually described as a 'radical', a 'crusading' editor, and 'a scourge of landowners'.[15]

His criticism of the Highland policies was harsh, and his defense of the Highlanders impassioned. By 1850, his paper even argued for land reform. In comparison, however, with other radical and crusading papers the *Witness* lagged behind by the 1850s. It was also primarily an ecclesiastical paper, first fighting for the Disruption and then devoting itself chiefly to the affairs of the Free Church. But during the 1840s debates over the Highlands, the voice of the *Witness* was weighty and sharply critical.

Hugh Miller was a man of many talents and contradictions. Born in 1802 in Cromarty, he was a Lowlander on his father's side and a Highlander on his mother's, but he considered himself more of a Lowlander. (In one of his writings he remarked that he was the only Lowlander among Highlanders.) Rising from the modest background of a stonemason, he became a geologist and writer, and editor of the *Witness*.

His knowledge extended to folklore, poetry, travel, history, science and religion. He was at the time among the best-known Victorian literary figures, 'admired by the likes of Thomas Carlyle, Charles Dickens and John Ruskin'.[16] He also played a leading role in the Disruption in 1843 second only to Thomas Chalmers.

Under his editorship, the *Witness* attained a circulation of over 2,500 making it the third largest Scottish newspaper after the *Glasgow Herald* and the *Scotsman*.[17] In his autobiography, Miller claimed that his paper had the highest number of university-educated readers among comparable Scottish newspapers.[18] Miller produced some of the best journalism in Scotland at the time, his writing exhibiting true literary merit. His descriptions were poetic and his arguments cogent.

But Miller's was a tragic intellect. Towards the end of his life his mind became unstable, he was tormented by nightmares, and, realising that he was going insane, he shot himself on Christmas Eve in 1856. According to his twentieth-century biographer, George Rosie, Miller was an enigmatic character. Throughout his life he battled with many dualities. He was simultaneously a 'romantic Scottish nationalist' deeply approving the Union, a bank officer writing sentimental verse, a fierce Presbyterian favouring Catholic emancipation, a 'radically-inclined journalist who savaged the gentry, but who despised the Chartists and the Socialists'.[19] George Rosie sees Miller as a man struggling with the contradiction between his sense of justice and his instinct for order and submission. Perhaps this also explains why Miller never became a persistently radical crusading journalist.

The first time Miller wrote in a critical vein about the Clearances and Highland destitution was in 1845 in his book *The Cruise of the Betsey*. It was originally written for the *Witness* following a tour around the Hebrides. Miller went with an old friend of his who was Free Church minister for the Small Isles. What he saw of the state of the people there appalled him. He saw miserable hovels with bed-ridden, poverty-stricken women in them, and people with shrivelled frames worn out by famine. He described his 'outrage' at the poverty of the people. But he was also appalled by what had happened to the land itself. In a brilliant passage, he first painted a poetic and romantic picture of the Highland landscape and then suddenly hit the reader with the disturbing reality of the Clearances and depopulation:

> The evening was clear, calm, golden-tinted; even wild heaths and rude rocks had assumed a flush of transient beauty; and the emerald-green patches on the hill-sides, barred by the plough lengthwise, diagonally, and transverse, had borrowed an aspect of soft and velvety richness, from the mellowed light and the broadening shadows. All was solitary. We could see among the deserted fields the grass-grown foundations of cottages razed to the ground; but the valley, more desolate than that which we had left, had not even a single inhabited dwelling: it seemed as if man had done with it forever.[20]

Miller then related how the land was given over to sheep and, while all the 'aborigines' of Rum crossed the Atlantic, the only population consisted of the sheep farmer and his servants. Soon, however, the depopulation was found too extreme, the place being 'too thoroughly a desert for the comfort of the occupant', and after Clearances in Skye some ejected families were given land on the coastal areas. Still, most of the island remained devoid of human habitation. The Highland Clearances were perhaps never more poetically described than in Miller's writing here:

> The whole of the once-peopled interior remains a wilderness, without inhabitant, – all the more lonely in its aspect from the circumstance that the solitary valleys, with their plough-furrowed patches, and their ruined heaps of stone, open upon shores every whit as solitary as themselves, and that the wide untrodden sea stretches drearily around.[21]

But a good poetic image was just one of the tools of Miller's writing. His critical edge worked with strong words. After the lengthy description of the cleared lands he simply called the whole process 'extermination' carried out thoroughly and 'on system'. He dismissed it as 'bad policy' and refused to be convinced by 'economists' who claimed that there were 'more than enough people in Scotland still'. Miller argued that this policy rid the country of a better class of men and to crown it all, it did not produce results. He cited the example of Rum again; the new sheep-farmer eventually was 'unfortunate in his speculations' and left the island. It was yet again up for sale and was about to be purchased by a wealthy Englishman who planned to turn it into a deer forest.

Miller's trip around the Hebrides took place in 1844 and 1845, and he witnessed much misery and desolation. With the outbreak of the potato famine in 1846 the Highlanders saw the coming of their worst crisis yet. During the peak years of the famine, Miller devoted much space in the *Witness* to the destitution in the Highlands and to criticism of the Clearances.

An editorial in November 1846 called the famine 'a solemn crisis', and called on every Christian Church to do their duty proving their 'Christian kindness and liberality' in the 'sad and trying emergency'.[22] Miller was aware, however, that in order to gain public sympathy he first had to demonstrate that the Highland Gaels were indeed worthy of sympathy and that the famine was not 'their own fault' arising from inherent laziness. He insisted that 'misapprehension' and 'apathy' in the public stemmed from ignorance of the true cause of the famine: that people had come to depend entirely on one vegetable alone.

The *Witness'* basic standpoint throughout the debates of the 1840s was that the people became solely dependent on the potato not because they were too lazy to do anything else but because they had no other choice under the circumstances which had engulfed them with the Clearances and with the mostly bad management of their landlords. In the current tide of public opinion, however, the *Witness* did not have many allies in the press. Apart from the small *Glasgow Argus* and a few other smaller papers like the *Scottish Herald*, the *Witness* stood quite alone in its battle with the hostile press's campaign on the inherent sloth and racial inferiority of the Celts.

Among the most influential articles to appear in the 1840s was a series of reports by *The Times* Commissioner in the autumn of 1846, reprinted and discussed in many Scottish papers.[23] Hugh Miller reacted to it in a lengthy editorial. Normally a severe and serious man, he started the article with unusual sarcasm. This opening paragraph ridiculed the accusations in *The Times*, which were also leveled by the *Scotsman* and other Scottish papers:

The late articles of the *Times'* Commissioner have excited a deep interest
over Scotland generally, and more especially in that northern portion of it to
which they chiefly refer. Our Highlanders, however, seem in degree
satisfied. They have been quite aware for some time past that they are
far from being a wealthy people, and the failure of the potato crop has cost
them many fears; but they deem it cold comfort to be told that their
depressing poverty arises, as a necessary consequence, out of their inherent
peculiarities as a race, and that if they were not Celts they would be quite
able without assistance to get over the loss of their potatoes. They derive no
solace from being informed, in their hour of calamity, that, were they
Saxons like the English, they would almost all, on a smaller or larger scale, be
capitalists, and in circumstances to live comfortably during one bad season
on the hoarded stores of previous good ones.[24]

Miller went on to say that it was a fact that the Celts were a different race,
and that indeed in modern times the countries of the 'Germanic family'
stood 'higher in the industrial virtues' than the Celtic. But, he warned, it
was exaggeration to say that the 'present condition of the Scotch Highlander' was a 'consequence of his blood and lineage', that he was exposed to
famine to such an extent because he was a Celt. Such accusations, Miller
argued, served the effect of 'diverting attention from the great economic
causes' which had dissipated the Celts' means and depressed their condition.[25]

These 'great economic causes' were the Clearances, according to the
editorial. After the Highlands had become the 'subject of the great clearing
experiment', the Highlanders lost all their former relative security, when
they had a few cattle or sheep to sell in times of scarcity. Driven out from
the interior lands on to 'unproductive patches of moor' their 'little capitals'
soon disappeared and fell into arrears. The editorial closed with impassioned sympathy:

> We have seen whole tracts of country on the north-western coast, in which
> the rents of five whole years hung in one hapless mill-stone of debt around
> the necks of the inhabitants. What wonder if, in such circumstances, the
> industrial energies of the Celt should be miserably overlaid? The real wonder
> in the case is that his moral nature should still stand erect amid the utter ruin
> of his means.

Miller's basic stance was reiterated in a three part series entitled 'Past and
Present Condition of the Highlands' written by 'A Highlander of the Old
School'. The Clearances and the bad management of the land were at the

'root of all misery, and wretchedness, of much of the indolence and sloth' of the Highland population, the writer claimed.[26] Formerly, the land was more evenly distributed, and although its system of farming was 'probably inferior in point of science', at least every family had a bit of corn land and a small stock of sheep or goats providing some dairy produce and wool. But the Clearances impoverished the bulk of the population:

> The Highlands have proved a fortune-making country to not a few adventurers; but exactly in proportion in which this has been the case, have they proved to the poor despised native a land of poverty, of want, and starvation.[27]

The writer painted an image of the Highlanders which was characteristic of most sympathetic papers: the Highlanders were the poor victims of a vicious system. They were 'hardy and peaceable, and kind-hearted', who suffered in silence the inhuman treatment of their expulsion from their 'lovely glens'. The '*horrid clearances*' reduced the Highlanders to a 'sad and melancholy' condition, as this 'Highlander from the Old School' put it. His condemnation of the landlords' clearances policy was harsh and strongly worded:

> It is assuredly a monstrous abuse of the rights of the property, and an equally monstrous neglect and omission of its duties, to depopulate whole islands and entire parishes, which contained a dense population, and to lease them to *one man*, – to drive scores and hundreds of families out into bays and creeks of sea to starve, and let their possessions, amounting, it may be, to from thirty to forty thousand acres, to *one solitary individual*.[28]

The writer hoped that the 'exposure' of the ill-treatment of the Highlanders might eventually lead to such measures on the part of the government and legislature as would ameliorate the situation. This was the point which perhaps motivated much of the crusading journalists' writings and the style they chose. What often seemed exaggeration to their contemporaries, as well as present readers, stemmed from their ardent desire to shake up public opinion and force change through the power of the press.

Apart from their desire to expose these wrongs, most sympathetic papers also came up with their own proposals for change. The *Witness* advocated improvement through the cultivation of more land and the abolition of 'old feudal laws'. In an article on 'Waste Land and Waste Labour', Rev. James Begg, – a well-known social reformer and Free Church minister, – made a survey of the state of land. With his Letter to the Editor, the *Witness* printed a large table drawn up by Begg, detailing how many acres of land in each county was cultivated, uncultivated and barren. The conclusion of his calculations was as follows:

> . . . of the 20,000,000 of acres in Scotland, only about 5,000,000, or *one-fourth*, is cultivated. Taking the population of the country at 3,000,000, there are fully *six acres* of land for every individual, man, woman, and child. Taking the families at an average of *five* individuals each, there are thus *thirty* acres of land for every family, of which *one half* is arable. Now, in Belgium, from *four to five* acres of land is, by spade husbandry, made sufficient to support a family. In such circumstances, it seems perfect folly to drive some of the very best of our people out of the country, and to suffer so many more to sink into hopeless pauperism.[29]

In short, there was enough arable land, he argued, but in the wrong hands. The majority of people existed on meagre lands or were driven off the land while most of the good land was in the hands of a few. The only solution therefore, said Begg, was the entire abolition of the 'preposterous feudal laws of entail and primogeniture'. Begg reiterated this argument a year later in a speech given at a meeting in Edinburgh, saying that the abolition of the law of entail and the free trade in land were essential prerequisites for more cultivated land.[30]

The solution the *Witness* itself urged was best summed up in a short editorial in September 1849. It started off by warning that the Highland landlords proceeded 'with great energy in driving their inoffensive tenantry into reluctant exile' while the eyes of the public were directed elsewhere towards the Continent where the Italian and Hungarian revolutions and wars of independence had recently come to tragic ends.[31] The editorial even made the point that while the public manifested much sympathy towards the 'Romans' and the Hungarians, they should also spare some for 'our noble Highlanders'.

The solution the writer suggested for the Highlands was essentially a different system of management under caring landlords and competent factors, where leases would be given to the tenants. Through this, the Highlands could not only retain their present population but maintain even more:

> It has been remonstrated by Mr. M'Ewen and others, that the Highlanders, if only properly managed, would become abundantly industrious and profitable at home, and that they have been reduced to their present position chiefly by the refusal of leases and the other infatuated policy of non-resident pauper landlords and incompetent factors. It is proved that the Highlands would sustain far more people, – that land subjected to sheep

and deer soon sinks in value, – and that, whilst native Highlanders cling with fond tenacity, from long habit, to their wild hills and islands, it will be next to impossible to replace them with another population.[32]

In the light of today's efforts towards 'Highland regeneration' and attempts to keep people on the land, this seems almost prophetic.

The above lines, however, also show that Hugh Miller did share the contemporary view that the Highland Gaels were lazy and indolent. They would have to be 'properly managed' to make them industrious. But Miller rejected the accusation that they were indolent because of their race: in his opinion they had been *made* lazy and degraded by a bad system. The Gaels had to be 'elevated' and rescued from their degradation, the *Witness* implied throughout its articles dealing with the issue.

The paper's longest and fullest series of articles on the Highlands ran in September 1849. Under the title of 'The Depopulation of the Highlands' it consisted of four lengthy articles in four consecutive issues. It was the last time that the *Witness* devoted considerable space in its pages to the Highland crisis. We can only presume that it was written by Miller since no other name was given and Miller would normally write most of the articles himself. The collective 'we' for editorials was also frequently used in the articles.

The first article focused on a general condemnation of the Clearances and depopulation. As in the editorial a few days earlier, this article also opened with reference to events on the Continent, drawing a parallel between the sympathy expressed towards the oppressed Hungarians and the oppressed Highlanders:

> The oppression of a great nation is a sad and grievous spectacle. But there is a sadder spectacle to be witnessed nearer home, – a spectacle which a man need not leave the territory of Britain to see, – we mean the gradual extinction of a high-spirited, loyal, and Christian people. And if we have sympathy for the oppressed Hungarian, – and who that is worthy to be called a freeman, has not? – surely we are not to close our hearts against all sympathy with the oppressed – the ejected Highlander.[33]

The comparison might seem exaggerated. At this time in Hungary, the Austrians having crushed the war of independence with the help of Russian troops on 13 August, launched a brutal retaliation campaign led by the ill-famed Haynau, the 'Hyena of Brescia'. Those who took part in the freedom fight were hunted down with great brutality, and hundreds were imprisoned. The bloody oppression of Hungary did excite much sympathy around Europe, and the Scottish papers were especially fascinated by the Hungarian case.[34]

What the *Witness* suggested here by the comparison between the bloody aftermath of the crushing of the Hungarian freedom fighters and the Highland Clearances was that although one happened on a much greater scale and was a more momentous event, the other was equally tragic in the nation's life. And it also warned that 'the greatness of the scale on which they have been exhibited' had served 'to exclude occurrences of apparently less moment'. The real danger threatening the Highlands now, the *Witness* argued, was nothing less than gradual but 'complete extinction'. This 'extinction' meant the depopulation of the Highlands, the gradual disappearance of the native population from its lands.

The second part of the series examined the reasons usually given for the 'ejection system' and rejected them one by one. The paper put the bulk of the blame on the landlords but it did not entirely condemn them. It suggested that some of them were also victims:

> . . . we write with no feeling of hostility to our Highland proprietors. We believe that many of them have acted in ignorance: they are strangers to the people, and they have been made the dupes of other interested parties. We do not say that this is excusable, but we believe it to be the fact.[35]

One accusation laid at the landlords' door was that they had encouraged over-population, which was now the chief reason given for the Clearances. During the years of kelp manufacture it was in the landlords' interest to have as many people as possible on their estates, while at the same time the agriculture of the land was neglected. In the *Witness*'s judgement, if the landlords at the time had taken the 'lion's share' of the benefits, they should now equally take their share in the 'subsequent disadvantages'.

The very assertion that the Highlands were over-populated was rejected by the paper. It called it a 'gross delusion', pointing out that many parts of the Highlands were not peopled at all, and insisted that 'ten times the present population could be maintained by the soil under a proper system'.

Another reason given to justify the ejection was the alleged indolence of the people, which the *Witness* yet again strongly rejected, reiterating the point that such accusations served to divert attention from the real causes:

> It is an old saying, 'Give the dog a bad name, and hang him.' Nothing is easier than to make such a charge as this; but even granting that the charge is true, as they mean it, we must remember that it may be entirely a relative one. The people may be slothful and inactive as agriculturists, but that does

not prove that they are inactive universally. It merely proves that agriculture is not the direction their activity takes. In the kelp manufacture, we are told of the Uist people, that they often work fifteen hours a day at a most labourious occupation.[36]

This was due, according to the *Witness*, to the lack of inducement and security they received. In a system where people have security and see their advantages they will naturally work 'like other men', the paper argued. It claimed that nine tenths of the rural population had no interest in the cultivation of the soil, being mere 'serfs'. If landowners and the government wanted to avoid the Highlands becoming 'a hot-bed for revolutions', they should give them 'an interest in the soil'.[37]

After examining and rejecting the explanations usually given for the Clearances, the *Witness* named what it saw as the real reasons. The first of these was 'the inexplicable craving on the part of some proprietors after large farms'.[38] The paper claimed that the landlords had 'adopted' the idea of joining field to field out of ignorance of their real interest. Large fields, according the *Witness*, did not bring larger rentals, but only increased waste lands with no people to cultivate them. The estates thus lay unimproved, the land falling back 'into its original state of wilderness'.

These proprietors were then able to pose as noble and glorious lords, the paper suggested:

> They can ride out of a forenoon with their visitors, and point out to them the splendid enclosures, or the extensive sheep-walks, or the well-stocked deer-forest, as they pass along, without once alluding to the amount of human suffering by which the whole was purchased. They want fine fields and fine forests. What care they for men! They want on their estates something worthy of their patrician greatness. What though hundreds or thousands of human beings should be wrenched from their beloved homes, and cast for subsistence on the cold world! Little do these men know what they are doing –.[39]

This picture certainly made the Highlands look like a playground for men posing as feudal lords and arranging the land as a stage to act out their fantasies. In an age of improvement and capitalisation, the impression from images like these was that time had stopped in the Highlands, and such images were quite characteristic of many sympathetic papers.

In its list of the real causes of depopulation policy in the Highlands, the *Witness* gave four more reasons. These were the 'competition for land among the larger farmers', the 'dread' of the New Poor Law, 'the uncomplaining character of the people' and their fear of God, which prevented them from 'revenge' on the oppressor, and lastly, the 'almost inextricable difficulties' of many landlords.

In the last part of the series, the paper drew up its list of remedies. One remedy, it proposed, was to 'agitate the question of the security of tenure generally over the kingdom', as part of a 'great national movement'.[40] Another remedy suggested was some sort of court action challenging the rights of the landlords. But, as the paper feared, the law courts were 'so completely made up of the privileged classes' and 'so thoroughly imbued with the spirit of the feudal law' that it did not hope for much success in that area.

The remedy which the *Witness* urged most strongly was the abolition of the laws of entail and primogeniture. It called these laws 'the curse of this nation', which 'fettered' the soil, and 'beggared' the proprietors and people alike. Only the total annulment of these laws would 'emancipate the soil', which was an essential prerequisite for the emancipation of the people.

In its closing remarks, the *Witness* assured its readers that it spoke 'in the spirit of the truest conservatism', and envisaged the changes being carried out constitutionally. It only desired 'to have all property under the control of a system of laws' which would 'secure the wellbeing of the nation'.

After the autumn of 1849, the Highlands did not occupy much space in the pages of the *Witness*. In 1850, not until December did a single article appear dealing with the Highlands in any form. This rather sudden stop came at a time when destitution was getting worse and when other sympathetic papers, among them two newly established ones, were leading loud campaigns in defense of the Gaels and doing battle with the system. Perhaps one explanation was offered in an article in the *Witness* in December 1850:

> We are aware that many of our readers look upon this continuous cry of Highland destitution somewhat in the light of that of 'Wolf, wolf', while the wolf never came.[41]

This might refer to an editorial decision not to 'overdo' the Highlands topic. However, silence throughout a whole year of crisis was perhaps more than this. While the paper did pick up the Highland issue in 1851, – urging aid for the famine, condemning the M'Neill report, and with Miller writing an overview reiterating the papers' old points[42] – it again went completely silent in 1852 and for most of 1853 and 1854. While other papers ran several crusading articles in each of their issues, the *Witness*, with the largest circulation and its weighty influence, remained mostly silent. And some of the most brutal Clearances, as in Knoydart and Greenyards, were not even reported in the paper.

In this light, the question can be raised of just how 'radical' Hugh Miller and the *Witness* were on Highland issues. How much of a 'crusading editor' was Miller when he kept the debate on the Highlands out of his pages when the crisis and the debate were hottest? And how much of an 'outraged' man was he, when during the crises in the early 1850s, he ran other people's letters but did not write editorials himself?

One answer that can be offered here is that Hugh Miller in his *Witness* was indeed a scathing critic, and when he did speak out he did so in radical tones. But the Highlands did not form a central issue in his paper and his campaigns, and Miller was far from a consistently crusading missionary journalist for the Highland Gaels. That battle was largely fought by others.

A more persistent crusading critic was Robert Somers in the *North British Daily Mail.* Somers was much less known than Hugh Miller, and rarely mentioned as a Highland critic. His writings are hardly ever quoted today, and were not even included in Alexander Mackenzie's famous *History of the Highland Clearances,* which gathered many of the defenders of the Gaels throughout the nineteenth century. This is all the more perplexing as Somers wrote one of the most comprehensive and longest-standing critiques of the Highland policies, in his series of letters published in 1848 under the title of *Letters from the Highlands.*[43] Moreover, he was quoted at length in no less a work than Karl Marx's *Das Kapital* in the chapter on 'Expropriation of Agricultural Population'.

Somers was also editor of the *North British Daily Mail* between 1849 and 1859, and under his editorship the paper became a highly critical forum for sympathetic public opinion. The *North British Daily Mail* was especially vigorous in campaigning in 1851 against the M'Neill report and the emigration schemes relating to it. It also ran articles by Donald Ross, the well-known crusading 'friend' of the Gaels. However, the paper also tended to patronise as well as romanticise the Highlanders. After 1851 it devoted more space for romantic descriptions of the Highlands than to their grimmer reality.

Born in 1822, Robert Somers was just twenty when he was already a well-known lecturer on social and political issues, and he published his first pamphlet on the Scottish Poor Law in 1844.[44] After this publication he was offered the editorship of the *Scottish Herald,* just founded in Edinburgh. For a brief period he was editor of the paper and when the management of the *Herald* was merged with the *Witness*, Somers became the colleague and assistant of Hugh Miller.

In 1847 Somers joined the *North British Daily Mail* in Glasgow and as a 'special commissioner' went to the Highlands on a 'Tour of Inquiry' into the distress there. He wrote as many as twenty-seven letters in a series of articles throughout the autumn. This was possibly the longest series on the condition of the Highlands ever published in the mid-nineteenth-century Scottish press. When they were published in book form in 1848 entitled *Letters from the Highlands*, four new articles were added.

In 1849 Somers began his ten years as editor of the *North British Daily Mail*. The paper was the first Scottish daily and by the 1850s it was thriving, attaining a circulation close to that of the *Witness*, making it the fourth largest circulation paper in Scotland.[45] Considering that the *North British Daily Mail* was a daily paper while the rest were twice or thrice weeklies, its readership was even higher. According to Jack's *Scottish Newspaper Directory* the paper's political principles were 'very undecided, sometimes Whig, sometimes Radical, sometimes neither', and it was usually considered the organ of the Whig party.

The Highlands occupied more of a central place in this paper than in either the *Argus* or the *Witness*. As Somers himself remarked in the preface of his book, the *North British Daily Mail* was 'a journal, which, since its commencement' had taken 'a marked interest in every question affecting the condition and prospects of the Highlands'.[46] Such a paper was a suitable forum for a missionary journalist like Somers. A newspaper any less interested in the Highlands was not likely to run twenty-seven articles in one series on the subject.

Somers set out on his Tour of Inquiry in October 1847. In his preface to the book he gave the gist of the crusading journalist's creed:

> To help forward the cause of the suffering Highlanders was the prime object
> for which they were written, and to that cause they are dedicated anew.[47]

The *Letters from the Highlands* was a complex work. Its arguments were powerful, its language strong and angry, and the proposals and demands put forward were often radical. However, it was also a rather strange mixture of impassioned defense of the Gaels with strongly patronising attitudes and sudden romanticising soliloquies.

Somers called the Clearances the 'heartless extirpation' of the people, and 'a policy of barrenness and barbarism'.[48] He described the process bitterly as a heartless 'business-like' operation in which people were cleared like trees in wasteland:

The clearance and dispersion of the people is pursued by the proprietors as a settled principle, as an agricultural necessity, just as trees and bushwood are cleared from the wastes of America and Australia; and the operation goes on in a quiet, business-like way, that neither excites the remorse of the perpetrators, nor attracts the sympathy of the public.[49]

This passage was quoted in Marx's *Capital* Volume II, published in London in 1884. In the chapter on the 'Expropriation of Agricultural Population', it was Somers Marx quoted most. Marx moved to London just one year after Somers' book was published and he might have come across it while he spent time in the British Museum. According to Marx, what the 'clearing of estates' really meant could be best seen 'in the promised land of modern romance, the Highlands of Scotland'.[50] There, he said, it was carried out in 'a systematic character' and on a very large scale, in areas as large as German principalities.

Marx also quoted Somers extensively on the question of deer forests, 'the second time the Gaels were hunted out'.[51] Somers devoted much space in his book to the issue of deer forests. He was especially furious at this new phenomenon. In this 'second Clearance' in which sheep and men were cleared to make way for deer forests people were yet again dispossessed, and this time for the sake of pure private pleasure and luxury. Somers was infuriated to see the vast lands of the Highlands turned into aristocratic playgrounds. If the forests continued to extend at such a pace the people would simply disappear, 'perish from their native soil'. This was one of Somers' angriest passages in the series, worth quoting at length:

The gigantic scale of their operations is incredible. New forests are rising up like mushrooms . . . Houses, roads, enclosures, cattle, men, – every work of time and of progress – the valuable creations of labour and the slow changes of centuries – are all extirpated by a word, in order that deer may enjoy the luxury of solitude, and sportsmen monopolise the pleasures of the chase . . . (. . .) It devotes land to private pleasure, the produce of which was formerly so much gain to the commonwealth; and even in its direct bearings upon the small tenants, it is attended with effects not much less injurious than a positive ejectment. It is curious, though painful, to trace the perversity with which the Highland people are pursued from bad to worse to worse again. In the first place, sheep were introduced into glens which had been the seats of communities of small farmers; and the latter were driven to seek subsistence on coarser and more sterile tracts of soil. Now, again, deer are supplanting sheep; and these are once more dispossessing the small tenants, who will necessarily be driven down upon still coarser land, and to

more grinding penury. Or, to speak more truly, the deer-forests and the
people cannot co-exist. One or the other of the two must yield. Let the
forests be increased in number and extent during the next quarter of a
century, as they have been in the last, and the Gael will perish from their
native soil.[52]

The result of the Clearances was devastation, turning the Highlands into a
desert and making the people paupers. There was less work to be done but
more people to hire themselves, 'grinding down small farmers into day-
labourers', while at the same time there were no great industrial operations
to absorb the unemployed, leaving people without resources. Apart from
the consequences of the Clearances there were 'daily oppressions' burden-
ing the people, Somers said. These included prohibitions against killing fish
in the river and wild beasts on the hills, or travelling through forests and
paths, and refusing church sites.

Somers depicted the whole scene of Highland oppression in images
evoking a race for life, a struggle for survival:

> Deer have received extended ranges, while men have been hunted within a
> narrower and still narrower circle. The strong man has fainted in the race for
> life. The old and tender have been left to die.[53]

These expressions went beyond simple journalism. Somers wrote here
metaphorically of men being hunted down and failing in a 'race for life'.
These images suggested that men had to compete with deer in a struggle for
life over the soil of the Highlands. A 'struggle for survival', in fact. These
were essentially Darwinian notions, although it was not until 1859 that
Darwin's famous book, *The Origin of the Species*, appeared. However, some
of his ideas had been 'in the air' long before in the intellectual climate of the
nineteenth century, in the theories of Thomas Malthus and Herbert
Spencer. And by the 1840s the notions of the 'survival of the fittest'
and 'struggle for survival' had been suggested by some economists, and
many Darwinian notions were present in the Scottish encyclopedist Robert
Chambers' *The Vestiges of the Natural History of Creation* in 1844.[54] All this
illustrates that the climate of opinion was quite 'Darwinian' by the 1840s
and that Robert Somers was aware of these ideas and applied them, to some
extent, to the Highlands.

Somers warned that if this 'hunt' of the people in this 'race for life'
coupled with 'daily oppressions' were pushed much further the overall
suffering of the people would reach a 'pitch' when 'action' would be 'the
plainest duty' and 'most sacred instinct'. In the light of the ensuing crofters'

resistance in Greenyards in 1854, and much later in Skye in the 1880s, Somers' words here proved to be prophetic. By calling action 'the most sacred instinct' when suffering reached intolerable levels, Somers implied that it was the right of the people to revolt and resist oppression.[55]

In some parts of the Highlands people did not wait until their condition became unbearable, but rather emigrated voluntarily. This 'voluntary' emigration, however, was not truly free and willing since people left in desperation seeing no other choice at home where life was made impossible for them, Somers asserted. This argument later became central in the debates and conclusions of the 1850s in many sympathetic newspapers:

> . . . the people emigrate voluntarily rather than settle down in a state of degrading wretchedness; but like other Highlanders, they are strongly attached to their native country; and the extensive emigration which has taken place may be taken as an index of the pressure which has been operating upon them of late years.[56]

Somers saw one of the most fundamental problems in the state of the crofters. They were not more than serfs, or even slaves, he claimed. This had several grave consequences. Apart from the wretchedness of the people, it meant that the crofters had no interest in working effectively, were not even given proper instruction how to improve their work, and remained wretched and degraded. Such a system was also disadvantageous from the landlords' point of view since slaves simply made bad workers with no interest in improvement. The following passage summed up well what Somers thought on this:

> Slave-labour, it is said, is dearer than free labour, and one reason of that must be, that the slave, conscious that he is plundered of the fruits of his toil, refuses to apply himself with energy and vigour to his work. But if this is the effect produced upon a slave, who is well fed and well clad at his master's cost, how natural must it be for the Highland cottar to hate and detest labour, when he feels himself bound hand and foot for the petty privilege of planting a few barrels of potatoes! It is vain to talk about indolence and laziness of the Highlanders so long as such a system continues. To the Highland cottar labour has hitherto been synonymous with robbery and oppression. He has never known its value – he has never tasted its rewards; and how can it be otherwise than that he should feel averse to it, and prefer to resort to more easy and more questionable means of livelihood?(. . .)It is preposterous to talk of slavery being abolished in the British dominions. The

Highland cottar groans under a bondage as oppressive and degrading as the feudal serf of the middle ages, or the negro slave of the present times.[57]

The above lines made it clear that Somers did share the opinion that the Highlanders were 'lazy' but he entirely attributed this to the system which did not motivate and teach them to work hard. The solution, he urged, was to give the people an interest in the soil by granting them leases and then instruct and educate them to improvement. Instead of driving people off their lands, their country should employ them at home, train them to industry, 'raise their standard of comfort' and 'increase their intelligence'.[58]

The first measure to take, therefore, was to give the people leases and more land. If they were given better lands with security, Somers suggested, they would work on it hard enough. No improvement was possible without 'a new distribution of soil', he insisted.[59] 'The cry for land' was already here in 1847:

> The cry of the people themselves is 'more land, more land!' and it must be re-echoed by their benefactors till the vast arena of opinion resound with the demand. There is no remedy but the cultivation of the soil. The famished people cling to their patches of land with the desperation of wrecked mariners to their last plank. Like the plank, these patches are narrow for them to stand upon, and they are like to be overwhelmed in the yawning gulph; but give them wider space – a broader deck – and they will breast the billows.[60]

The landlords, however, were decidedly unwilling to grant leases or more land. Somers explained this with a rather striking theory, involving certain 'secret hankerings' of the landlords.[61] He claimed that the landlords never really wanted to keep people on the land but to 'clear them from the soil' and 'sweep them from the country'.

If they had had enough money they would have shipped everyone to a foreign shore all at once. But the expense of such an emigration was 'too much for their slender means, and the project had to be abandoned'. Instead, they introduced the croft system 'as a temporary expedient to facilitate the clearances', and to provide 'a refuge to the outcasts till an opportunity should arise to transporting them to their allotted homes in Australian or Canadian wildernesses'. The landlords had only been waiting for an opportunity to be able, with Government or public funds, 'to ship away the miserable population which swarms along their shores'. In order to do this they had to ensure that the people were only 'loosely' tied to the soil, and leases would have been 'awkward barriers'. People were therefore kept deliberately in a state in which they could be shipped off easily and in a condition which could justify the necessity, Somers claimed:

> Why attempt to ward off the evil tendency of a system which is already doomed? Why make an effort to improve the condition of people who are on their march to another hemisphere, and from whom we have nothing either to hope or fear? Leave them to themselves. Let them marry, subdivide and multiply, till they are ready to eat each other up in the struggle for existence. When things are at the worst they will mend. The more deplorable and hopeless the extremity to which matters come, the more cogent the reasons for wholesale expatriation, and the more urgent the necessity for the Government to interfere, so that when the night is darkest then will come the dawn. These are the silent cogitations and the secret hankerings in the minds of the Highland lairds, which paralyse improvement, which wither up the soul of the enterprise, and which undermine every humane and every patriotic resolution.[62]

The charge he made here was one of the harshest ever brought against the Highland landlords. It certainly had an element of conspiracy theories, and at first might have sounded like madness to many. However, there was a grain of truth in it. To many landlords the people on their estates were indeed a heavy, unwanted burden, and when in the 1850s the Government came up with emigration schemes many landlords were relieved to be able to ship off hundreds of people at public expense. In the 1850s many sympathetic campaigners echoed Somers' theory and carried it even further, accusing the landlords of deliberate 'exterminating' policies.

In the concluding Letter, Somers gave a review of the sources of Highland destitution and made detailed proposals for possible remedies. He summed up the sources in five points: 'waste of land' (by sheep walks, deer forests, natural wastage, and imperfect cultivation), 'waste of manure', 'waste of capital', 'waste of labour' and 'waste of time'.[63]

Somers proposed four basic remedies: 'liberal and effectual poor law', 'law for the unemployed', 'law of entail entirely abolished', and 'greater and better means of education'. It was under the 'law for the unemployed' where he put forward his most original proposals. 'Liberty to work is a natural right', was Somers' motto here:

> Let it never be said that liberty to work for daily bread is a boon – a charity – conferred upon the labouring man by society. It is a natural right; and society is as richly blessed by its exercise as the labourer himself.[64]

The notion of the 'right to work' was around by this time in France, originating from Pierre Joseph Proudhon in his *Qu'est-ce que la propriété?* (What is Property?) published in 1840, and taken up by other French socialists, such as Louis Blanc. Proudhon's main aim was to abolish unproductive property and to establish 'mutualist' farmers' or workers' co-operatives as an answer to economic injustices.[65] It was also in this work that Proudhon put forward the concept of the right and freedom to work as everyone's natural right. This concept became law in the 1848 Revolution in France when in February the Provisional Government issued a decree about 'the right to work' and National Workshops served as extensive projects of unemployment relief.

Proudhon's work was not published in English until 1876, but as there was considerable contact between the French socialists and the British Chartists, his ideas might have had some influence on certain thinkers in Britain. Somers could either have read Proudhon's work in French, (he was well-educated) or could have read about it while he was a young lecturer on social and political questions, or perhaps simply he was aware of the concept in the general intellectual climate during the 1840s. There was certainly a detectable influence of Proudhon and French socialism on Somers' ideas, not only in the concept of the right to work but also in his vehement opposition to unrestricted property, and in the employment proposals he outlined as one of the remedies for the Highlands.

As the first point of this scheme, he recommended a law which would give 'a right to employment' from the parishes for those able-bodied people who were deprived of their lands and could not find work.[66] According to Somers, there was abundant employment to be found in the Highlands on the vast uncultivated lands. The question was, as he put it, 'exceedingly simple'. The land and labour were both there, all that was wanted was the 'necessary funds to maintain the labourers during the initiative stages of the works'. This necessary startup capital should come from a 'an improvement tax levied upon property'. It was 'reasonable', Somers said, that those productive properties which yielded an annual rental of more than half-a-million should be charged with the 'preliminary expense of improving the remainder' which was waste and unproductive. The planning and organisation should be done by a Board of Works with the parochial boards assisting with a committee of works. The reclaimed land would then be purchased from the proprietor for the parish.

There was another side of the coin in Somers' scheme. Providing employment was not only necessary because it was everyone's natural right and because it could regenerate the Highlands, but it would also serve the educational purpose of 'training' the people to industry and hard work. Abundant employment opportunity would leave 'no excuse for idleness', Somers reckoned. His scheme of public works would give 'an excellent field for drilling the Highlands in industry', for 'inuring them to hard labour', and for training them in 'habits of steady perseverance and self-exertion'.[67] The public works would also give the Highlanders 'masters', who, Somers thought, were necessary 'to direct their operations, and to keep them steadily at work'.[68]

So vehemently was Somers urging the Highland Gaels to take up hard work that at one point he plunged into a long sermon addressed directly to the Highlanders:

> Hercules only helps those who help themselves. This is a maxim which cannot be too deeply impressed upon the Highland mind. The Temple of Plenty can only be entered through the Porch of Labour. In sunny and genial climes, where the earth sends forth her fruits in spontaneous profusion, men may eat the bread of idleness with comparative impunity; but in the Highlands, with its cold blasts, its deluges of rain, and its iron soil, life can only be sustained by hard and perserving exertion. Highlanders! this is the condition imposed by that land of mountains and storms you love so well, and it is the part of true patriotism to submit to it. If you would cling to your native country, you must labour unceasingly to improve, adorn, and replenish her waste places. You must build up her ruined walls. You must renew and recultivate her obliterated fields. You must drain her marshes. You must economise and develop her resources. *You must work, work, work, and work as you have never worked before*, till her face is irradiated with the smile of plenty, and her very deserts rejoice and blossom as the rose.[69]

Somers' crusading criticisms were therefore directed not only against the landlords' 'evil' policies but also against apparent Highland indolence. But he made it plain that the regeneration of the Highlands he envisaged was only to be achieved through mutual 'exertions' on all sides. In his final judgement, however, Somers clearly put the bulk of responsibility on the landowning class:

> . . . as I have often remarked, the indolence of the monied classes of the Highlands is a worse obstacle to improvement than the indolence of the poor. The same evil taint infects society from its top to its base, being the more fatal and inexcusable the higher it is found on the social scale.[70]

Throughout most of his *Letters*, Somers maintained his argumentative and impassioned style, dealing with many concrete points of the grim reality of the Highlands. Amidst these stood out a long passage of pure romantic fantasy. It was a blend of exhilaration inspired by the beauties of Highland scenery and an Arcadian notion of turning the Highlands into some poetic land of idyllic peasantry. Somers was carried away into dreaming of re-establishing the mystical 'Golden Age' in the Highlands. In his imagination he arranged Highland cottages as if he held a painter's brush in his hands creating a romantic scenery. This was 'improving' in a poetical vein. It was quite a remarkable chain of thought:

> For an instant a thin vapoury cloud would pass between the sun and the earth, and fall in light dewy showers, like the momentary blush which steals over a maiden's cheek and vanishes in tears. My road lay through a forest of natural wood, the openings of which afforded sweet glimpses of the Loch; and upon entering the more fertile glades, I was frequently surprised to find myself in the presence of a group of cottages, with plots of corn ground, enclosed from the wood by small wicker fences. Here might be seen the shepherd's hook; here also was the forest shade, the gurgling stream, and the wooly flock. *I fancied to myself that if Arcadian bliss could be realised on earth, it might be here.* The Highlands offer the most splendid attractions to that class of improves who delight in developing the poetry and romance of rural life. The external formation of the country affords the best possible opportunities for embellishment and effect; the cottages might be placed in the most beautiful and fantastic situations; the imagination of the people themselves is poetical, and would really strike in with any scheme of improvement which was poetical in its tendencies. If the work of Highland regeneration be ever taken up with rigour and earnestness, the Highlands, without hyperbole, may become the most enchanting country, and the Highlanders the finest peasantry in the world.[71]

This apparently strange blend of severe criticism and romance did not only characterise Somers' *Letters from the Highlands* but the whole of the *North British Daily Mail* under his editorship. Often on the same page as strongly critical articles written in a dark foreboding tone, the paper ran travel pieces on the picturesque beauties of the Highland scenery written in a light, romanticised style. There was something bizarre in one article bitterly attacking the 'extermination' of the native Highlanders and the depopulation of the land, while another would find the barrenness of the land scenic and picturesque.[72]

The romantic side of this paper's split personality was becoming dominant, especially after 1851. Before then, however, the *North British Daily Mail* produced a particularly fierce campaign against plans for extensive emigration schemes from the Highlands and became one of the main opponents of the M'Neill report and the ensuing Emigration Act.[73]

After the publication of Sir John M'Neill's report, which prescribed extensive emigration from the Highlands, the *North British Daily Mail* ran six long articles within less than two weeks vehemently attacking it. Every second issue – that meant every second day – contained a long editorial on the subject virtually tearing the report to bits, ridiculing M'Neill and loudly protesting against the proposed emigration plans. Many of Somers' arguments from 1847 were also echoed in these articles.

The paper's indignation was first directed at the speed at which Parliament was passing through the Emigration Advances Bill following M'Neill's recommendations. The Bill passed through the House of Commons in four days without questions or amendments. The *North British Daily Mail* was appalled, and compared the Government to the Roman dictator Julius Caesar. As the second editorial put it with irony:

> Caesar's conquest of Britain when he came, and saw, and conquered, was not a more wonderful feat than that of the Whig Government in conquering Highland destitution.[74]

Two days later the paper's indignation grew even more; this time the editorial emphasised that the London Parliament was simply 'trifling' with Scotland's interest:

> It is expected to regenerate the social condition of half a kingdom, and yet it is a subject of less examination and criticism than an English Parochial Vestry Bill (. . .) the House takes no notice of it, never dreams of inquiring whether it is suitable to the end in view (. . .) but allows it to be hurried through its various stages as if it really felt that the Bill and all whom it concerns were utterly beneath its notice. It is impossible not to feel indignant at this scandalous trifling with our dearest interests; . . .[75]

M'Neill's recommendation to the Government that only extensive and government-assisted emigration could be any remedy was simply dubbed by the paper as a 'plot' for the 'deportation' of the entire population to foreign shores.[76] It claimed that M'Neill was 'hood-winked' by the Parochial Boards, which consisted mostly of factors, graziers and 'the mere tools of these parties'. These, the paper went on, had a 'rooted aversion to the people' and had been 'intriguing indefatigably for the last six years to effect their entire expulsion from the country'.[77] This echoed Somers' accusation in 1847 that the landowners only waited with 'secret hankerings' for the opportunity to get rid of their unwanted burdensome tenants.

From the actual Bill as it was passed the paper did not expect 'much evil'. The implementation was 'guarded by too many checks', it said, to produce much good or harm. It depended on the people's willingness to emigrate, on the readiness of the landlords to burden their estates, on the Treasury advancing the money and on the Land and Emigration Commissioners' acceptance of the people as emigrants. It was going to be a 'machine with many drags' moving 'slowly and imperfectly', the editorial pointed out.[78]

It warned, however, that precisely because of the way the Bill was passed, the landlords would do everything to make life difficult, so that the people would not want to remain on their lands any more:

> . . . a cruel effort will be made in various quarters to render the Highlands too hot for its inhabitants. 'Old as I am,' said an aged crofter in Skye to Sir John, his heart heaving with agony, 'I would rather go, if I find the means, than remain *with the prospects before me*.[79]

The *North British Daily Mail* was not, however, opposed to emigration as such. It gave its support to a 'natural, gradual, wholesome' emigration, as 'one of the essential measures' to Highland improvement. This was another reason, according to the paper, why the Emigration Bill should have been made more 'safe and sure'. The editorial voiced its strong concern that the Bill did nothing to prevent landlords clearing people in order to push them off the land and force them to emigrate. The paper urged provision for the settlement of those who emigrated and measures for the protection and improvement of the Highlanders who remained at home.

In addition to the numerous editorials, the *North British Daily Mail* also ran a six part series on M'Neill's report. The series' aim was to disprove M'Neill's explanations and conclusion, by comparing his points with those given by the witnesses and by the paper's own observations.

As the articles took M'Neill's points one by one the paper was highly derisive, going as far as ridiculing M'Neill's intellectual capability. At one point, it talked about 'Sir John's intellect' having 'evidently become obfuscated in this mysterious passage of the Report'.[80] At another point, it complained of having to read 'a whole congeries of causes contributing to Highland destitution, in the utmost irregularity and confusion'.

The paper's main contention was that M'Neill misrepresented the evidence given to him, and mixed up cause and effect. First it quoted at length from both M'Neill's conclusions of the Report and the evidence given by crofters. 'The be-all and the end-all of Sir John M'Neill's theory of Highland Distress', the paper said, was over-population and he attributed to this all other causes, such as want of capital and land. The crofters' account, however, gave a different picture from M'Neill's, with which he had 'amused and exercised his imagination', the paper argued, once more in ironic vein.[81]

In the final part of the series, the paper summed up its verdict. 'We charge Sir John M'Neill', it said severely, 'with having returned a Report to the Government' which was not only 'unsupported, but directly contradicted by the Evidence given him in the Highlands'.[82] M'Neill misplaced '*effects for causes*', and through this, he virtually deceived the Government, keeping the 'true and fundamental sources of destitution out of sight' to win support for his own 'favourite remedy of emigration'. In order to make its point abundantly clear, the *North British Daily Mail* drew up a list here, summing up in seven points the causes of Highland destitution according to M'Neill and according to the evidence of witnesses. This list provides a good summary of the arguments on both sides of the 'Highland Question':[83]

CAUSES OF DESTITUTION ACCORDING TO SIR JOHN M'NEILL.

1. Want of land sufficient to maintain the population.
2. Want of capital among the crofters to occupy and cultivate the soil.
3. Bad climate, rendering crops in the Highlands scanty, precarious, and unprofitable.
4. The system of small farming, under which nearly every man depends for his food on the produce of land occupied by himself.
5. Indolence and Incorrigibility of the people.
6. Imperfect execution of the Clearance Policy in the remote parts of the Highlands and Islands.
7. Want of Intercourse with the Lowlands.

CAUSES OF HIGHLAND DESTITUTION ACCORDING TO SIR JOHN'S MINUTES OF EVIDENCE

1. Monopoly of the soil by Sheep Graziers, and consequent pressure of the people into mosses and on small and barren patches of land.
2. Exorbitant rents of Crofts, paid and payable in Kelp-making times, and under a system of potato culture, but totally disproportionate to the fair value of the soil under the new circumstances, which have arisen since the cessation of the Kelp-manufacture, and the failure of the potatoes.

3. Inferior Cultivation of the Soil, and unsuitable Crops.
4. Concentration of the old moderately sized farms into a few large sheep-walks, and the consequent extremes of too large holdings on the one land, and too small holdings on the other.
5. Want of leases, of education, and industrial training.
6. Violent dispossession of the small tenants, and consequent accumulation of poor, unemployed, and destitute persons in the towns and villages.
7. The necessity imposed upon the people, by the inadequacy of their crofts to maintain them, to remain idle during a great part of the year, or wander up and down the country in search of work, when they should be attending to their own fields and crops.[84]

It was easy to see where the two sides differed. What Somers' paper condemned most was that M'Neill overlooked the 'huge monopoly of the soil' and that he not only kept silent on the 'swallowing up' of moderate-sized farms but he actually supported 'the execrable clearance policy'.

The solution the *North British Daily Mail* urged was radical. It amounted to nothing less than the re-distribution of the soil by taking land back from the sheep farmers to be given to the people again:

> If the land in the possession of the people is too small for their support, a portion of these sheep grazings should be opened up to them; and if this is a measure against which landlords and graziers revolt, we cannot see how they can escape from the alternative of supporting the poor and able-bodied destitute out of the profits of that favourite system, upheld for their interest, and against the interests of the people.[85]

What was at issue here was the capitalist interests of landowners and their human responsibility to take care of those at whose expense their profit was made. In the value system of the *North British Daily Mail*, the interests of humans came before the interests of capital.

After this heavy and impassioned campaigning against the M'Neill Report, the paper turned down the intensity of its crusading journalism. It started to run more of the romantic travel pieces and sometimes, as in 1852, the topic of Highland destitution had all but disappeared from its pages. However, the case had not been abandoned completely, and when new crises arrived with the brutal clearances in Knoydart and Greenyards the paper ran the reports of the radical Donald Ross. At the same time, there were no more impassioned editorials accompanying these reports. The commitment to the Highlands had waned considerably after 1851.

The *North British Daily Mail* was indeed a radical critic of the Highlands when it decided to devote its attention to the issue. It was not, however, a persistent crusader with a thorough dedication. This task was taken up by two new papers in the early 1850s, which were established partly in order to campaign for the Highlands.

II. The Crusaders of the 1850s

What crusading journalism really meant was shown on the pages of the *Inverness Advertiser* and the *Northern Ensign* in the 1850s. In their editorial content and in the number of articles they ran with 'investigative' pieces by 'special correspondents' these two papers went far beyond any other sympathetic papers. The two papers taken together produced three times as many articles on the Highlands as the *Witness* and the *North British Daily Mail* together in the 1850s.

While the papers of Hugh Miller and Robert Somers had only occasionally taken up the issue of the Highlands, the *Inverness Advertiser* and the *Northern Ensign* were primarily established in order to fight oppression, advocate human rights and deal with the Highland question. They were literally 'dedicated to the Highlands'.

These two papers also provided a forum for all the most radical critics of the Highlands. There were times when the *Ensign* ran in one single issue articles from Thomas Mulock, Donald M'Leod and Donald Ross. Both the *Advertiser* and the *Ensign* were fiercely critical, and concentrated their attack on Highland landlordism.

The *Inverness Advertiser* was a liberal weekly paper founded in June 1849, with an average circulation of 1200.[86] It was partly founded as a Free Church journal and partly 'to expound Highland grievances'. On ecclesiastical questions it 'introduced a new acerbity', and it was the 'most authoritative voice' on Highland distress.[87]

In its introductory issue, the paper claimed it wanted to become 'a true local Highland newspaper'. It apologised to its readers for the fact that the journalists themselves were not from the Highlands, that they were 'strange in a great measure to their men and things'. However, the editors expressed their determination to learn everything, and recommended themselves to the readers' 'Highland generosity'.[88]

The paper vowed thorough political independence, becoming

'partisans of no particular set of men'. Its philosophy was summed up as serving 'the public good', all that was of mutual interest in society. Agricultural and manufacturing interests were bound together and none of them should be sacrificed for the sake of the other, the editorial said:

> Truly understood, the interests of all classes are inseparably bound up together. The prosperity of one, is the prosperity of all, and only measures just to all, shall receive our support.[89]

The *Advertiser*'s radical criticism of the Highland landlords partly stemmed from this philosophy. It saw an unjust imbalance of interests in the Highlands, where the prosperity of one class was entirely sacrificed for another, the interests of the landlords ruining the lives of the crofters. Taking this basic philosophy further, the paper also pledged its duty to come to the defense of 'the weaker party':

> . . . our single object is to give added solidity and cohesion to the foundation of the social fabric where they have gone out of joint. Were the fair and just rights of property or capital invaded, were they the weaker party, we should just as earnestly and energetically defend them, as we now espouse the cause of the injured peasantry. . . . God helping us, we shall not flinch from the position we have taken up, but shall continue to lift up testimony, sincere, however humble and feeble, against oppression.[90]

This was true missionary journalism. 'Espousing the cause of the injured' and upholding a testimony against 'oppression' summed up what crusading was about. The solemn oath of not flinching from the fight with God's help also revealed a crusading spirit. From its very beginning the paper recruited fierce fighters, first Thomas Mulock, then Donald Ross.

The *Inverness Advertiser* did maintain its fight during the 1850s, even when all other papers, except the *Northern Ensign*, were all but silent. Throughout 1850, for instance, the *Advertiser* assigned its 'own commissioner' to investigate 'Highland Destitution' in the western Highlands and Isles, and ran a long series with an article in almost every issue until mid-1851. On most major events, like the North Uist resistance and the Greenyards evictions, it reported from the scene. Its readers' correspondence was substantial and well written.

The *Advertiser*'s fellow crusader, the *Northern Ensign*, joined the battle in June 1850. It too solemnly vowed to defend the weak, and uphold society's mutual interests. Its motto came from the Greek Solon: 'An injury done to the meanest subject is an insult upon the whole constitution'.

The *Ensign* was a weekly, neutral paper based in Wick, at the northern end of the Highlands. Its average circulation of 1100[91] was similar to the *Advertiser*. Like the *Advertiser*, it also declared complete independence from any party or influence in its opening editorial:

> Without desiring to adopt a mere braggadocia style, we wish it to be distinctly understood, that we are neither at the bidding of any man, at the mercy of any sect, or tied to the chariot-wheels of any party. We demand the liberty which Milton claimed, 'to think, to argue, and to utter,' according to our conscience.[92]

Among its declared principles the paper listed 'private character as sacred', admiring and respecting 'dignity of labour', the right of private judgement in every matter, and the principle of public men being public properties and journalists' right to 'canvass their public actions'. The paper also declared the brotherhood of all men, their interests mutually linked:

> We regard all men as brethren, as children of one common parent, as branches on the same tree, and, as, therefore, deeply and mutually interested in each other. This great truth we will especially endeavour to enunciate and enforce.[93]

This egalitarian spirit naturally led to the paper taking up the cause of the 'suffering Highland Gaels' and going into battle against 'landlord oppression'. From the start the *Ensign* had Thomas Mulock at its helm to fight this battle. Seven months after its launch, the New Year editorial already talked about 'espousing the cause of the oppressed' and 'exposing the doings of the oppressor'. The paper claimed that it had a fiercer battle than other papers because with its 'unyielding independence' it provoked more opposition than others did:

> From the position we took up at the commencement, that of stern, unyielding independence; from the circumstance of our having been called upon to do battle against 'wickedness in high places', and to expose misrule and mismanagement in influential quarters, we have evoked a spirit of reckless and powerful opposition which has condescended to the basest and yet the silliest antagonism it is possible to conceive of.[94]

The 'opposition' against the *Ensign* only grew stronger, and by the end of 1851 the paper had been threatened with nine libel prosecutions. In the end, an editorial boasted, none of them had gone to court, and in only one case did the paper feel a duty to make an apology.[95] Even more telling was the fact that seven out of those nine cases had been 'intimately associated with the questions regarding the Highlands'.

From its start, the *Ensign* had become the most active champion of the Highlands. It was especially fierce and uncompromising in its first year and a half while it employed Mulock to lead the fight, but after his departure the paper sustained its campaign with Donald Ross and Donald M'Leod. Throughout the 1850s the editors maintained their policy of opposing tyranny by 'whomsoever perpetrated', and vowed to remain an organ of 'human rights':

> Having nothing to regret in reference to our advocacy of human rights, we have only to pledge ourselves that we shall adhere to the course we have pursued.[96]

In addition to its clear and determined editorial philosophy, the *Ensign* also produced professional journalism. Its composition was among the best of its time, with clean headlines and an easy layout. Its articles were generally well written and showed uniform editorial style.

The paper was also very 'reader centred'. It had the liveliest correspondence among the Scottish papers. The reply section of its 'To Correspondents' was much longer than in other papers, and it was also much more entertaining. A few examples give an idea of the paper's general tone with its readers:

> A Boy – Try again. Don't aim at being a poet. Try useful, practical writing, and, by perseverance and industry, you may be a great man yet.
>
> An Observer – has erred in his observations. He will require to make better use of his eyes.
>
> A Moderate – is exceedingly immoderate both in tone and manner . . . If other people abuse you, that is no reason why you should follow their example.[97]

The *Ensign* sought to entertain as well as educate its readers. It had a small section each week on 'Things to smile at' and 'Things to think about'. Its wisdom included observations on the foolishness of love, on how people only noticed other people's faults, and how one should not dwell too much on life, but participate and be less contemplative.

In just four pages, the *Ensign* managed to give good foreign and domestic news coverage, entertain its readers, and devote a large section to the issue of the Highlands. In some cases, the Highlands took up one whole page. No other paper had such concentration on the state of the Highlands.

The *Inverness Advertiser* and *Northern Ensign* together provided a most suitable forum for all crusading journalists like Thomas Mulock, Donald Ross and Donald M'Leod. It was a fortunate meeting of opportunity and talents.

'Notorious', 'eccentric', 'unblushing egotist', 'troublesome and unmanageable' were just some of the words his enemies found appropriate to describe Thomas Mulock. His admirers spoke of him as the true 'friend' of the oppressed Highlanders, as a man of 'talents and humanity', and as 'a household word' among the Highlanders, who had struck 'terror in the minds of the ruthless oppressors'. He saw himself as the fearless champion of the 'oppressed' Highlanders, truly devoted to their defence. As he summed up his mission: '– my business lies with the poor and the oppressed, and if I overcharge my statements of their case, I confess myself open to the censure of aggrieved proprietors'.[98]

Thomas Mulock was the most controversial character of the Scottish press at the time. He stood apart from all other journalists. His was a markedly different style: his language fiery, his arguments stubborn, ruthless in his sarcasm and boastful of his own significance. He saw himself as the sole champion in 'conflict with Scottish oppression', and looked down on other 'scribbling combatants'.[99]

He joined battle with everyone from landlords to the government, and with other newspapers. He delighted in controversy as if it gave him an opportunity to sharpen his arguments and display his brilliance. As his main paper, the *Ensign*, said of him, he smiled 'with contempt' at 'pigmy' attempts to belittle him for his 'sparkling wit, fiery rodomontade, and caustic philippies against all and sundry'.[100]

Mulock was an angry and passionate man, firmly convinced of his own truth. He was also a master of language, which he used as his main weapon. Alliterations and strong words were fired at his opponents like bullets from a gun. The following passage was characteristic of Mulock's style and temperament:

> In these days of puffery, clap-trap, and scheming sordidness, it is not to be expected that simple, straight-forward appeals on behalf of truth and justice will produce any very powerful effect on the public mind, or indeed that the Press can be made the medium of any such honest appeals. Of all the high-flown nonsense babbled by brainless chatterers, the most execrably sickening is the lying self-laudation regarding the independence of the Press![101]

Despite all the theatricality, Mulock was by far the sharpest and most ruthless commentator on the Highlands, and eventually his main arguments were proved right even by his opponents. Years after Mulock had left the scene, Donald Ross and Donald M'Leod arrived at very similar conclusions.

Lord Byron, the poet, whom Mulock had also attacked, thought him a tragic figure with ability, ambition but no discipline:

> I thought there was something of wild talent in him, mixed with a due leaven of absurdity, as there must be in all talent let loose upon the world without a martingale.[102]

Perhaps because of his unruly talent and temperament, Mulock has been largely forgotten by posterity. He was dismissed as an eccentric, someone who dared to attack even 'the immortal Hugh Miller', and the fact that his views about the Highlands were most radical and still relevant years later did not weigh heavily enough. When in 1883 Alexander Mackenzie compiled his popular *History of the Highland Clearances*, which was supposed to include all major sympathetic writers, Thomas Mulock was quoted only very briefly in the collection.

Mulock was an outsider among the crusaders not only in his individual style and temperament, but also in his background. He was an Anglo-Irish journalist who spent most of his life outside Scotland. He was an outsider, a stranger, and he drew on this position as an advantage when looking at the Highlands. He thought this provided him with more objectivity on Scottish matters. It also added to a certain sense of uniqueness and mystique which he liked to see around him. In a passage where the *Ensign* described his arrival on the newspaper scene, his image evoked a noble crusading knight suddenly appearing from afar to save the suffering Highlanders, all on his own:

> After an era of oppression and tyranny, almost unparalleled in the history of a civilised nation, and after every effort had been made to keep the press silent on the subject – with a degree of success but too well known – a stranger, stuck with wonder at the system which had obtained in certain northern districts, uninfluenced by malice, and instigated only by an unquenchable desire to benefit the suffering, came forth, and with eloquent pen exposed and denounced the system under which greater parts of the Highlands have been made a scene of woe and sorrow fitted to awaken the sympathetic indignation of every lover of man.[103]

Mulock arrived in Scotland in 1849 when he was already sixty. He was tall, handsome and witty, and 'a darling at conversation provided nobody interrupted him'.[104] By then, he had a rather stormy career behind him.

Born as a son of a Stamp Office Controller, he showed promise at Oxford, became a close friend of George Canning, read for the Bar, opened a law firm in Liverpool but soon turned to literature for greater excitement. He lectured to the Pitt Club, attacked the Whigs and Byron, and acquired a nickname of 'Bloody Moloch'.[105] After his marriage to the daughter of a tanner, he left England and appeared in Geneva and Paris giving lectures on English literature. Thomas Moore found these lectures irritating, in which, characteristically, Mulock dismissed a large part of English literature:

> He talked of persons going to the well-spring of English poetry in order to communicate what they have quaffed to others . . . Dryden was no poet. Butler had no originality, and Locke was of the school of the devil![106]

After the failure of his lectures, Mulock tried divinity and entered a Baptist Ministry, founding a chapel in Stoke-on-Trent. As with other areas of his life, he ran it in his individual way. He created his 'own elect' because he resented privilege by birth or wealth. Among this righteous 'elect' he also included his creditors. He was always in debt, mostly due to libel cases arising from his writings in the press. In 1831 he left Stoke, to reappear in Liverpool writing for the *Chronicle*. This time his attacks were directed against the Duke of Newcastle, Thomas Carlyle, Disraeli, and Prince Albert.

By August 1849 his name appeared on the pages of the *Inverness Advertiser*. He spent only two years in Scotland but during these two years he became a persistent crusader for the Highlands, and earned his 'notorious' reputation. He dedicated most of his time and prodigious energy to the issue of the Highland Clearances, first in the *Inverness Advertiser* then in the *Northern Ensign*.

In his very first article, which appeared with his name written from Skye, Mulock stated firmly the nature of his 'mission' and launched an attack on forced emigration. 'My proper mission is to listen to the cry of the oppressed', was his motto, in the true 'crusading' journalist vein.[107] He expressed his conviction that all the emigration movements were connected with 'injustice, compulsion, ferocity and fraud'. He called the allegations that the Gaels were willing exiles from their land 'monstrous misrepresentations' and 'vile cheats'. Petitions to emigrate did not reveal the real causes, they merely disguised the fact that the people felt forced to go:

> However coloured the immediate proceedings may be, by petitions to proprietors, &c., the real springs of emigration movements must be sought for in the sordid oppressions to which the wretched holders of petty portions of land are subjected, by the different instruments of ill-administered property.[108]

Mulock was already showing some of his typical tactics: the vigorous language where almost every word hit home ('sordid oppressions', 'petty portions of land'), the suggestion that he could unveil the real reasons below the surface, and of course his mastery of alliteration. A typical 'Mulockian' passage would always have a high number of alliterating words, fired like bullets from the page, greatly increasing the effect of anger and indignation.

After his opening piece, Mulock was soon in North Uist, the scene of recent evictions and crofters' resistance on the estate of Lord Macdonald.[109] At the time Mulock arrived there in September the crofters who had taken part in the resistance had just been taken to court. Now Mulock decided to subject Macdonald himself to investigation and scrutiny in the pages of the *Advertiser*. He wrote a series of articles to the paper from Uist addressed to 'the Right Hon. Lord Macdonald'. Mulock's sense of social justice and disregard for privilege were clearly put forward here:

> No privilege of your order can avail you here; and in your character of proprietor you are as amenable to the principles of truth and righteousness, as your captive tenants were to the common law of the land.[110]

Mulock charged Lord Macdonald with 'incorrect statements' when alleging that the land at Sollas was unsuitable for tenants. Mulock argued that with proper management and encouragement, and above all, with a reduction of rents and enlargement of crofts, the people could become 'thriving' there. Lord Macdonald had the 'remedy' at hand and could have made the right decision, Mulock suggested. Instead, he partitioned the district among two or three tacksmen, 'who had found favour' with his functionaries. As Mulock boldly affirmed, these 'monstrously unjust pre-arrangements' were 'at the root of all the systematic clearances'.

In his second letter Mulock went further and accused Lord Macdonald of using the police force, money from public charity and a loan from the government to carry out emigration schemes, in order to force the tenants 'to become despairing emigrants'.[111] Mulock also accused the landlord of 'spreading a salutary terror among the refractory non-emigrating of other clearing proprietors', by using harsh police tactics against the tenants who had refused to emigrate.

One of Mulock's most persistent points was that emigration from the Highlands, even if seemingly voluntary, was in fact forced, because people were either frightened into emigration or their conditions were rendered such that it was better to leave. Mulock stressed throughout his two year campaign that he was not opposed to genuine voluntary emigration where people chose freely to leave their lands for another country. However, what was happening in the Highlands was not truly voluntary but a result of various forms of persecution.

He claimed that Highland emigration was in fact covert compulsion:

> What I assert is this – that, in nine cases out of ten, the emigration of a large number of families is, however cloaked, in fact and truth, a compulsory proceeding. The poor exiles are not captured, chained, driven to the coast, and forcibly shipped, like gangs of negroes on the slave shore; but their condition is rendered miserable and hopeless in their native land. . . . Men's minds were harrassed – their lives embittered – their expectations totally crushed, by the persevering impolicy of their formerly kind landlord; and when a letter arrived from some refugee in America, recommending expatriation, the prospect then held out was seized on, as a raft is betaken to by shipwrecked mariners.[112]

He persisted in his argument of the essentially enforced nature of Highland emigration with growing force and angrier tone. At one stage he compared the expulsion of the Highland Gaels to the expulsions of the Jews from Spain and the Huguenots from France. The following passage was one of his most emotional, evoking universal images of the suffering of outcasts and refugees:

> When I see all the arts of persecution employed to impoverish, degrade, and render miserable the smaller tenants of an estate, with the view of making them vacate their little lands to swell the grazing solitudes of some insatiable sheep-master; when I hear of ship-loads of these poor expatriated creatures departing from their native coast, stripped of their substance to pay the price of a compulsory passage – leaving land, and stock, and crop, in the clutch of an inexorable factor; and pursuing them to their despotic destination – when I find them vomited out upon some unfriendly shore – harassed, hopeless, and pennyless – can I hesitate in affirming that these results are the product of tyranny and covetousness – excluding all semblance of free agency on the part of the unhappy victims of a ruthless and . . . an utterly unwise system?[113]

Mulock stoutly refused to accept the usual allegation of 'over-population' as the main reason for emigration. He called it 'the babble of Malthusian deprecators of progeny' and the 'moan of philanthropic proprietors'. He did not deny that people were indeed crowded on narrow patches of land, but this, he said, was a consequence of the clearances, of 'agrarian tyranny', and not of genuine over-population. The solution was not forced emigration but more land for the people, and checks on the 'tyrannical' powers over the land. 'What the people really require is *land*', he said emphatically:[114]

> I maintain that the people are not too many, but that their holdings are too small – their rents are too high – their oppressions innumerable – their encouragements *nil*. Impounded in sterile spots, which even the tacksman forbears to envy; their industry is checked by the total absence of all efficient incentives to exertion; they plod painfully on the thorny path of hopeless penury, drenched in debt, which, at length, has its issues in ejectment and emigration. All this accumulation of wrongs and neglect on the part of the unworthy proprietors is, forsooth, to be huddled out of thought and sight; and the whole evil to be accounted for by Malthus's infidel doctrine, denouncing early marriages, and progressive population – (. . .) My Lord, I treat with the scorn it deserves the trashy theory with which oppressors of the poor seek to cover their agrarian tyranny.[115]

Mulock was vehemently anti-aristocratic, his anger often reminiscent of French revolutionary radicals. At one point he would suggest evicting the aristocracy from their palaces and clearing them out of the land, they being the truly useless part of the population. He said that the real surplus population was in fact the 'idle, improvident or insolvent landlords', those who were tyrannical, those who were mere absentee landlords 'grinding down the faces of the poor Highland tenantry in order to support a shabby splendour in London or Brighton'. Mulock proposed that it 'would be desirable to check a population of *this* sort'.[116]

Mulock's anti-aristocratic feelings extended beyond the Highlands. In the whole of his contemporary society he saw a more universal social inequality, where 'the neglect of the poor' threatened to destroy the entire foundation of the social system. In Mulock's philosophical view of his age, the rich became mostly 'oppressors', and their 'epidemic blindness' and selfish 'hardness of heart' were to hinder any true national prosperity.

Mulock's view here recalled the *Advertiser*'s editorial philosophy of mutual interests in society, and it was also the creed the *Ensign* avowed a few months later. Mulock, however, was the fiercest advocate of these views, and he freely vented his anger against the upper classes of society. He had no pity for the 'slothful, sleepy sons of aristocracy' and argued that they would be no great loss, whereas degrading the productive classes of society would do fatal harm. For Mulock, what was happening in the Highlands was a case study of more universal injustices. The following extract from an

article on the parochial poor gives a good insight into Mulock's wider
views:

> The interests of the rich seem to be the exclusive care of conservativism,
> while, in fact, the neglect of the poor is destroying the entire foundations of
> the social system. The wealthy have their assigned position: they are
> stewards, administrators, responsible trustees of property, with a bounteous
> proportion for their own superior support and gratification; but if they
> selfishly appropriate *all*, they risk the loss of *all*. There is nothing new in
> selfishness. 'All for ourselves, and nothing for other people, has been in all
> ages', says shrewd Adam Smith, 'the vile maxim of the masters of mankind.'
> And our times are rife with this wickedness. In every city, town, village,
> hamlet or isolated abode of poverty, we can trace the operations of that
> insatiable covetousness, which prostrates the poor beneath the feet of
> opulent oppressors. The indigent have their share of sin and guilt – they
> are partakers of the same evil nature that incurably taints the more fortunate
> classes; but, still, it is to be remembered, that the productive labour of
> society is supplied by those who, if we may so speak, are nearest the earth,
> who till and sow, or toil and spin. Remove the slothful, sleepy sons of
> aristocracy, *summa papavera carpens*, and the damage can be readily repaired,
> for the artificial orders of society can re-constitute themselves; but, if the
> great body of the people be crushed into the degradation of absolute
> pauperism, we may be assured that, whatever be the seeming splendour of a
> great country, the real springs of national prosperity are fatally dried up.[117]

Mulock's anti-landlord feeling drew strength from his crusading mission, as
the defender of the weaker party. '*The rich hath many friends*', he wrote
emphatically and added that those who are in important positions had
'weightier responsibilities', therefore more blame should be put on the rich
than the poor.[118] Mulock's anti-landlord stance, however, was primarily
directed at the whole system of landownership by which the proprietors
were allowed excessive powers which they used for 'gross mal-administra-
tion of property'.[119] Mulock argued that the whole system was at fault
when a landlord had more power than an Austrian or Russian autocrat. He
claimed that no European monarch had 'a tithe of the potency to persecute'
that a Highland proprietor had.[120]

This comparison between Russian and Highland despotism was not
entirely new. A few years before, in 1845, the idea had already appeared in
the Scottish press, most likely originating from Hugh Miller. He
compared James Loch to Peter the Great, and Sutherland to a sort of
Russia 'on a small scale', waiting to be civilised by himself.[121] The same

comparison was also made in the London *Atlas*, reprinted in the *Times* in 1845, depicting Sutherlandshire as 'a sort of Russia, to be handed over to the autocratic civilisation of another Peter in the person of Mr Loch'.[122] From the closeness of the two versions it seems likely that the passage which the *Atlas* and the *Times* quoted was in fact from the *Witness* and Hugh Miller. It showed that the comparison with Russia gained wide circulation at the time, and Mulock must have been aware of it. In true 'Mulockian' vein, however, he did not stop at likening the Highland proprietors to 'small scale' Russian despots but, as was often the case, took up arguments put forward by other crusading journalists and boldly radicalised them.

In December 1849 Mulock took over the editorship of the *Advertiser* following the sudden death of the previous editor, James M'Cosh. He led the struggling paper for four months before he left it for the newly launched *Ensign*. During these four months Mulock's vigorous pen was largely directed against the Highland Destitution Relief Board and its new 'Labour Test'.[123] He condemned the Test, designed to exact maximum work for minimum food, as nothing better than starving off the Highlanders after the Irish fashion 'upon grounds of Celtic affinity', and heavily criticised both Sir Charles Trevelyan and Captain Elliot for what he saw as an inhuman system.

Mulock's energy, however, was mostly occupied by his editorship of a paper in crisis. What happened at the *Advertiser* during these few months can only be pieced together from the various articles which the *Ensign* and the *Advertiser* threw at each other in the ensuing row between them over Mulock himself.

After James M'Cosh's death, Mulock was asked by the family and the paper's publisher to take up the *Advertiser*'s editorship. According to Mulock he was unwilling to accept it but eventually bowed to the wishes of the 'imploring' family. The publisher and Mulock never reached any agreement over extra pay for the editor's job, with the publisher insisting that Mulock's 'services' should be 'ex gratia'. It appears that Mulock eventually decided to leave the paper in April or May 1850, mainly because he was not paid for his editorial responsibilities and had disagreements with the publisher.

Once Mulock was with the new *Ensign* – and obvious rival to the *Advertiser* – he was angrily attacked by his old paper which accused him of being an 'unmanageable' and 'troublesome' editor demanding 'both power and payment'.[124] He was depicted as an unbearable despot, who cunningly made himself editor and dared to demand extra pay during hard times at the paper. It was immoral, the *Advertiser* suggested, that an editor should demand money from a paper in severe difficulties. Mulock and the *Ensign* replied with no less vigour to the 'vulgar attack' of 'the unprovoked assailant', and the two papers continued their row until the end of the year.

One other feature that Mulock must have found irksome in the *Advertiser* seemed to be a certain degree of censorship. This was implied in one of his retorts to the *Advertiser's* campaign against him. He said that before he wrote for the *Ensign* his articles had been 'treacherously garbled to suit sinister purposes'.[125] He also revealed here that the condition he made to the *Ensign* on joining it was that he would not be censored and his articles would be published unedited, uncut, in their 'integral form'. The *Ensign* granted him this condition, and, as a result, Mulock's communications had 'flowed in uninterruptedly' to the *Ensign* readers. Such freedom put Mulock in an exceptional situation. Enjoying the right of unedited publishing was a rare privilege for any journalist, and still is even today. This undoubtedly gave Mulock a unique position in the Scottish press at the time.

It also meant that in the *Ensign* nothing could stop Mulock's radicalism. His writings reached their peak during the fifteen months he spent with the paper. From June 1850 to August 1851 Mulock wrote at least one long article in almost every issue, and sometimes he would take up a quarter of the paper with several articles on one page. Not only in the quantity but also in the quality of his polemics Mulock was at his best in the period he spent with the *Ensign*: at his angriest, sharpest and most uncompromising.

His opening piece, entitled 'Fresh Barbarities connected with Compulsory Emigration', set the tone for his forthcoming flood of angry articles. He threatened the landlords, whom he simply dubbed 'Caledonian Caligulas', with 'avenging exposure' and 'vengeance of divine judgment'. They wished secretly, he said, the 'extermination' of the Gaels. This echoed with greater force the 'secret hankerings' theory put forward by Robert Somers a few years before:

> Men who are capable of perpetrating the clearances which we have tracked in the Highlands and Islands, are in truth a sort of Caledonian Caligulas who, if the secret of their hearts were known, would wish the peasant population had but one neck, that the sword of extermination might leave a wilderness for 'sheep-walks or shooting'. Upon all such, the vengeance of divine judgment cannot fail to descend.[126]

For Mulock, Highland 'oppression' and 'tyranny' meant that the proprietors were free to do anything they wanted to their tenants, throwing them out of their houses or forcing them onto emigration ships. He insisted throughout his writings that such actions were unacceptable in any circumstances since they violated basic human rights and were against the law. Compulsory emigration was but a 'lawless attempt', he said:

> No factor, nor sheriff, nor minister of state – no, not Queen Victoria on her
> throne – possesses a particle of just power which can compel British subjects
> to be huddled in an emigrant ship, in order to transport them to some
> colony where the lazaretto and the ditches dug for the dead await them![127]

Mulock 'fearlessly' asserted that in this system of abuses the poor could attain no justice against 'the rich and powerful' in the Highlands. Like other crusaders, he believed that his task was to expose and condemn injustice in the name of 'Christian championship of universal equity'.[128]

One of Mulock's methods of exposing Highland abuses was to take a 'case study' from which he made more general observations. One example of this was his investigation of the Strathaird clearances on Skye in the summer of 1850.

The proprietor of the Strathaird district of eight farms was Mr M'Alister. He was renowned for philanthropy and described as an 'amiable man', Mulock said, adding that it simply meant that M'Alister did 'all his harsh deeds by deputy'.[129] Some of the tenants on the estate were in arrears, while others were willing and able to pay. Most of the arrears, amounting to £450, were confined to a few crofters on parochial relief, whom M'Alister planned to clear and ship off to America.

Tenants on four farms, amounting to 477 people, were given notice in June. They were also issued with a sort of 'manifesto' stating the need for emigration. The people, however, refused to emigrate and the factor, sheriff and some sections of the press feared that there would be disturbances similar to the one in North Uist a year before.

M'Alister was willing to spend £1200 for the emigration project, a sum more than double the money he was owed. Mulock pointed out that without compulsory emigration the cleared people would fall on the poor rate, which would have to be paid by the proprietor and which would decrease the value of the estate. This was the real rationale of M'Alister's 'grand plan', Mulock said. The amount of money M'Alister was to 'sacrifice' for this 'humane object' could have discharged almost three times the accumulated arrears and would have enabled the people to cultivate their lands, he argued angrily. The real object of the Clearances and compulsory emigration, Mulock suggested, was to get rid of the burdensome tenants instead of finding ways to keep them on the land. True humane considerations were non-existent here.

To illustrate more sharply the inhumanity and outrage of compulsory emigration Mulock turned the Clearances upside down and played with the idea of the landlords being cleared off their estates. He wrote in true revolutionary spirit here, even evoking images of the French Revolution:

> Ah, Mr M'Alister of some Argyle *ilk*, how should you like to be transported against your Scottish will from Torrisdale to Toronto? How painful would be the compulsory packing up of a laird's moveables, bairns inclusive! Stars and garters! just imagine the Duke of Sutherland under orders for a backswood location – Trentham and Dunrobin receiving a new possessor – the mistress of the robes breathing a mournful adieu to the 'old country', and about to exchange Almack's for a tea party in an improvised log-hut! Worse things have been within memory. French Dukes and Marquises have cleaned shoes in London, under the pressure of 'compulsory emigration'.[130]

No other crusading journalist went this far by suggesting, even if only perhaps as a rhetorical tool, that it was the landlords who should be cleared off the Highlands. Elsewhere he proposed with less rhetoric that those proprietors who managed their lands badly should be compelled to give up their estates to people who would properly administer them.

Like other Highland critics, Mulock regarded the land question as central to the solution of Highland problems. The *Glasgow Argus*, the *Witness* and Robert Somers all shared the view that one of the reasons why most crofters were destitute was the lack of good land, which was itself a consequence of the Clearances. Mulock also took up this point but, as was usual with him, he radicalised it to some extent. He was adamant that the root of all evils in the Highlands was in the landlords 'despotically' driving people off good arable lands and forcing them onto rocky soil unfit for agricultural improvement. Everything else was a consequence of people having been deprived of the land, therefore the only good solution would be to give people good lands and not to force them into expatriation. If crofters were given 'sufficient land to cultivate' there would also be marked agricultural improvements, Mulock argued.[131]

All the talk about the 'Celtic sloth' was also a consequence of the lack of land and not of some racial inferiority, Mulock said. He pointed out that the argument that the Highlanders would become more industrious in foreign lands in fact carried in itself the proof that only sufficient land could make people want to work. In his usual style of turning arguments upside down, ridiculing landlords and questioning ruthlessly, Mulock again made his point strongly and vividly:

> Queerly enough, too, all these emigration sticklers are confident of the prosperity of the expatriated Highlanders. At home, the Celtic sons of poverty are, it would appear, incorrigibly idle, and implacable foes to all industrial development, but if shipped across the Atlantic they shake off sloth, and manifest every active quality which secures success for the possessor. And why this signal change? Because they exert their energy on adequate allotments of land, and because they are assured of enjoying the fruits of their labour! Is it really so, philosopher Macleod? [Macleod of Macleod, proprietor in Skye] then pray tell me what is to prevent a Highland landlord in Skye or Sutherland, with thousands upon thousands of spare, cultivable acres, from allowing men to live and thrive here, instead of packing them off to some region of the globe? 'Strict entails,' quoth one, 'mortgaged estates', whimpers another, 'implacable trustees,' cries a third; and all agree that to strip the land of cultivators is the only remedy remaining to distressed proprietors. To which I boldly reply, If the case be come to this extreme issue, it were better that the land should change its proprietors than lose its people.[132]

To keep people on the land to be self-supporting by giving them enough land was what Mulock and other crusading journalists primarily fought for. Emigration was an abhorrent policy in their eyes. But something had happened by April 1851, and Mulock made a stunning about turn. He was now advising the Gaels to go, to escape for their lives.

Thomas Mulock gave up. He became embittered and disillusioned by what he had seen in Highland landlords' policy, and drew the conclusion that battling against the Clearances and forced emigration was hopeless: the landlords were not going to change. The only solution would have been to give land to the people instead of driving them off but by the spring of 1851 Mulock bitterly concluded that this was just not going to happen. Therefore, people would do better to run for their lives and escape from such a hopeless country. Mulock recommended emigration now, not because he agreed with it but because he saw no other option. His tone of writing changed too, there was a darkness descending over his words.

Mulock explained that his conclusion arose from a 'saddening but sober and thoughtful survey of Highland landlordism' and only a 'sense of hopelessness' could ever 'wring' it from him. The most radical crusader's final conclusion was perhaps the most startling and saddening in the sympathetic press at the time:

We advise them to think seriously of VOLUNTARY EMIGRATION, renouncing all expectation of having their miseries mitigated by an up-springing of justice and liberality on the part of the proprietors of the soil. *Escape for thy life*, we would solemnly say to every poor Highlander ground down by heartless landlords and fraudulent factors. All the ancestral amenities which bound together the cordial chieftain and his devoted clan are gone – never to return! . . . Fly, then, ye poor and needy, from the face of the proprietors who deem you to be nuisances on their possessions, and seek on far distant shores the bare subsistence which is cruelly denied you at home. Yield to the wicked wishes of the arch-designers of desolation, and as they would leave the peasantry without land, leave them a land cursed with the want of cultivating peasantry![133]

Mulock only grew firmer in his conclusion during his last few months on the Scottish newspaper scene. In several articles he reiterated his points with growing force. The 'great experiment' of 'complete depopulation' was unstoppable, and the powers pursuing it too 'overwhelming in influence'. 'Extermination is the order of the day, *pur et simple*', he concluded bitterly.[134]

He also continued to explain to the readers why he arrived at this view. He described how he had battled against the Clearances and 'tyrannical' landlords, and how he eventually came to realise that the battle was hopeless in the face of the powerful majority of supporters of the system. The landlords persisted in refusing the people any prospect of true improvement, Mulock argued. Larger holdings of land were 'inflexibly denied', small tenants-at-will could be turned out any time, and employment prospects were hopeless following the 'avowed adoption of universal sheep-farming'. No other means of escape were thus available for the Highlanders except 'the sorrowful succour of immediate expatriation', Mulock said.

The M'Neill report published in July 1851 only made Mulock's conviction stronger. It was a curious fact that on the surface both M'Neill and Mulock urged the same thing: emigration. Yet, the differences between what the two men were saying were enormous. M'Neill asserted that emigration was in fact the only solution, Mulock insisted that the real solution would be to keep people on the land, but because this was stoutly resisted the only choice remaining was emigration.

Mulock was naturally most angered by the M'Neill report and attacked it with his usual ferocity. He called it a 'snake-like report' designed to protect the rich and cast off the suffering poor. M'Neill's allegation that the cause of Highland destitution was over-population and therefore the only remedy was extensive emigration was angrily repudiated by Mulock. The real cause was the clearance system, he reiterated in a passage ridiculing M'Neill as blinded by 'Malthusian glasses':

All he deigns to impart is his absolute affirmation, that the Western Highlands and Islands are over-peopled; and that except this plethora of population be speedily removed, the most appalling destitution will surely prevail. To all which heartless rigmarole we reply, as we have done scores of times, that nothing can be more untrue than the assertion of a positive overpopulation being existent in the Highlands. What a man having eyes in his head, but unobscured by Malthusian glasses, will not fail to observe is this, that cultivation is systematically sacrificed in order to promote sheep-feeding, and that the peasantry, having been driven from their former holdings, are now huddled into miserable masses, and located upon petty patches of the very worst land.[135]

Mulock went on to point out that what the landlords were really afraid of was a new poor law provision which would put the burden of sustaining the able-bodied poor on the owners of the land. To avoid this 'ruinous result of their own oppression and short-sighted rapacity' the Highland landowners were determined to expatriate the people from their lands. This was the real motive behind the emigration policy. This only reinforced his belief that the Highland proprietors were so set on executing the emigration schemes that nothing would change their minds. And now with the M'Neill report's recommendation the 'emigration remedy' received official sanction. The lesson was clear, Mulock suggested: there was nothing left for the Gaels but to abandon the land which did not want them. This was his farewell message:

On these oracular sayings being interpreted, the pith of the whole matter comes out to be, that the Highlands and Islands *must* be dispeopled of their Celtic inhabitants. The owners of the soil are resolved to clear their possessions of unfortunate beings whom they have deprived of all sufficiency of land, and for whom they open no sphere of industrial occupation; and the Government, void of wisdom and effective vigour, suggests no remedy which would stop short of depopulation. Emigration, therefore, is the only alleviation of present distress and deeper prospective calamity, and in the total absence of all domestic hope, we must honestly exhort the poor Highlanders, whose fast friend we have shown ourselves to be, to prepare for eternal exile.[136]

The most radical and fiery crusader for the Highland Gaels thus left the field in bitter disillusionment, giving up the fight.

Although Thomas Mulock was gone from Scotland by the end of August 1851, controversy still raged around him in the sympathetic press. He was attacked in the *Witness* and other apparently sympathetic papers for his alleged 'inconsistency', blamed for having abandoned the Highland cause and labelled as a 'strange fish swimming in the waters of Celtic strife'.[137] The accusations reached him in England from whence he returned one more retaliatory blow, this time not only at the Highland 'oppressors' but the Scottish press and the whole Scottish nation.

Mulock was bitingly angry and outraged at not being appreciated and recognised as the only true champion of the Highland cause. Calling himself a 'retired soldier' (*miles emeritus*), he asserted the right to 'stand at ease' after his two year 'conflict with Scottish oppression' in which he declared he had stood alone with no other fighters around him. He went on to say that while he alone advocated 'the truth and justice of the Highland cause' others were silent but now they rose up from their 'heathery brakes like Roderick Dhu's hidden henchmen' and instead of fighting the oppressors they joined battle against himself.

One of his attackers charged him with inconsistency by referring to him as 'Et tu Brute', 'exclaiming with the Roman emperor'. This was an easy target for Mulock, who first pointed out that Julius Caesar never was an 'emperor' (he never held the title, only successive rulers adopted it), then went on to say how this 'bit of nonsense' was wound up 'with another classic confusion about Pyrrhus and his elephants' (Hannibal and the battle of Pyrrhus mixed up here). All this 'illiterate rubbish' was designed to show, he said, how he was trampling down on friends instead of foes.

Mulock asserted that his identity was indisputable, his consistency unimpeachable, and insisted that he had been 'one of the best and most consistent friends of the distressed Highlanders'. He gave a summary of his views and arguments from attacking 'tyrannical proceedings of some Highland proprietors' which were tantamount to compulsory emigration, to his protests against the Clearances and depopulation.

He saw, however, that his appeals were generally disregarded, and his efforts 'utterly unseconded by the Scottish press'. It became clear to him, he explained again, that the proprietors were 'inflexibly intent upon clearing their lands of all peasant population', and that no concessions would be made for improvement. Destitution advanced, the remaining resources were fast disappearing, and there was no help or hope in sight. It was in the light of all this that he had decided, 'after the maturest reflection', to recommend voluntary emigration, which he had never opposed anyway. He added that by this time the tide of thought had turned and people were becoming more willing to emigrate on hearing favourable news from emigrants.

Mulock accused those journalists of irresponsibility who opposed voluntary emigration under such circumstances. He called them 'shallow scribblers' and a 'band of blockheads', who could offer no real practical prospect, only 'false and foolish advice'. In a country with such a press, Mulock suggested, it took an outsider to 'hammer' the truth and, inevitably, he was to become misunderstood. Mulock by this time felt betrayed not only by the Scottish press but by the Scots themselves. This was the complaint of a 'great man' confronted by an uncomprehending narrow audience:

> . . . the real explanation of the distastefulness of my interposition in Scottish matters is the narrow-mindedness of the Scotch themselves, who, being puffed up with undue national pretension, are prone to undervalue whatever is not hammered upon their own anvil! I was not disposed to be a fighter for the Free Church, nor a partisan for any Caledonian *clique*, and, as a consequence I have been snarled at by divers parties who are incapable of appreciating the high-minded zeal that springs from genuine independence and impartiality.[138]

Thus the 'notorious' Thomas Mulock disappeared from the Scottish press. For a while, the sympathetic campaign for the Gaels was maintained by other crusaders who continued to believe that it was possible to influence public opinion and force changes from the government and from the landlords. However, just a year later, the very opponents of Thomas Mulock eventually had to admit him right when they arrived – similarly sad and bitter – at the same conclusions.

Donald M'Leod and Donald Ross are perhaps the best known defenders of the Gaels, even today. They were both prolific writers and their pamphlets were extensively reprinted in Alexander Mackenzie's *History of the Highland Clearances* in 1883, thus securing a more lasting influence.

The two men were the first journalists writing about the Highlands who were actually from the Highlands – simple Gaelic-speaking 'natives' themselves.[139] Donald M'Leod came from Strathnaver in Sutherland and not only witnessed the infamous Loch Sellar clearances but was a victim of them as well. Later he became one of the best known pamphleteers, attaining fame with his personal account of the Sutherland Clearances in the 1810s, which was serialised in 1840 in the *Edinburgh Weekly*

Chronicle and then published as the *History of Destitution in Sutherlandshire* in 1841. Donald Ross was from Ross-shire, probably from Dornoch, and became a lawyer in Glasgow. He became the only journalist to engage in practical campaigning for the Highlanders. Ross was best known for his accounts of the Knoydart eviction and the 'Greenyards massacre'.

The background of these two men defined much of their thought and style as writers. They made no pretensions to literary merit, although they exhibited a fair amount, and their missionary zeal as crusaders was imbued with their sense of commitment to their own people. This also meant that their writings were often characterised by a tendency to romanticise the Highlanders and to depict their former life as some 'golden age'. Their language was also highly sentimental and emotional. They wanted to raise public opinion first and foremost, and felt that the plight of the Highlands could not be exaggerated or overstated.

Donald M'Leod was the calmer crusader of the two, especially by the 1850s when he was in his mid-fifties and had written most of his major works. He was not so prominent on the newspaper scene as Donald Ross. His name only appeared in the 1850s on the pages of the *Northern Ensign*, which gave a forum for all the major sympathetic journalists during this period. While Thomas Mulock and Donald Ross dealt with many specific cases, campaigning and making wider observations from them, Donald M'Leod was more of an general analyst.

The thrust of M'Leod's thoughts on the Highlands was the notion that the Gaels were being 'exterminated' and were threatened with extinction. Considered a lower race, they were allowed to starve and were hunted down and forced to emigrate:

> Highland destitution and famine have become proverbial and so familiar that people think and speak of them as a calamity hereditary to the Highlanders, and indeed, since they have become so burdensome to the public for the last half century (keeping them alive upon charity), the more fortunate portion of the Christian world are beginning to think, and say, that they should not exist any longer, and that the sooner they are exterminated the better. The appellation Gael, Celt, or Gaul, has now become a reproach. . . . in return for their ancestors' services to the nation, they, the progeny, are doomed to die by famine, or be exterminated from the land, so dear to them by many sacred ties, by compulsory emigration . . . [140]

These were strong words but by no means unique to M'Leod. Many others, from Hugh Miller to Robert Somers and Thomas Mulock, had

used expressions like 'extermination' in describing the clearances and
emigration.

To a late-twentieth-century ear the word 'extermination' sounds
extreme, having been applied to the genocide of Jews in Hitler's
Germany. In this context, to apply the same word to the Highland
Clearances seems exaggerated, as no attempt at the complete physical
destruction of the Gaels ever took place. However, it was the complete
rooting out and disappearance of the Gaelic people that contemporary
crusading journalists most feared, and that is what they meant by
'extermination'. From the seventeenth century onwards the word 'extermination' already denoted 'destroy utterly'.[141] In Donald M'Leod's
writings in the 1850s the notion that the complete destruction of his race
was a real danger was constantly recurring.

In 1851 M'Leod published a four-part series of an essay entitled 'The
Progress and Civilisation in the last half century – taking Sutherlandshire as
a criterion'. The series ran in the *Northern Ensign* from the end of October
1851 to February 1852, and was essentially more of a loud lament and cry for
help than a strong argumentative piece.

The last half-century only brought ruin and tragedy for the Highlands,
destroying a 'once happy life', M'Leod said. He depicted the old life in the
Highlands as an era of a 'golden age'. The images here were strongly
coloured with nostalgia:

> I am now advanced in years, and have a pretty correct recollection of passing
> events and of the movements of society for the last fifty years. At that period,
> and down to the period at which the calamities accompanying the *clearing*
> system overtook us, and before we came under the *Loch* iron rod of
> oppression, and drank of that *bitter* cup of many withering ingredients
> which accompanied that ever *cursed and condemned by God* system, I say that
> we lived what might be termed a happy life, when compared with the
> present. Some years our corn would fail, but we had cattle which we could
> sell, and purchase food with the price of them; we had sheep and goats
> which we could take and eat; we had salmon and trout for the taking; we
> had abundance of milk, butter, and cheese; and none of us ever died by
> famine. To the stranger every door was open; to the lame, needy, and poor
> every hand was stretched with relief; to the sick and afflicted every breast was
> full of sympathy.[142]

His people were now hunted down, cleared and banished by oppressive
landlords in order to save themselves from the poor-rate, to satisfy their
'boundless ambition' and to 'gratify a deep-rooted and long-cherished

animosity towards the *Celtic* race'.[143] This was all the more terrible a tragedy, he suggested, because it affected a 'peaceable, inoffensive and once brave people', who had brought so much glory for Britain. The race of the famous Highland soldiers was now being betrayed and driven off to foreign lands, he complained. M'Leod was crying out to the whole of Britain to notice what fate the Highlanders were suffering:

> . . . we have a more heart-rending result to record; we have a brave, peaceable, religious, and moral peasantry ruined, dispersed, and murdered. Those who were once Scotland's yea Britain's pride in the hour of danger and of need, are now in thousands, dying by inches the agonising death of famine, upon the bleak unproductive shores of the north and west coast of Scotland, and as many of them sharing a similar fate among the inhospitable wilds and climes of Canada. Oh! Christian Britain, ruler of the ocean, can it be possible that these are thy sons and daughters, who are dying by famine within thy hearing and seeing, on thine soil, and perishing, homeless, houseless, and meatless, far from their home, upon a foreign inclement strand? If it is, I ask who have made you a great and glorious nation? Who have established thy throne? Hearken to me. Was it the depopulators of great Highland dominions? .. Was it those who made such a great nation of you upon such a small speck of the earth, so that you are the admiration and terror of Europe? I answer in the negative, No! These are and were comparatively the drones and cankerworms of society.[144]

This was desperate pleading. M'Leod was primarily trying to appeal to the conscience of not only Scotland but Britain. He was not arguing about the economics and agriculture of the Highlands, but spoke in moral terms on the grounds of basic humanity. As if fearing that the Highlanders' simple humanity was not enough, he made a case out of their merits and services for Britain, their military fame and excellence. The frequent reference to the 'peaceful nature' of the Highland Celts also implied that unlike the 'rebellious' Irish Celts they were not a threat to Britain and therefore deserved to be treated much better.

M'Leod was appalled by the Government's emigration scheme following the M'Neill report in the summer of 1851. In giving assistance to landlords to help people emigrate M'Leod saw nothing but the promotion of depopulation and expatriation. This would only lead to 'lingering' and 'agonising death' on a foreign shore. Stretching the point to its utmost, M'Leod said that even shooting 'these poor old men' would be 'more humane' than deporting them.

M'Leod was certainly a man of exaggerations, and it was perhaps, and still is, easy to dismiss him. His strong words, however, should not necessarily be taken literally, like the words of critics such as a Hugh Miller or Robert Somers. It should not be forgotten that Donald M'Leod was one of the Highland people with a different language, coming from the very scene of the Clearances.

He spoke a different language in more than one sense. He was a stonemason from Sutherlandshire, so his mother tongue was Gaelic. Even once he learnt English, his native Gaelic language must have affected the form and choice of his words. Gaelic was a very descriptive, poetic and essentially oral language, and someone with such a background would tend to express thoughts differently in English. His repetitive style with many synonyms, for instance, was a typical Gaelic feature.[145] M'Leod apologised frequently for not having the mastery of English, saying that he could 'not lay much claim to grammatical or literary qualifications', being a simple native stonemason from Strathnaver.

He spoke a different language on another level too. He was of the people of the Highlands and had a different set of values and emotions. For him, the cause of the Gaels was not some worthy cause to be taken up from the outside, but the cause of his own closest people, and from that perspective he saw things differently. M'Leod wanted to plead for his people, to raise public awareness for their suffering, and in this he was an early propagandist. Propaganda required a different sort of language from that of criticism and discussion: it demanded an emotional tone, applying for the empathy and sympathy of those who listened.

M'Leod was certainly a master of emotional language. While for Mulock's combative style, the mastery of alliteration produced a forceful effect, for M'Leod's purposes, repetition and synonyms in long sentences were quite effective. The following passage might sound too flowery for today's ears but it was written for an audience more than a hundred years ago when these words sought to awaken the conscience and sympathy of the outside world:

> Hear the sobbing, sighing, and throbbings of their guileless warm *Highland hearts*, taking their last look, and bidding a forever adieu to their romantic mountains and valleys, the fertile straths, dales, and glens, which their forebears for time immemorial inhabited, and where they are now lying in undisturbed and everlasting repose, in spots endeared and sacred to the memory of their unfortunate offspring, who must now bid a mournful farewell to their early association, which were as dear and as sacred to them as their very existence, and which had hitherto made them patient in sufferings.[146]

In the end, Donald M'Leod himself bade farewell to his country. Little is known about why and how he left.[147] After 1851 his name disappears from the newspaper pages and by 1853 when Harriet Beecher Stowe made her visit to Sutherland, from which she later published her *Sunny Memories*, M'Leod was already in exile in Canada. From there his name once more appeared on the Scottish scene with his angry reply to Stowe's book, and the subsequent publication in 1857 in Canada of his *Gloomy Memories*, a selection of his earlier writings.

One more crusader was gone from the battlefield. Another Highland native, however, remained firmly on the scene and through the untiring *Northern Ensign* sustained the battle throughout the first half of the 1850s. This last remaining crusader was Donald Ross.

Donald Ross was the most energetic and idealistic journalist of the 1850s. Although very little is known about him, not even his date of birth, there was something youthful both in his character and his writings. He was tireless in his campaign against the Clearances, even when he had to overcome his own disillusionment. He had enough energy and faith to flood newspapers with his long articles, to go on investigative trips, to organise practical aid for the destitute, to set up charity schemes, and to publish pamphlets and books based on his newspaper articles.

Ross was the only journalist at the time who not only wrote about the Clearances in indignation but actually went out to find tents and blankets for evicted people: a practical '*engagé*' journalist.

He also differed markedly from other journalists in his style of writing. His investigative journalism produced an early documentarist genre, which was unique at the time. He tirelessly recorded cases of abuses and evictions, with long and detailed descriptions. This factual documentarist style, however, was mixed with frequent romanticising passages both about the bygone 'golden age', and about the Highland people themselves.

Donald Ross first appeared at considerable length on the Scottish newspaper scene in the pages of the *North British Daily Mail* and the *Inverness Advertiser* in 1850. He wrote from the Isle of Skye from a trip he made there in order to examine the condition of the people and the capabilities of the soil. He argued that the land would be capable of sustaining the people if there was 'a proper system of management' providing leases for encouragement and helping to teach people the necessary skills and reformation of their 'habits'.[148] Agreeing that the people did have 'indolent' habits, he said that this was not their fault but derived from the lack of leases which would provide incentives to work and improve their lands. The 'evil' here, Ross said, was the '*want of fixity of tenure*', which was coupled with a constant threat of eviction.

Shortly after Thomas Mulock left the *Northern Ensign* in the summer of 1851, Donald Ross appeared on its pages and remained one of the paper's most prolific writers in the first half of the 1850s. It was almost like a takeover at the *Ensign*: one crusader leaving the battlefield as another raised the banner. From August of 1851 Donald Ross became the *Ensign's* 'frontline fighter'.

After Mulock had left, giving up hope of protesting against the landlords and keeping the Gaels on the land, Ross took over, representing a different opinion. He was still hopeful and optimistic that something could be done to stop the Clearances and emigration. He was 'fresh blood' infused into the *Ensign*, whose editorial opinion differed from Mulock's final view. In fact, in the very same issue where Mulock voiced his advice for the Highlanders to escape for their lives and emigrate from a hopeless land, the editorial article expressed the opposite view. 'With all due respect to the opinion of many valued friends', the leader began with this probable reference to Mulock, and went on to say that the fight should not be given up against emigration and the M'Neill bill. The first article in the *Ensign* from Donald Ross went along the same line. It was the new battle song of a fresh combatant:

> None but cowards will say that it is now hopeless to plead the cause of the poor Highlanders, or expect any improvement in their condition in their own native land. While I find that there are in the Highlands of Scotland about 500,000 acres of good land fit for cultivation, yet still lying waste, I hold that it is a wicked fallacy to assert that there is no room in the Highlands for the present population, and therefore I look upon the scheme now in progress for expatriating the people as one not only impolitic in many respects, but one grossly unjust towards the poor peaceable and God fearing Highlanders. It would be folly, therefore, to expect that real friends of the Highlanders and true patriots should be found silent, and, as it were, giving their consent to the provisions of this iniquitous bill. No, no; sooner let the tongue cleave to the roof of the mouth and the right arm lose its strength, than that we should keep silence at this important period. Let us protest against the measure, and shew to the world that we are sincere in our advocacy, and that we are right at heart in the cause of the poor Gaels.[149]

In the spirit of this battle song, Ross engaged himself both in a sustained campaign against the Emigration Bill and in trying to prove that improvement was still possible in the Highlands. People could and should be employed at home, he insisted.

One example he gave was based on a pamphlet written by Robert Brown, the commissioner of the Duke of Hamilton, on adapting 'flax culture' in the Highlands. Ross hailed this work as proof that there could be labour provided for the people on the land, which would benefit both landlord and tenants. In Brown's theory, the ten thousands of acres of Highland land, now lying waste, were suitable to grow flax and other crops. Britain, however, was still paying 'eight millions sterling of money' to foreign countries for flax.[150] Produce flax at home, at a cheaper price, on land lying waste which could employ people to keep them on the land and no emigration schemes would be necessary.

Brown also asserted in his pamphlet that contrary to popular theories the Gaels were not indolent and lazy 'whenever they had an opportunity of exerting' their industry. This was another point that Ross passionately maintained. 'The Highlander is not *lazy*, but the oppressors of the Highlander are lazy', he put it simply. The key factors could only be to give them sufficient land with security and encouragement:

> The means of cultivation are on the land, and if the people who are now destitute were to have fair portions of it, and leases, and if their exertions were properly directed, I have no doubt whatever that they would soon raise themselves high up above their present condition, be a source of profit and credit to their proprietors, and of far more value to this kingdom than the sheep, deer, and game, on a thousand estates.[151]

Another reason why it was a bad policy to pursue extensive emigration from the Highlands was that it deprived the country of its best soldiers, Ross argued. The Highlanders had been traditionally the best fighting men of the British army, bearing hardships well and possessing 'instinctive courage'. Already in 1851, Ross warned that Britain had many potential enemies from France to Russia. He cautioned that Russia had 'immense dominions', 'the largest army in the world' and had 'no friendly feelings' towards Britain. In such circumstances, driving away the cream of the British army was against the national interest, Ross warned. In the light of the Crimean War erupting in 1854, this was good prophecy.

Amidst his journalistic writings, Ross was busy with practical schemes to campaign for the Highlands. An advertisement appearing on the front page of the *Northern Ensign* in January 1852 revealed a project similar to modern charity organisations' activities. Donald Ross and the 'Hebridean Industrial Society' advertised 'a large quantity of socks and stockings knitted by Poor

Destitute Females' in the Hebrides.[152] The socks and stockings were of 'most excellent quality and beautiful', the advert said. The purchase, though, would have a humanitarian purpose as it would promote the employment of destitute Highland women and help them to escape starvation:

> Parties desirous of seeing the work done by these poor Hebridean females, and who may feel disposed to encourage this branch of industry, whereby many poor creatures are enabled to save themselves from starvation by their own labour would do well to give their countenance and support to this benevolent undertaking.[153]

What became of the project is not known. The advert disappeared from the front page of the *Ensign* after a few runs. What was certain, though, is that Donald Ross also disappeared from the pages of the *Ensign* until the end of the year. It can only be guesswork now whether his absence was due to being busy with practical projects, or whether the failure of such attempts left him struggling with disillusionment.

When Ross returned to the *Ensign* in November 1852, he was a changed man. This most idealistic of crusaders, who passionately had taken over from the disillusioned Thomas Mulock only just over a year ago, had now arrived at the same bitter conclusion. He also gave up any hope that the government or the landowners would ever reverse their policies. They had turned 'a deaf ear to all appeals', he concluded. In an open letter to his 'fellow-countrymen', the Highlanders of Scotland, Ross recommended to them the same 'escape for thy life' solution:

> I think the time has fully come when all true Highlanders should leave the Government and the landholders to the consequences of their blind and infatuated policy, and betake themselves to countries where there is sufficient reward and encouragement given to honest labour.[154]

This must have been a sad and most difficult point to arrive at for a man like Donald Ross. While Mulock was bitter with his own futile struggle but above all angry at the unbending landowning class, Ross sounded a sad and shaken man here. In his explanation of how he reached this conclusion he was apologetic, confessing failure. Accepting, however unwillingly, the 'cruel reality', he was now resolved to advise emigration from a country which 'despised' and made life impossible for its people:

> Whilst there was a ray of hope I ceased not (in season and out of season) to point out the necessity of earnest active measures on the part of the

Government and of the landlords, to rescue the poor Highlanders from
the alarming destitution which threatened and still threatens to destroy
them; but I must confess, that not only my own labours this way, but
those of valuable and distinguished coadjutors, have in a manner entirely
failed – for never, so far as I can learn, have the poor Highlanders'
complaints and appeals, whether directed to the legislature or their own
landlords, been so cruelly and so recklessly disregarded as at present. . . .

To the Highland labourer, whose capital is in his strong arms and ten
fingers, and whose value is not appreciated at home, I say, without any
hesitation, that he should *immediately leave a country where he is starved
and despised.*[155]

For eight months Ross disappeared yet again from the *Ensign*. When he
reappeared he did so under the pseudonym of 'Scotus'.[156] His reappearance
did not mean that he was again more hopeful about the possibility to
influence landlord policies. His initial optimistic idealism was gone, and a
new tone appeared in its place.

It was from this time, from the summer of 1853, that Ross began his
documentarist genre in a markedly darker tone, often in a rather naturalist
style. Having given up campaigning for change, he now resolved to expose
the abuses and the increasing brutalities accompanying the evictions of 1853
and 1854. The Knoydart and Greenyards evictions were some of the most
brutal in the history of the Highland Clearances, and there was also a new
phenomenon of crofters' resistance emerging with them. Ross felt he could
not remain silent at times like these.

The Knoydart clearances in 1853 and the Greenyards evictions were
undoubtedly the two most famous cases Ross documented.[157] While there
were a number of newspapers which reported on the Knoydart evictions, it
was only Ross who spent a long time on the scene to take the testimonies of
the evicted and hunted people.

Ross's journalistic motto by now was that facts were 'better than remarks
or reflections'. In this vein, most of his articles on the Knoydart evictions
consisted of stories of the individual cases of those who were hunted down
by officers after they refused to go on the emigration ships. There was a
man, without arrears, who refused to leave because his wife was sick. His
house was pulled down, and with his wife and six children he was hiding in
a wretched hut, which was demolished by the officers. There was an old
widow who had to be dragged out by force from her house, and who had
then spent the night in the rain staring at the ruins. There was an old
widower who slept in the open air, on cold grass and hard rock, and an old

sick woman who was thrown out of her sickbed by the levelling officers. The list was long. The details of more than fifteen cases certainly made harrowing reading.

However much Ross vowed to use only facts he often could not resist bursting into indignation and sorrow over 'man's inhumanity to man':[158]

> The scene upon the whole was heart rending – a sad blot upon our humanity and civilization. John M'Kinnon finds more sympathy from the swallows which his presence amid the ruins of the sanctuary annoys and disturbs, than from his proud superiors.[159]

The case of a 'fine Highlander', Allan, especially aroused Ross's indignation. He and his four children were also thrown out by the officers, and he was losing his 'wits' at what happened. Ross related with bitter irony that back in 1823 when King George made his famous visit to Edinburgh, Allan was selected as 'a truly noble specimen of the real Highlander' for the pageantry in the king's honour. Now, he was 'doomed to perish', Ross said, 'in a hut where no gentleman would for one night risk the life of his dog'.[160]

What happened at Knoydart was in essence an utter disregard of humanity, on a land where human lives had become worthless, Ross declared:

> Had Allan and his children been deer, they would have a hearty reception and permanent comfortable residence on Glengarry. Poor Allan, however, in this advanced age of civilisation, is so unfortunate as to be a *man* – so unlucky as to have a parent's affection, and so awkwardly placed as to feel and think for himself.[161]

In his pamphlet entitled *The Glengarry Evictions*, Ross further developed this thought, putting in even harsher terms how humans were in fact 'sacrificed to the god of sheep-farming and expatriation'.[162] In fact, this idea had its roots in the popular Gaelic concept that they were betrayed because for the landlords 'sheep were more valuable than men'. Since Donald Ross himself was a Gaelic speaker from Ross-shire, it was no surprise that the concept was deeply rooted in his mind:

> Within the last 30 years *man* has fallen off dreadfully in the estimation of highland proprietors. Commercially speaking, Allan M'Donald has now no value at all. Had he been a roe, or a deer, a sheep, or a bullock, a highland laird in speculating could estimate his 'real' worth to within a few shillings, but Allan is *only* a man. Then his children they are of no value, nor taken

into account in the calculations of the sportsman. They cannot be shot like hares, blackcocks, or grouse, nor yet can they be sent south as game to feed the London market.[163]

For Ross, the suffering of the Knoydart people was essentially a humanitarian question, which left 'a deep stain on the humanity of the British nation'. However 'maudlin and canting' Ross's writings were, as the *Inverness Advertiser* remarked, there is no doubt that any humanitarian organisation today would agree with his indignation.

Ross was a forerunner of modern humanitarianism in practical ways as well. During the Knoydart evictions he tried to organise tents for those people who were exposed to the harsh October weather. He wrote to obtain permission from the factor, who sent him to the agent of the estate curators. The agent refused saying that the people must not remain on the land, but at least should go to a nearby town for shelter and relief. Ross rejected this, arguing that moving people to a town would be part of the forced evictions in which he did not want to assist.[164] Ross also tried to appeal for immediate food aid for people, but it is not known how successful he was.

While the Knoydart case excited quite a lot of press interest, even from the *Scotsman* and *Inverness Courier*, a year later the violent evictions and crofters' resistance were almost solely reported by Ross. The violence and brutality following the crofters' resistance to the evictions in Greenyards surpassed any reported cases at the time.[165] If Ross was outraged at the treatment of the Knoydart people a year before, now, when women were battered with batons by policemen, left lying in blood and some of them taken to prison, he was almost mad with anger. He could not find words strong enough to convey his outrage and cry out to the public. In the first of his series of articles on Greenyards, Ross simply called the case 'a savage butchery':

> Even on the most favourable view of the recent procedure on the part of the factor and sheriff-officers, and the constables, it cannot be described by any other name than that of *savage butchery*. The very idea that there are dozens of poor females whose flesh is mangled, and whose bones are shattered, owing to the blows inflicted upon them by a set of men let loose (after being regaled at a public-house) to carry out the wishes of the managers of the Kindeace estates, is enough to make one's blood run cold. It is all very well to talk of the 'rights of property', and the 'majesty of law', &.c; but surely some respect ought to *have* been shown to the *lives* of those who are sought to be evicted. The cavalier manner in which it is boasted in some papers, of

the business-like way and the cleverness with which the officers and
constables handled their batons in breaking the backs and in smashing
the skulls of defenceless women – while they, the constables, it is said,
escaped unhurt, shows a cool-hardiness, which could scarcely be passed over
in a wild Kaffir from Africa or in a savage from Terra-del-Fuego! . . . The
men who can hold up their heads, and brag that they maimed, and bruised,
and levelled to the ground, with their sticks, so many females in half-an-
hour, are a disgrace to a civilized and Christian country. The Red Indian
would turn aside in disgust from such men, and the wild men of Timbuctoo
would refuse to associate with them.[166]

In his other reports Ross gave details of each injury, and even collected for
evidence 'patches of scalps of skin with the long hair adhering to them' and
bloodstained pieces of clothing found on the field. However, not even his
own paper, the *Ensign*, was willing to credit his account fully. An editorial
said that they had in fact 'modified' to a large extent one of Ross's articles as
they found the conduct of the constables described in it 'almost incredible'.[167] Ross replied angrily, finding the editorial procedure 'very queer',
and insisted that he did not 'over-state' but rather 'under-stated' the facts.

Avoiding any editorial censoring, Ross published a pamphlet entitled
The Russians of Ross-shire, on what he called 'the massacre of the Rosses',
later in the year in 1854. Here he gave the full account of as many as twenty
cases with graphic descriptions of their beatings and injuries. It made
harrowing reading. This was just one passage among the many similar, or
worse:

Elizabeth Ross, aged 22, daughter of Alexander Ross, tenant, at Amat-na-
tuath, was struck most violently on the head with a baton, and was kicked
on the breast and shoulders while lying on the ground. There is a deep cut,
$3\frac{1}{4}$ inches long on the crown of the head, which shattered the skull, and
destroyed a portion of the frontal and parietal bones, causing concussion
and compression of the brain. There is another cut in an opposite direction
on top of the head, and in the direction from ear to ear. It is fully $2\frac{1}{4}$ inches
long, and very deep. She has also severe bruises on her arms and shoulders.
The marks of the tacks of the policemen's boots were still visible on the
breast and shoulders of this girl. The kicks were given to her after she was
lying on the ground. Her clothing was completely red with blood. Pieces of
the skin of her head was stript off with the batons of the police, and her long
hair, clotted with blood, could be seen in quantities spread over the
ploughed land.[168]

With so many eye-witness details and almost medically precise descriptions, it was hard to suppose that it was all in Ross's imagination. The twenty similar case descriptions one after another could produce a shocking effect on the nineteenth-century reader, who at that time was not accustomed to everyday news coverage of large quantities of blood and dead.

Yet no public outcry followed, and the Greenyards case seemed to have disappeared from the newspaper pages, even from the ever-combatant *Ensign*. The attention of public opinion and the press was now suddenly directed elsewhere.

The Crimean War, which broke out in March 1854, brought the end of a phase in press attitudes towards the Highlands. The immediate result was that attention was all but gone from the Highlands, with hardly any articles on them in most newspapers, with the exception of the *Ensign*. However, this changed by 1855 and the Highlands were back in the news, but this time with a different emphasis. Suddenly, many were asking: 'Where are the Highlanders?' Simply, there were not enough of them when they were now needed for the British army fighting in the Crimea and suffering great losses. This focused attention again on the Highlands, and this time Clearances and depopulation became less easy to defend.

One of the first journalists to raise the new issue was Donald Ross, the only crusader still fighting on. He recalled in an article at the end of 1854 that there were up to 30,000 able-bodied Highlanders fit for military service back in 1745, and now there were not even 3,000 men. There were many districts which had formerly provided 500, 700 or 800 soldiers and these now were 'without a single human being in them, but one or two shepherds, and a brace of gamekeepers'.[169] Only a 'wreck of population' was left behind, the others had been driven across the Atlantic and were now 'feeding the strength of other lands', Ross added bitterly.

By early 1855 it was clear that recruiting attempts in the Highlands had failed. Not only were there not enough men to enlist but even those who were there refused to enroll. Ross reported in the *Ensign* how crofters in Skye and Sutherland simply told their landlords and the recruiting officers that they felt they did not have a country to fight for and did not forget how they had been treated in the past decades. They also told them they saw no guarantees that on returning from the war they would not find their homes levelled and their families evicted.

Ross quoted an excerpt from a statement which a committee of crofters

in Sutherlandshire sent to several newspapers explaining the reasons for
their refusal to enroll in the army:

> We do not know what we are to come forward for. We have no country to
> fight for, as our glens and straths are laid desolate, and we have no wives or
> children to defend, as we are forbidden to have them. . . . For these wrongs
> and oppressions, as well as others which we have long and patiently endured,
> we are resolved that there shall be no volunteers or recruits from Suther-
> landshire.[170]

This was perhaps a surprising turn for many landlords and government
officials. The consequences of the past decades' Clearances and depopulation became suddenly quite tangible.

All the critics and crusaders in the sympathetic press since the mid-1840s
had been warning against the rash policies of Clearances and forced
emigration, and had been urging ways to keep people on the land by
giving them more land and security. Most crusaders had given up during
this battle, including Donald Ross. He repeated bitterly in 1855 what he
realised a few years earlier, that the Highlanders had no other hope and
prospect than to be destitute in their homeland or 'escape for their lives' to
more appreciative continents:

> . . . Highlanders idolise their native soil and hills, and nothing but dire
> necessity could force them from it. As matters now stand the Highlander has
> no alternative but to starve in or fly from his native land.[171]

In the end, in the battles of the sympathetic critics and crusading journalists
it was the 'notorious stranger' Thomas Mulock whose conclusion proved to
be right and enduring – at least for some time to come.

Notes

1. *The Glasgow Argus*, Leader, 18 January 1847.
2. The paper says this of itself in its 'Farewell Address', 29 November 1847.
3. Cowan, *The Newspapers in Scotland*.
4. *Waterloo Directory*.
5. *Argus*, 'Our Farewell Address', 29 November 1847.
6. *Argus*, Leader, 7 December 1846.
7. 'Destitution in the Island of Skye' (Letter from a Highlander in Glasgow), *Argus*,
   15 February 1847.
8. 'The state of Ireland and the Highlands', *Argus*, Leader, 8 October 1846.
9. *Argus*, Leader, 18 January 1847.

10. A.W.B. Simpson, 'Entails and Perpetuities', in: *Juridical Review*, 1979, 9.

11. 'The Famine in Ireland and the Highlands', *Argus*, Leader, 14 January 1847.

12. *Argus*, 14 January 1847. Italics are mine.

13. 'The Highland people and their landlords', *Argus*, Leader, 8 February 1847.

14. 'Our Farewell Address', *Argus*, 29 November 1847.

15. G. Rosie, *Hugh Miller: Outrage and Order*; Dr James Robertson in his introduction to Hugh Miller, *My Schools and Schoolmasters*, Edinburgh, 1993.

16. Robertson, Introduction, *loc.cit.*

17. Jack, *Scottish Newspaper Directory*.

18. Hugh Miller, *My Schools and Schoolmasters*, 535.

19. Rosie, *Hugh Miller: Outrage and Order*, 16.

20. Hugh Miller, *The Cruise of the Betsey*, Edinburgh, orig. 1845, Edinburgh, 1858 ed., 152

21. Miller, *Cruise* . . . 153.

22. 'Destitution in the Highlands and Islands', *Witness*, 25 November 1846.

23. See page 54.

24. '*The Times*' Commissioner', *Witness*, 21 October 1846.

25. *Witness*, 21 October 1846. This argument was echoed a month later by the *Argus*.

26. 'Past and present condition of the Highlands', *Witness*, 12 December 1846.

27. *Witness*, 12 December 1846.

28. 'Past and present condition of the Highlands', *Witness*, 6 January 1847. Italics as in text.

29. 'Rustification of the Poor – Waste land and waste labour', *Witness*, 10 February 1849.

30. Mechrie, S., *The Church and Scottish Social Development*, Oxford, 1960, 120–121.

31. 'Highland Clearings', *Witness*, Leader, 8 September 1849.

32. *Witness*, 8 September 1849.

33. 'The Depopulation of the Highlands', *Witness*, 12 September 1849.

34. See page 79.

35. 'The Depopulation of the Highlands', *Witness*, 15 September 1849.

36. *Witness*, 15 September 1849.

37. 'The Depopulation of the Highlands', *Witness*, 19 September 1849.

38. *Witness*, 19 September 1849.

39. *Witness*, 19 September 1849.

40. 'The Depopulation of the Highlands', *Witness*, 22 September 1849.

41. 'The Barra refugees', *Witness*, 18 December 1850.

42. This article is published in Rosie's book on Hugh Miller, but in the light of the previous articles it did not add anything new and was not drastically different, or more radical in style than the writings discussed above. Its basic points were that the potato famine struck an already exhausted population with no capital, that the Highlanders were not naturally lazy but they were given no land as inducement, that emigration only took the best people away, leaving pauperism behind.

43. His book has recently been reprinted (1977).

44. *Dictionary of National Biography*.

45. Jack, *Scottish Newspaper Directory*. By 1853 the circulation figures were as follows:

Glasgow Herald: 4505, *Scotsman*: 2924, *Witness*: 2657, and the *North British Daily Mail*: 1253.

46. Robert Somers, *Letters from the Highlands*, (Inverness, orig. 1848.), 1977 ed., Preface.
47. Somers, *Letters*, Preface.
48. Somers, *Letters*, 23 and 133.
49. Somers, *Letters*, 12.
50. Karl Marx, *Capital*, Vol.II (London 1887), 752.
51. Marx, *Capital*, 755.
52. Marx, *Capital*, 25–26.
53. Marx, *Capital*, 28.
54. R.N. Stromberg, *European Intellectual History since* 1789 (New Jersey, 1986)
55. This belief that action against oppression was a sacred instinct and right of the people echoed Jacobin ideas in the French Revolution.
56. Somers, *Letters*, 29.
57. Somers, *Letters*, 89.
58. Somers, *Letters*, 116.
59. Somers, *Letters*, 31.
60. Somers, *Letters*, 82.
61. Somers, *Letters*, 97–99.
62. Somers, *Letters*, 97–99.
63. Somers, *Letters*, 165–167.
64. Somers, *Letters*, 176.
65. Stromberg, *Intellectual History*, 87.
66. Somers, *Letters*, 175.
67. Somers, *Letters*, 178.
68. Somers, *Letters*, 63.
69. Somers, *Letters*, 171.
70. Somers, *Letters*, 171.
71. Somers, *Letters*, 155–156.
72. An analysis of tbe attitudes of 'romance' is given in Chapter Four.
73. On details of the Sir John M'Neill report see page 83.
74. *North British Daily Mail*, 28 July 1851.
75. *North British Daily Mail*, 30 July 1851.
76. *North British Daily Mail*, Leader, 26 July 1851.
77. *North British Daily Mail*, Leader, 28 July 1851.
78. *North British Daily Mail*, Leader, 30 July 1851.
79. *North British Daily Mail*, Leader, 30 July 1851.
80. *North British Daily Mail*, 'Sir J. M'Neill's Report on the Hebrides', 1 August 1851.
81. *North British Daily Mail*, 'Sir J. M'Neill's Report on the Hebrides', 1 August 1851.
82. *North British Daily Mail*, August 9, 1851.
83. As this was one of the best summaries given in the press at the time of the issue, it is worth quoting at full length.
84. *North British Daily Mail*, 9 August, 1851.
85. *North British Daily Mail*, 9 August, 1851.
86. Jack, *Scottish Newspaper Directory*.

87. Cowan, *Newspapers in Scotland*.
88. *Inverness Advertiser*, Leader, 19 June 1849.
89. *Inverness Advertiser*, 19 June 1849.
90. 'North Uist', *Inverness Advertiser*, 31 July 1849.
91. Jack, *Scottish Newspaper Directory*.
92. 'Opening address', *Northern Ensign*, 6 June 1850.
93. *Northern Ensign*, 6 June 1850.
94. 'A happy new year', *Northern Ensign*, 2 January 1851.
95. 'Ourselves', *Northern Ensign*, 20 November 1851.
96. *Northern Ensign*, 20 November 1851.
97. Selection of 'To Correspondents', *Northern Ensign*, 1850–1855.
98. *Inverness Advertiser*, 4 November 1849. Quoted in Mulock, *The Western Highlands and Islands of Scotland, socially considered with reference to proprietors and people: being a series of contributions to the periodical press* (Edinburgh, 1850).
99. 'Mr Mulock's alleged inconsistency on the subject of emigration from the Highlands', *Northern Ensign*, 4 September 1851.
100. 'Our own commissioner', *Northern Ensign*, 21 November 1850.
101. 'Highland Destitution', *Northern Ensign*, 2 January 1851.
102. Quoted in Prebble, *Highland Clearances*, 240.
103. 'Mr Mulock's book', *Northern Ensign*, 4 September 1850.
104. Prebble, *Highland Clearances*, 239. Prebble does not give a source for this description.
105. All details of Mulock's biography up to 1849 come from Prebble, *Highland Clearances*. Unfortunately, Prebble does not name his sources.
106. Prebble, *Highland Clearances*.
107. 'Highland Clearings', *Inverness Advertiser*, 28 August 1849.
108. *Inverness Advertiser*, 28 August 1849.
109. For the details of the evictions on North Uist see page 78.
110. 'The Sollas Trials', *Inverness Advertiser*, 25 September 1849.
111. 'The Sollas Trials', Letter II, *Inverness Advertiser*, 2 October 1849.
112. 'Notices of Lochalsh and Glenelg', *Inverness Advertiser*, 18 December 1849.
113. 'Highland Depopulation – The Sollas Trials', Letter III, *Inverness Advertiser*, 23 October 1849.
114. 'Notices from Lochalsh and Glenelg', *Inverness Advertiser*, 18 December 1849.
115. *Inverness Advertiser*, 18 December 1849.
116. *Inverness Advertiser*, 18 December 1849.
117. 'The neglected state of the Highland parochial poor', *Inverness Advertiser*, quoted in Mulock, *The Western Highlands and Islands*.
118. 'Notices of Lochalsh and Glenelg', *Inverness Advertiser*, 18 December 1849.
119. 'The Emigration from Lochalsh, Glenelg, and South Uist', *Inverness Advertiser*, 25 December 1849.
120. *Inverness Advertiser*, 25 December 1849.
121. Quoted in Rosie, *Hugh Miller*, 122. No date of publication is given.
122. 'Highland Clearances', *The Times*, 26 May 1845.
123. For a detailed description of the operations of the Relief Board, see Chapter Two.
124. 'The Northern Ensign – Mr Mulock', *Inverness Advertiser*, 11 June 1850

125. 'The Inverness Advertiser and its 'own commissioner', *Northern Ensign*, 5 December 1850.

126. 'Fresh Barbarities connected with Compulsory Emigration', *Northern Ensign*, 20 June 1851.

127. *Northern Ensign*, 20 June 1851.

128. 'Compulsory emigration', *Northern Ensign*, 4 July 1850.

129. *Northern Ensign*, 4 July 1850.

130. *Northern Ensign*, 4 July 1850.

131. 'Practical suggestions for the immediate and economical relief of Highland destitution', *Northern Ensign*, 23 January 1851.

132. 'Macleod of Macleod's attempted refutation of Mr Mulock's statements', *Northern Ensign*, 16 January 1851.

133. 'Gairloch – the failure of a project founded on false principles', *Northern Ensign*, 10 April 1851. Emphasis as in the original.

134. 'Extension of emigration from the Outer Hebrides', *Northern Ensign*, 3 July 1851.

135. 'Sir John M'Neil's report and the Peterkin parenthesis', *Northern Ensign*, 7 August 1851.

136. *Northern Ensign*, 7 August 1851.

137. 'Mr Mulock's alleged inconsistency on the subject of emigration from the Highlands', *Northern Ensign*, 4 September 1851.

138. *Northern Ensign*, 4 September 1851.

139. It could be argued that Hugh Miller was also from the Highlands, but he was, on the one hand, only half a Highlander, and on the other hand, Cromarty was not exactly the most deprived Highland area itself.

140. 'The treatment of the Highlanders', *Northern Ensign*, 24 July 1851.

141. *The Concise Oxford Dictionary of Word Origins*, ed. by T.F. Hoad, 1993.

142. 'Progress and Civilisation in the Highlands for the last half century – taking Sutherlandshire as a criterion', *Northern Ensign*, 30 October 1851.

143. *Northern Ensign*, 27 November 1851.

144. *Northern Ensign*, 27 November 1851.

145. I am grateful to Hedda Macleod from Gaelic & Features Television for pointing this out to me.

146. *Northern Ensign*, 18 December 1851.

147. Even Prebble is vague on this, and there is also no mention of the circumstances of his exile in Mackenzie's book. According to Professor Ted Cowan, M'Leod wound up as a newspaper reporter in Woodstock, Ontario.

148. 'The condition of the people in the Highlands of Scotland', letter to the Editor of the *Daily Mail* [*North British Daily Mail*], reprinted in the *Inverness Advertiser*, 27 August 1850.

149. 'The Emigration Advances' Bill', *Northern Ensign*, 14 August 1851.

150. 'A Cure for Highland Destitution', *Northern Ensign*, 28 August 1851.

151. 'Highland Destitution', *Northern Ensign*, 16 October 1851.

152. *Northern Ensign*, 20 January 1852.

153. *Northern Ensign*, 20 January 1852.

154. 'To the Highlanders of Scotland', *Northern Ensign*, 11 November 1851.

155. *Northern Ensign*, 11 November 1851. Italics as in original.

156. Proof that 'Scotus' was indeed Ross comes from the fact that these articles had a lot of common points both in style and arguments with some of his published pamphlets, and from the fact that the *Inverness Advertiser* once identified him as such: 'Mr Donald Ross (writing under the signature of Scotus) . . .' (*Inverness Advertiser*, 25 October 1853).

157. For the details of these two evictions, see page 87.

158. 'The Glengarry Clearances', *Northern Ensign*, 20 October 1853.

159. *Northern Ensign*, 20 October 1853.

160. *Northern Ensign*, 20 October 1853.

161. *Northern Ensign*, 20 October 1853.

162. Donald Ross *The Glengarry Evictions, or scenes at Knoydart*, Glasgow, 1853.

163. *The Glengarry Evictions.*

164. Early on during the Yugoslav war in 1992 it was one of the moral dilemmas of humanitarian and refugee organisations whether to accept people who were 'ethnically cleansed' from their lands, since by taking these people on they in fact also assisted ethnic cleansing by facilitating the movements.

165. For the details of the Greenyards evictions, see page 87.

166. 'The Greenyard evictions', *Northern Ensign*, reprinted in the *Inverness Courier*, 20 April 1854.

167. 'The Strathcanon tragedy', *Northern Ensign*, 11 May 1854.

168. Donald Ross, *The Russians of Ross-shire*, Glasgow, 1854.

169. 'Depopulation of the Highlands', *Northern Ensign*, 14 December 1853.

170. 'Recruiting in the Highlands', *Northern Ensign*, 8 February 1855.

171. *Northern Ensign*, 8 February 1855.

CHAPTER FOUR

Romance

I. Romantic elements in the press

Not all the press depicted the Highland Gaels as either members of a 'vicious race' or a pitiful peasantry. While views of contempt and sympathy were by far the most powerful ones in mid-nineteenth century Lowland public opinion, the romanticisation of the Highlands proved enduring enough, and was often strangely mixed with the other two attitudes. Romantic notionss did not form an entirely separate group but rather permeated and coloured the two main views. The romanticisation of the Highlands was nothing new. It had been a recurring feature since the eighteenth century. It can be said with some confidence that ever since the *Ossian* controversy Scottish literature in particular tended to romanticise all aspects of rural life, including the Highlands. This tendency only grew stronger and more prevalent by the mid-nineteenth century – ranging from tourist accounts to popular literature – and appeared frequently in the pages of the contemporary press.

Those papers contemptuous of the Highland Gaels, such as the *Scotsman*, the *Fifeshire Journal* and the *Inverness Courier*, were still prone to romanticise the past of the Highlands; the bygone era of 'colourful' clan history. These papers reported with considerable delight on many Highland Society and Braemar gatherings, becoming great promoters of the new 'Highlandism' fashion. On such newspaper pages the Highlanders were now being turned into some kind of museum or souvenir curiosity: kilted clansmen, safely placed in the past. While the present Highlanders were thought despicable, deserving only to be sent off their lands, the Highlanders of the past were seen as more colourful and much less troublesome.

It seemed as if two parallel views of the Highlands existed, even within one newspaper and one editor. Leading articles condemning the Highland Gaels as racially inferior ran in tandem with reports of splendid Highland gatherings with Highland 'clansmen' described as a hardy and gallant race.

When in 1845 the *Inverness Courier* joined the pro-Clearances campaign it argued that since the Highlanders were lazy and had 'slumbered' in a 'semi-barbarous state' the Clearances could only improve them. Along with articles in this vein, however, it also published enthusiastic reports about the yearly Braemar Gathering of 'admirably' contesting 'clansmen':

No one cloud obscured the happiness of the meeting, and the Highlanders of the two districts swore lasting friendship, and henceforward to go 'shoulder to shoulder'. In the evening, the clans and their sweethearts joined in the merry dance; and next morning the hardy chief of Athole and his trusty guard marched off to their native glens to the sound of the pibroch.[1]

An idyllic picture indeed. However, it did not seem to bother the *Courier*'s editor that the Clearances he advocated effectively drove away those 'gallant', 'trusty guards' of the 'hardy chiefs', and that the clan system was long over even before the era of the Clearances.

It was equally odd that many Highland landowners took an active part in the various Highland societies, which avowed to 'preserve the nationality of the Highlands', with its 'national spirit' and habits.[2] In the light of press reports, the Highland Society mainly tried to achieve this task by having rounds of pipers, claymore brandishing, numerous Highland toasts and Scottish songs during the dinner evenings.

The 'chief' of the Highland Society was Prince Albert himself. The speech he gave at a society dinner in 1847 – after bagpipe performances from the pipers of the Queen and the Duke of Sussex – summed up well some of the typical 'Highlandism' images. This time, it was the *Scotsman* reporting the event:

> It is impossible for any one to go to that country, to breathe its fresh air, to see its beautiful scenery, and live among the simple, hearty, and kind people of Scotland, without receiving the most favourable impression.[3]

In one world, the people were 'hearty and kind', in the other world they were burdensome and 'inherently lazy', best transported to faraway countries. A few years later Prince Albert was also patron of the Highland Emigration Society. 'Highlandism' became more and more fashionable in the 1840s, especially in London. A yearly festival, the 'Scottish Fete', was a virtual revelry of Highlandism under the direction of the Scottish Society of London. It included a 'competition in archery', a 'Scottish national sports and pastimes' competition, Highland flings, sword dances, and bagpipe bands in abundance.[4] It was also a pageant of the 'fine Highland race'. The correspondent of the *Inverness Courier* wrote most enthusiastically about the pleasing sight of the 'handsome Highlanders':

> One of the most gratifying features of the exhibition was the sight of so many stout, well-made, handsome Highlanders, with plenty of bone and muscle, but no fat. The soldiers of the Guards – all picked men, I presume –

were taller, but had not such a girth round the breast. As one old stalwart Highland piper stalked past, with the stately step and proud bearing of Hardicanute, some one observed – 'There, now; see to what perfection the human frame may be brought by the joint operation of pure air, constant exercise, and oatmeal.' 'Come, come,' said another, 'that won't go down. The oatmeal is all very well in its way, but I am much mistaken if heather-fed mutton, a deer from the hill-side, and a salmon from the loch, have not had some considerable share in perfecting such a physical structure.'[5]

When these comments were made in London at this exhibition of Celtic manhood, most of the members of this picturesque species were suffering from famine. Perfecting their physical structure with heather-fed mutton and salmon was far beyond their reality. However, the romantic Highlander was a more successful and certainly more poetic topic than the problems of Highland destitution.

The sympathetic newspapers primarily romanticised the landscape of the Highlands. In a strange twist, the emptier the Highlands became the more romantic they appeared. 'Barrenness' now provided grand 'solitude' for the Lowland townspeople escaping from the greyness of industrialism. The uninhabited glens and straths were seen as covered in solemn grandeur. The history behind the 'romantic barrenness' was largely ignored and evaded. There was something odd and absurd in how the sympathetic press placed romanticising articles and poetry next to dire accounts of destitution and Clearances.

'Tours', 'trips' and 'rambles' in the 'classic Highlands' were becoming frequent by the 1850s, and accounts of such trips were widely published in the press. Most of these articles were tourist writings, describing in enthusiastic tones the 'celebrated beauties' of the land and the wild but 'picturesque' scenery. The 'charm of the Trossachs' and the 'enchanting' Staffa were a 'must' tourist destination by this time.[6] One traveller spoke of 'hosts of visitors' around these localities, crowding every 'place of resort'.[7]

The images of the Highlands in these tourist pieces were the clichéd, familiar ones: rugged mountains, wild scenery, romantic isolation, nature in its sublime beauty. These few passages from a 'Six Days Tour in the Highlands', published in the *North British Daily Mail*, were quite characteristic:

> The glen through which the road now ran for many miles is *as desolate, black, and wild as could be desired.'*
>
> The distance from Ballachulish to the termination of the glen beyond the Devil's Staircase is about nine miles, but the last three should be walked both ways, so as to enable the visitor to examine the wild beauties of the glen

in detail and in leisure, as they successively open to the wonder and awe-struck gaze of the admirer of all that is wild and sublime in natural scenery.'

Nothing we take it, in Scotland can be found more grandly sublime than the Pass of Awe; and we are only surprised that its beauties are not more generally appreciated and known. What a glorious sail would it be from end to end of this magnificent, wild Highland Loch, in a small steamer; and what hosts of tourists would such a reasonable facility induce.[8]

Throughout these descriptions the human inhabitants were conspicuously missing, as if the land had no people on it at all, as if it existed for the very purpose of providing thrilling scenic experiences for the travellers and tourists. History and present day reality behind the Highland scenery were ignored. In the few instances when there were references to the inhabitants they were either made in connection with some lack of 'facility' that should have been provided for the tourists, or as a passing remark about 'the poor sparse population'.[9]

Those who did pay more attention to the inhabitants saw them as 'natives', who only confirmed the general prejudices about their 'natural laziness'. There was a hint of annoyance here of a traveller who saw his perfect scenery ruined by the unfitting ugliness of the 'natives':

> We were now in the Highlands, and everything was highland enough: Bluebonnets, here and there a kilt on a gilly, and Gaelic everywhere. The accounts we got of the indolence of the inhabitants of the Mull of Cantyre generally, were by no means flattering. An extensive landed proprietor of the district stated that, in carrying out extensive improvements in draining, &c, he found the greatest difficulty in inducing the natives to work.[10]

II. A 'gloomy' and 'doomed' people

While the barren landscape was made appealing and poetical it was also depicted as a land of gloom, especially in popular literature appearing in the newspapers. Much of this popular poetry contained laments conveying a strong sense of doomed fate. The themes and images showed a world that was disappearing, or even dying. The romanticisation here was part of the wider sense of giving up on the Highlands, present both in the contemp-tuous and the sympathetic press.

The mood of gloom and lament was all-prevailing in the poetry that was published in the press under the heading of 'popular poetry'. Lament over something or someone gone, dead, never to return. Lament over loss. Essentially, lament over a vanishing world. There were poems about a chieftain's death, with whose body his spirit had also passed away,[11] about the old glory of fighting for Prince Charles,[12] about grief over the loss of a child,[13] about tears and lost happy times,[14] to cite but a few.

One of the poems in the newspapers at the time which expressed best this overall mood of lament and death was published anonymously,[15] with the title of 'The Garden Revisited'. Already the title conveyed the idea of the lost Garden of Eden, and the nostalgia of remembering it, 'revisiting' it. Although there was no specific reference in the poem to either place or time, certain expressions evoked strong images of the Highlands, with the 'vale of tears', a 'departed spring', of friends who were now gone, and 'a cherished past' that could not last. 'The Garden Revisited' was one of the most strongly expressed examples of the sense of lament and loss. At the end of the poem there was a request for a Gaelic translation:

> *The Garden Revisited*
> Alas, how soon this life appears
> A wilderness – a vale of tears!
> The joys our youth and childhood knew,
> How like a dream, how fast they flew!
> While oh, how many sorrows low'r
> O'ershadowing each succeeding hour!
> There's not a scene that long ago,
> In infancy, we used to know,
> Which know, when gazed on, does not bring
> Sad thoughts as of departed spring.
> Yet-sweetest flowers around may rise
> Beneath the light of summer skies,
> Ev'n mid the warmth of July's breeze
> A wintry feeling seems to freeze;
> We feel life's early blossoms shed,
> And fancy's brightest garlands dead,
> And the remembrance clouds our brow
> Of friends who were, but are not now.
> Yet, every spot to memory dear
> Tells us our home must not be here;
> Here ev'ry charm our senses meet,
> Flowers of bright dye, and odours sweet,
> And melody from bird and rill,

> When all around is hushed and still
> All bring to mind some cherished past,
> As sweet, that would not, could not last.
> Flow'rs, odours, sound from bird and stream,
> Whisper that life is but a dream,
> Its evanescent charms but given
> To point our hearts and hopes to heaven.
> There memory shall never deplore
> A past to be enjoyed no more.[16]

Lament over the lost past was more specifically expressed in poems about emigration and exile. Several 'exile' poems appeared mostly in the sympathetic papers during the 1850s, under such titles as 'The Exile',[17] 'The Emigrant Ship',[18] 'My Fatherland',[19] or 'To a Scottish Exile'.[20] Most of them were either anonymous or written by lay poets. These poems spoke of the pain of leaving the homeland, of the hopelessness of finding home and friends on distant and foreign shores, of 'cruel' ships tearing people away from scenes of cherished happiness, and of the native land as their only home, which was now gone.

The compelling force behind emigration and the Clearances appeared in few of the poems. One such work was reviewed and quoted in the *North British Daily Mail*. The 'Raid of Albyn – Historic Poem' by William D. Campbell and his co-author father aimed to be more than a lament. It was written as an impassioned protest against the Clearances and depopulation. In this sense, it was a 'crusading' poem, composed by poets who saw themselves as the conscience of the nation, – a very romantic notion. The main object of the 'Raid of Albyn' was 'to create a feeling of re-action in the public mind' and 'to arrest the attention of our legislators to the horrors of the system', said the *North British Daily Mail* in its review.[21] It was also for this purpose, it added, that the poem was dedicated to the periodical press.

What can be pieced together today from the poem comes from the review itself and from the extracts, which were published alongside. According to the review, the poem had no plot or any consecutive historic narration. It consisted of 'a series of detached sketches, episodical in their nature' intended to portray 'the genius and virtues of the Scottish Celt'. There were sketches of the Highland landscape, and of the 'domesticities of Highland life'.

The poem was divided into six cantos. The introductory canto started with the meeting of an old and a young bard, which turned into a lament over bygone days. The young bard, called Carril, envied the old one for having had a much more pleasant mission, singing of 'bright' and 'serene'

days. He had to sing of the 'wrongs' and the oppressions. His mission was
to battle for his people:

> The friendless minstrel of a friendless race;
> I sing the wrongs of Albyn's ancient line,
> And fearlessly unmask the oppressor's face.[22]

The first canto then continued with some 'beautiful pictures of Highland
landscape with a deer hunt', and with an episode of a window and a young son.
Canto II was a 'spirited' description of the battle of Inverlochy. Canto III
related the story of the 1745 rising led by Prince Charles. In canto IV the young
bard reappeared again and came forward with 'an indignant verse' on the
instigators of the clearance system. He stated that Sutherland used to contain
15,000 'brave inhabitants' forty years earlier, but their reward was expulsion,
leaving them 'homeless in their own dear land'. Canto V described an emigrant
ship with the evicted exiles, and the sufferings and hardships they endured on
the journey. Canto VI contained 'an appeal to the nation on behalf of the Gael'.
This was the part from which the review quoted at most length:

> Our country once was great indeed, but now
> The laurels fade and rot off her brow;
> Her chiefs are Moloch's grown, to glut whose greed,
> A silent sacrifice, the people bleed;
> While rack-rents and oppressions waste the lands,
> By open fraud committed to their hands;
> And they in blood-bought garments strut and shine,
> The basest worshippers at Folly's shrine.
> . . .
> Give us our rights, we do not ask for more;
> Let us but live as we have lived before;
> This much at least, our country should demand,
> That no proud chief dare desolate his land.
> . . .
> Is there no voice in Britain's courts to-day,
> To plead for those who live the spoiler's prey!
> Is there no heart so generous and high
> As to denounce those deeds of blackest dye;
> To rend the mask from falsehood's face, and tell
> The tale our wasted forms express too well!
> Oh! if there be, for honour's sake sound forth
> And plead the cause of Justice and the North![23]

Many of the laments and accusations were familiar here, from the notion that the people had been 'sacrificed' by careless and heartless landlords to the call that Clearances should not be allowed. The strong demand of 'give us our rights' was, however, a new tone. It foreshadowed a more confident and more combative way of fighting for the land in the Highlands.

The review remarked at the end that the poets' concept was to maintain the old patriarchal system, which, in their view, was the 'best suited to the development of all manly virtues'. The reviewer refrained from discussion of the argument, implying that it was a rather naive one.

The 'Raid of Albyn' also contained notes, which gave such 'harrowing descriptions' of the clearances that they made 'the blood run cold' and were 'a disgrace to the age which witnessed them'. Whether or not the 'Raid of Albyn' was but a pure propaganda piece, it was certainly one of those relatively few poems which dealt with the issue of the Clearances.

The theme of dispossession was a prevalent one in Gaelic poetry,[24] but less so in Scottish poetry in general. There were many laments and nostalgic yearnings for the bygone era, but except for a few poems, such as Charles Mackay's 'Lament of Cona',[25] there were no powerful streams of clearance poetry.[26] Given that the Clearances constituted one of the gravest traumas in nineteenth-century Scotland, this was a strange and disturbing omission, or at least a subconscious evasion. Even when poems dealt with emigration, exile, and the Clearances, their basic tone was that of resigned lament rather than combatant anger, accepting as fate that there was nothing to be done.

The idea that the Highland Gaels were doomed irreversibly was not present only in the popular literature of laments. The same notion lay behind the arguments of the contemptuous press when it insisted that the Celts' racial inferiority predetermined them to eventual extinction. While the contemptuous section of the press more or less welcomed this idea, the romantics lamented and wept over it, but both considered the Celtic doom inevitable.

The doom concept, however, spread further. It penetrated the thoughts of even such sympathetic writers as Hugh Miller. He also saw a sort of fulfilment of a 'prophecy' of nation decay and death in the depopulation of the Highlands. In a remarkable passage from a supposedly early article on the depopulation in the Highlands published in the *Inverness Courier*, Miller described in eerie terms the scene of a cleared land. He was struck then by the thought that all the decay and desolation was in fact the result of some fatal prophecy, of some inevitable doom:

As we advanced we saw the ruins of deserted cottages, and perceived that the patches adjoining had once been furrowed by the plough. All was solitary and desolate. Roof-trees were decaying within the mouldering walls; a rank of vegetation had covered the silent floors, and was wavering over hearths the fires of which has been forever extinguished. A solitary lapwing was screaming over the cottages, a melancholy raven was croaking on a neighbouring eminence, there was the faint murmur of the stream, and the low moan of the breeze; but every sound of man had long passed from the air, – the tones of speech and the voice of singing. Alas! we exclaimed, the Highlander has at length been conquered, and the country which he would have died to defend is left desolate. The track of an eastern army can be traced many years after its march by ruined villages and a depopulated country. Prophets have described scenes of future desolation, – lands once populous grown 'places where no man dwelleth nor son of man passeth through,' – and here in our native country is a scene calculated to illustrate the terrible threatening of prophecy, and the sad descriptions of Eastern historians.[27]

The reference to Eastern historians suggested that Miller was writing in a wider context, influenced by European thinkers. What this influence largely was became clear from another passage in the same article. Miller discussed the concept of how the age of nations was comparable to the ages of the individual, and as such, nations would also become extinct at a certain stage. His wording was clear: '*Nations, like individuals, become old, and they at length expire*'.[28] This was almost an exact reiteration of the concepts of the late-eighteenth-century German philosopher, Johann Gottfried Herder.

Herder believed that the life of nations was similar to the individual, having childhood, adulthood and old age, and eventually nations could die out. 'Every nation has periods of growth, flourish and decline; no nation can remain in static condition', he said in his seminal work *Auch eine philosophie der Eeschichte zur Bildung der Menscheit* (The historical philosophy of the progress of humanity) in 1774. Around the world the various nations were in different stages of their life and development, some were still young, some in their maturity, and some in their old age, Herder said elsewhere.[29] This close parallel between the life of the individual and the nation penetrated his whole philosophy.

This 'Herderian' thought was very clearly present in Hugh Miller's writings. The following passages were almost literal translations from Herder:

> There are stages of development in the immature youth of individuals,
> that seem to correspond with stages of development in the immature youth
> of nations.
>
> There is a poetic age in the life of most individuals, as certainly in the
> history of most nations; and a very happy age it is. . . . but the poetic age is
> ever a credulous one, as certainly in individuals as in nations: . . .[30]

Contrast this passage with these lines from Herder:

> Just as individuals, mankind had a childhood as well./The Greeks repre-
> sented the youth of mankind, the Romans its adulthood./Every nation has
> its period of growth, flourish and decay . . .[31]

Herder's influence was direct here. However, many of Herder's other ideas
also sounded familiar and relevant in the Scottish context.

Herder was most famous at the time for his concepts on the *Volk*, on
'nation character', on *Zeitgeist*, and on language as prime carrier of the
nation's identity. His theory on *Volk*, (the word 'people' in its collective
form is the closest to the original meaning) was central in his philosophy.[32]
The *Volk* had a distinctive collective consciousness, which Herder also
called 'national spirit' or 'national character', which stemmed from its
language together with social customs, folklore, literary traditions. This
collective consciousness was what forged people with common language
and culture together, Herder said:

> This is the invisible, hidden, medium that links minds through ideas, hearts
> through inclinations and impulses, the senses through impressions and
> forms, civil society through laws and institutions, generations through
> examples, modes of living and education. It is through this medium that
> we actively establish a continuum between ourselves and those that follow.[33]

This was a radically different idea from the old Enlightenment view, which
identified culture with civilisation rather than being based on such a natural
endowment as language. Language was absolutely crucial, in Herder's view.
It was the embodiment of the 'soul' of the nation, as language was also an
expression of an individual, unique personality.[34] There was no *Volk*, no
nation without its own language – losing it eventually destroyed the 'soul'
of the *Volk*, and the *Volk* itself. Even if the *Volk* lost its state it could survive
if it retained its distinctive language.

Herder's views had enormous influence on the development of nationalism – as tenets for the establishment of nation states – especially in central
and eastern Europe, and on other 'peripheral', 'small' nations. Preserving

language with its cultural traditions now became tantamount to ensuring the survival of the people, of the *Volk*. This gave rise to immense philological research, language modernisation, and folklorist movements around central and eastern Europe, becoming integral parts of the awakening nationalisms. The phrase that 'the nation lives in its language', was a commonplace among many Hungarian writers.

These Herderian theories, however, also meant that it was conceivable that a nation could lose its language and eventually disappear, die out. The concept of 'nation-death' was very forcefully introduced by Herder. He even predicted the death of certain nations, among them, the Hungarians. He first predicted the Hungarians together with their language disappearing in the sea of many nations in central Europe, then he feared that the forceful Germanisation of the Habsburgs would destroy the language and national character of not only the Hungarians but of other nations as well.[35]

Herder's prediction had an enormous impact in Hungary. The Hungarian world view had been pessimistic anyway after a succession of defeats and occupations throughout their history,[36] coupled with the fact that the Hungarian language was different from all the surrounding languages.[37] Herder's prediction completely darkened the horizon for many thinkers, and the idea of 'nation-death' kept recurring throughout the nineteenth and twentieth centuries. Doom, decay and death were also present in Hungarian poetry in the 1830s and 1840s – a few decades before similar moods were struck in the Celtic Highlands. From a poem in 1831:

> We've seen the dismal nation-killing danger
> Coming over us as dark deluge
> With ravens' terrifying shrieks
> It howls: 'Hungarian! You are obliterated![38]

From a poem in 1845:

> There's no joy in your past
> No hope in your future,
> My decaying nice homeland,
>
> You waves-beaten island,
> Predicted as sinking
> by thousand oracles[39]

Herder's impact in Europe by the mid-nineteenth century stretched from the Italian nationalist Mazzini to Pan-Slavism and Czech national aspirations. His influence has not been noted in France or England,[40] but this is perhaps not surprising since both nations lived in fully-fledged nation states with no threat to their language or culture. However, on the peripheries such as Scotland, Herderian theories could have carried more significance.

This is not to argue that Herder had wide-ranging direct influence in Scotland – apart from the close parallels between some of his theories and a few passages in Hugh Miller's works. Nevertheless, the fact that some Herderian ideas did appear in the writings of such figures as Hugh Miller suggests that there was some measure of influence. Considering that the issues which Herder addressed – from language survival to national character and identity, and from aspirations to nationhood to the decay of peoples – were also of no small interest in Scotland at the time, some Herderian impact would be no surprise. At least, there were detectable echoes of Herderian theory in mid-nineteenth century Scotland, especially when it came to the issue of the Gaelic Highlands.

While the idea of nation-death appeared in Hungary in very sombre and strident tones, leading to determined fights for survival,[41] in Scotland the idea of a doomed Celtic race was expressed through lament and sad abandonment to fate. This mood was present in the mid-nineteenth century popular poetry and, to some extent, it was behind the disillusionment and surrender of some crusading journalists.

Although the 1850s were not yet the age of the 'Celtic Twilight', the seeds were already there. The images of decay and death would later be taken to the extreme at the end of the century in 'twilight' works like *The Mountain Lovers* by William Sharp (alias Fiona MacLeod). In this novel of 'sado-masochistic luxuriance in vague and Ossianic cloudiness', the Gaelic Highlands were shown as dying of some 'inherent decadence'.[42] Reality was completely absent by this time, there was nothing either about exiles or clearances, there was not even lament over the decay. By this time, in this work, the death of the Gaelic land was overlaid with some thrilling mist – it was used for aesthetic purposes.

The emergence of a framework for the 'Celtic Twilight' and the legitimisation of the decay of the Celtic race were of earlier date. The basic mood of gloom and doom over the vanishing Gaeldom was already established in the pages of the newspapers in the mid-nineteenth century.

Notes

1. 'Braemar Gathering', *Inverness Courier*, 2 September 1845.
2. 'The Highland Society', *Scotsman*, 27 March 1847.
3. *Scotsman*, 27 March 1847.
4. 'Scottish Fete in London', *Inverness Courier*, 28 June 1849.
5. *Inverness Courier*, 28 June 1849.
6. 'A six days tour in the Highlands', *North British Daily Mail*, 11 September 1852.
7. *North British Daily Mail*, 13 September 1852.
8. *North British Daily Mail*, 13 & 22 September 1852.
9. *North British Daily Mail*, 23 September 1852.
10. 'A Trip to the West Highlands', *North British Daily Mail*, 15 September 1851.
11. 'Clanranald's Lament', by 'Gael', *Inverness Courier*, 6 August 1845.
12. 'The Raising of the Standard', by 'Gael', *Inverness Courier*, 3 September 1845.
13. 'The child and the mourners', by Charles Mackay, in Wilson, *Poets and Poetry of Scotland*, 383.
14. 'O Ye Tears!', and 'Remembrances of Nature', both by Charles Mackay, in Wilson, *Poets*, 383.
15. It was only revealed that the poem was by the 'author of "Mary, my Mary"', 'Garden Revisited', *Inverness Advertiser*, 8 October 1850.
16. *Inverness Advertiser*, 8 October 1850.
17. *Inverness Advertiser*, 13 January 1851.
18. *Inverness Advertiser*, 18 January 1853.
19. *Inverness Advertiser*, 12 November 1850.
20. *The Witness*, 14 December 1850.
21. 'Literature; "The Raid of Albyn",' *North British Daily Mail*, 1 April 1854.
22. 'The Raid of Albyn'.
23. 'The Raid of Albyn'.
24. MacInnes, 'Gaelic poetry in the nineteenth century', in: *The History of Scottish Literature*, vol. 3, ed. by Douglas Gifford.
25. Quoted in Wilson *Poets and Poetry of Scotland*.
26. This claim is based on a survey of general trends in Scottish poetry as given in Gifford, *The History of Scottish Literature*, on the survey of poems collected in Wilson's *Poets*, and in consultation with Prof. Douglas Gifford.
27. Quoted in Bayne, P., *Life and Letters of Hugh Miller*, London, 1871, 261–263.
28. Bayne, *Life and Letters*.
29. *Briefe zu Beförderung der Humanität*, (Reflections on the History of Mankind), 1793–97.
30. Miller, *My Schools and Schoolmasters*, 39, 187.
31. From *Auch eine philosophie der Geschichte zur Bildung der Menscheit*, 1774. Own translations from Hungarian text of the German 1891 ed.
32. Herder has been accused sometimes of being one of the influences on Nazism. However, the organic 'Volk' concept of the Nazis was based on race and not on culture and language. Nothing was further from Herder's mind than the idea of master races, and racism. Diversity was crucial to the world's culture, he believed,

and he refuted any idea of inferior races. He was also vehemently anti-colonialist, and saw the European domination of the 'third world' as detrimental to the free flourishing of national characters and cultures there.

33. F.M. Barnard, *Herder's Social and Political Thought, From Enlightenment to Nationalism*, 117.

34. Barnard, *Herder's Social and Political Thought*, 59.

35. *Ideen zur Philosophie der Geschichte der Menscheit* (Outlines of a Philosophy of Man), 1784–1791. Vol II. ed. 1978.

36. These included Mongolian invasion, Turkish occupation, Austrian subjugation, and a couple of lost uprisings and freedom fights.

37. It belongs to the Finno-Ugric language family, and has no relation to the German or Slavic languages. This has always made the Hungarians feel set apart, without 'relatives' or 'brothers' around them.

38. Mihály Vörösmarty, 'V. Ferdinánd királyhoz', 1831; 'To the King Ferdinand V', own translation.

39. J. Bajza, 'Sóhajtás', 1845, 'Sigh', own translation.

40. Barnard, *Herder's Social and Political Thought*, 167–168.

41. Including a successful movement of language renewal, to decades of reform movement in order to bring the country into the world of progress to ensure its survival in Europe, and eventually it culminated in revolution and a war of independence.

42. Gifford, *The History of Scottish Literature*.

Conclusion

The Highland Gael was viewed and reported in widely different, often directly opposing, ways in the pages of the mid-nineteenth century Scottish newspapers. He was despised and glorified, hated and pitied, abandoned and fought for, abhorred and romanticised. Which of these views was dominant had changed by the end of the ten-year period between the outbreak of the potato famine and the years of the Crimean War.

In the second half of the 1840s contempt was by far the commonest, proclaiming the 'inherent laziness' and 'racial inferiority' of the Highland Gaels. These voices – mostly expressed in the pages of the *Scotsman, Glasgow Herald, Inverness Courier* and medium-size local papers – generally supported the clearance system, and the principle of work-for-food during the Famine, and later they also advocated compulsory emigration as the only possible solution for the Highland question.

According to these views, the problem lay essentially in the nature and character of the Gaels, instead of in the actual land policies and proprietors' management. The Gaels were declared hopeless and useless, therefore it was thought best to drive them away to a far-off country. When compulsory emigration attained official policy status following the M'Neill report in 1851, the 'majority of the Scottish journals' raised 'a blatant shout of welcome', observed one reader at the time.[1] 'Removing the diseased part'[2] was the solution these papers advocated as the suitable remedy for an inferior Celtic race.

Opposing these views of contempt were a few emerging voices of sympathy. Those sympathetic journalists who first went into battle with the ruling opinion were sharp and scathing critics, attacking both contemptuous opinion and the landowners' policies. The Glasgow *Argus*, the *Witness* with Hugh Miller, and the *North British Daily Mail* all vehemently opposed the Clearances and depopulation, and were highly critical of the landlords for not exercising their duties, for not doing enough for the people. They all believed that the Highlands were 'improvable', and the now 'degraded' and 'lazy' (but not because of their own fault) people would become a fine peasantry if only they were given encouragement and education.

In the 1850s the battle between contempt and sympathy became more fierce, as a new type of journalist emerged on the scene: the 'crusading journalist'. Crusaders like Thomas Mulock, Donald M'Leod and Donald Ross were angry and passionate men. They were hammering away at the landlords, at the government, and at other papers as no other critics had done before. Their newspapers, mainly the *Inverness Advertiser* and the *Northern Ensign,* maintained a persistent campaign on behalf of the Highlands.

They shared many points with the more balanced and calmer critics but at the same time they radicalised the arguments. They argued not that the people were too numerous but that there was not enough land for them, and they urged land reform through land redistribution. Only security of land or landownership would bring improvement to the Highlands. Thomas Mulock even suggested that the landowning class was the really useless one, and instead of the people being cleared off the land, the landlords should be turned out of their palaces.

All the crusaders angrily rejected the accusation that the Highlanders were lazy. They were as industrious as any other people provided they saw the fruits of their labours. According to Mulock, the whole charge of 'sloth' was just an excuse made up by the landlords in order to facilitate evictions.

Both the calmer critics and the angrier crusaders repeatedly warned that depopulation would have disastrous consequences, and would eventually lead to the 'extinction' of the Celtic race in the Highlands. They saw what was taking place in the Highlands as the 'extermination' and 'destruction' of the Gaels, and prophesied in vivid terms how the Highlands would become nothing more than a desert and a dead land. Their protest was a desperate attempt to stop the process, but in the end, even the most determined crusader, Donald Ross, had to give up. They became embittered as they saw thousands leave the land, and felt their own voices becoming weak and ineffective.

What seemed a futile struggle at the time, however, was only so for a while. Although the sympathetic press could not halt the Clearances, and could not force any land reform, at least public opinion was changing. By the mid-1850s there was a marked shift towards sympathy for the Highlanders.

With the outbreak of the Crimean War, they were suddenly considered useful again, and many formerly contemptuous papers now exclaimed, as if awakening from a dream: 'where are the Highlanders?' The formerly divided Scottish press was now unified in 'one spontaneous burst of sympathy with the Gael', as one reader remarked in 1855:

. . . our country being engaged in a bloody, disastrous, and uncertain contest with a giant power, it is truly amusing to observe how all those newspaper anomalies to which I have alluded have, within these few weeks, been fused into one spontaneous burst of sympathy with the Gael – one harmonious call for the condition of the children of the hills being examined into, and *land lots conceded to them* . .[3]

Sympathy was thus winning eventually, even in calls for land reform. By the 1880s, the demands of the radical land reform movement could no longer be ignored. When the Napier Commission took evidence from crofters around the Highlands, the grievances and arguments for land strongly echoed those already made by radical journalists back in the 1850s:

What we desire . . . is a reasonable share of the land, whereof we can make a livelihood, without being obliged to go to distant parts of the country to earn a living . . . There is sufficient land to distribute, and land formerly cultivated by tenantry, but of late converted into sheep farms.[4]

Although the demands of the Highland Land Law Reform Association mainly followed those of the Irish Land League, they included an added call for 'such an apportionment of land as will promote the welfare of the people throughout the Highlands and Islands'.[5] This clearly suggested land redistribution – a demand which had been widely advocated in the sympathetic press in the 1850s.

The result of the 1880s land reform movement, the 1886 Crofters' Act, did not meet the demand for land distribution. It made little provision for making more land available, and it did not restore the cleared lands to the people.[6]

Many of the proposals and demands made by the critics and crusaders of the 1840s and 1850s still remained topical. If nothing else, sympathy, at least, was now the dominant public attitude. In this sense, the sympathetic journalists proved in the long run victorious in the battles of the mid-nineteenth century.

It could be argued, however, that this 'victory' was rather belated, coming as it did more than thirty years after the period when many people believed that it was already too late to stop the depopulation of the Highlands. Thousands of people had gone already, and vast areas of land were lying waste and empty. In the 1850s Scotland seemed to stop caring about the people on half of its land. The sense of turning away from the problems, of giving up on solving them seemed all-powerful. Some contemporaries felt this very strongly, as this letter in the *Northern Ensign* showed in 1855:

> To appeal to Scotland, however, would be a mere waste of time. Scotland does nothing, and can do nothing, to save the Highlands from utter depopulation. In fact, a quiet belief has settled down on the minds of most Scotsmen, that the Highland population is ruined beyond recovery, and that the sooner the landlords make short work of the remnant that remains, the more merciful will be the operation. Scotland has become accustomed to scenes which remind one rather of the horrors of war carried on by barbarous people, than of the even administration of law in a civilized country . . .[7]

The 'quiet belief' that the Highland population was 'ruined beyond recovery' produced far-reaching consequences. On the one hand, it meant that unpleasant thoughts about the problem of the Highlands were banished from public consciousness, being replaced with a more comforting picture of the romanticised Highlands. If the real Highlands were doomed anyway, then there was room enough in the imagination to find new uses for them. 'Celtic Twilight' romances, 'Highlandism', romanticised images, and the poetry of doom and lament were all products of this outlook. Harsh realities were now swathed in romantic mist. The Gaels were represented as a vanishing, 'twilight' people, on the edge, disappearing.

This distortion and evasion of the realities of the Highlands served as a sort of 'mental clearance'. The Highland Gaels were cleared and exiled not only from their lands but also from the minds and consciences of their fellow-countrymen.

This 'mental clearance' of the 'doomed' people also proved to be a cunning weapon for wider landlord and government policies. In effect, it served as a 'permission for decay', where an already marginalised culture was allowed to die.[8] This sort of mystification was used by government and proprietors since it raised the responsibility from their shoulders. If the Highland Gaels' doom was inevitable, then there was no need to worry about policy there, no need to justify the failure to counter it.[9] In other words, the idea of Gaeldom decaying from 'an inner flaw, an inherent decadence' was a 'more politically acceptable diagnosis for the period'.[10]

Many argued at the time that the only solution was to give more land to the people. This, however, would have meant taking land from the landowning aristocracy, which would have amounted to a social revolution. But this the Highland landowning class was not prepared to allow.

In many continental countries, meanwhile, the power of the landowners was dwindling, and even in central and eastern Europe landlords were beginning to see that curbing their own power would lead to the progress of their country. In Hungary, for instance, throughout the Reform Age in the 1820s to the 1840s, great landowning aristocrats *themselves* were advocating peasant landownership, distribution of common fields, taxation of land-lords and the surrender of many proprietorial rights.

Similar moves in Scotland, however, seemed like a utopia, born only in the minds of such wild men as crusading journalists and sympathetic readers who believed in the equality of the Highland Gaels. For any fundamental change in Highland policy to have occurred, the first step would have been a change in the basic perception of the Highlanders. As one 'Lowlander' reader put this vividly and humanely in the pages of the *Inverness Advertiser* in 1851:

> *Let not the inhabitants any longer be regarded and treated as a proscribed and degraded race* – a race incapable of improvement – whose utter extinction is considered as alone compatible with the prosperity of the proprietors. Let not obstacles be thrown in their way. *Give them fair and even-handed justice – such a prospect of rising as is given to the southern.* . . . I have, sir, been grieved to see that too many of those who come from the south to the Highlands have been actuated by a spirit similar to that with which the proprietors and their agents have regarded the natives. They have affected to despise them and to look down upon them as an inferior race; and many of those who are far inferior in moral worth, character, and talent to the Highlander, would think that they degraded themselves if they made him their companion. This has been the cause of the ruin of the Highlands – a spirit that has travelled downwards from the managers of the estates to the poorest operative who they may chance to bring from the south. If, then, the improvement of the Highlanders is sought, *let him be placed on the same level with the southern – open up the land to him – break down the sheep farms* – let it be proclaimed and acted upon that there is in the future to be no barrier thrown in the way of the native – *that he is free to rise as any other – that he is to receive the same fair play* – that the farms are open to him as to another – that if he perseveres in industry, no obstacle shall be thrown in his way, but that any farm in the country may yet become his.[11]

The real cause of the ruin of the Highlands was deep down, rooted in the image of the Gaels, this reader believed. It could be argued that at the heart of the whole problem was the question of human and social equality, or rather inequality. In the mid-nineteenth century, the Highland Gaels were viewed in many ways – from inferior race to picturesque and poetic heroes – but, with a few exceptions, they were never seen as equal, fellow human beings.

Notes

1. 'The case of the west Highlands', *Inverness Advertiser*, 5 August 1851.
2. See page 77.
3. 'The Scotch Newspaper press and the Highlanders', *Northern Ensign*, 4 January 1855. Italics in original text.
4. Quoted in Hunter, *The Making of the Crofting Community*, Edinburgh, 1995, 126.
5. Quoted in Hunter, *The Making of the Crofting Community*, 143.
6. Hunter, *The Making of the Crofting Community*, 143.
7. 'What has become of the Highlanders?', *Northern Ensign*, 29 March 1855.
8. A phrase from Prof. Douglas Gifford.
9. I owe the crystallisation of these thoughts to Prof. Douglas Gifford.
10. Gifford, *The History of Scottish Literature*, 235.
11. 'The case of the Highlands – Remedy', letter to the Editor of the *Inverness Advertiser*, 2 September 1851. My own italics.

Bibliography

Manuscript Sources

National Archives of Scotland (formerly Scottish Record Office), Edinburgh
HD Highland Destitution. Major collection of government correspondence and all
material relating to the activities of the Edinburgh Section of the Central Board, its
officers and local committees, 1846–1850
HD 4/1–6. Papers of the Highland and Island Emigration Society, 1851–59

Mitchell Library, Glasgow
MS 21506. Letterbook on Highland Emigration of Sir John McNeill, 1852

Government Records and Parliamentary Papers

Hansard's Parliamentary Debates
Report to the Board of Supervision by Sir John McNeill on the Western
Highlands
XXVI. (1851) IV.
The New Statistical Account of Scotland
1835–1845, 15 vols.
The Statistical Account of Scotland
1791–99, ed. by Sir John Sinclair, 20 vols.

Newspapers and Periodicals

Aberdeen Free Press
Aberdeen Herald
Aberdeen Journal
Athenaeum
Atlas
Banffshire Journal
Berwick Advertiser
Blackwood's Magazine
Caledonian Mercury
Carlisle Journal
Dumfries Courier
Edinburgh Advertiser
Edinburgh Evening Courant
Edinburgh Evening Post

Edinburgh Review
Edinburgh Weekly Chronicle
Edinburgh Weekly Journal
Elgin Courier
Fifeshire Journal
Glasgow Argus
Glasgow Chronicle
Glasgow Citizen
Glasgow Constitutional
Glasgow Courier
Glasgow Herald
Glasgow Sentinel
The Globe
Greenock Advertiser
Illustrated London News
Inverness Advertiser
Inverness Courier
Inverness Journal
John O'Groat Journal
Morning Chronicle
Noncomformist
North British Daily Mail
North British Review
North Briton
North of Scotland Gazette
Northern Chronicle
Northern Ensign
People's Journal
Perth Constitutional
Perth Courier
Quarterly Journal of Agriculture
Saturday Post
Scotch Reformers' Gazette
Scots Magazine
Scotsman
Scottish Guardian
Scottish Highlander
Spectator
Stornoway Gazette
Tait's Magazine
The Times
Transactions of the Highland and Agricultural Society of Scotland
Westminster Review
Witness

Contemporary Commentaries

Alison, W.P., *Observation on the Famine of 1846–47 in the Highlands of Scotland and Ireland*, Edinburgh, 1847

Alison, W.P., *Letter to Sir John MacNeill on Highland Destitution*, Edinburgh, 1851

Allister, R., *Extermination of the Scottish Peasantry*, Edinburgh, 1853

Andrews, Alexander, *History of British Journalism*, London, 1859

Anon., *Depopulation System in the Highlands*, Edinburgh, 1849

Anon., *Extermination of the Highland Clans*, Edinburgh, 1854

Anon., *Extracts from Letters to the Rev. Dr MacLeod regarding the Famine and Destitution in the Highlands of Scotland*, Glasgow, 1847

Anon., *Observations on the Causes and Remedies of Destitution in the Highlands of Scotland*, Glasgow, 1837

Bain, Donald, *Observations upon the Potato Disease of 1845 and 1846*, Edinburgh, 1848

Bakewell, Thomas, *Remarks on a publication of James Loch Esq.*, 1820

Barron, J., *The Northern Highlands in the Nineteenth Century*, Inverness, 1903–1913

Bayne, Peter, *Life of Hugh Miller*, London, 1871

Bentham, Jeremy, *A Fragment on Government*, 1776

Birkbeck, G. (ed.), *Letters of Samuel Johnson*, Oxford, 1892

Boswell, James, *Journal of a Tour to the Hebrides with Samuel Johnson*, 1785, Penguin ed., 1989

Bruce, J., *Letters on the Present Condition of the Highlands and Islands of Scotland* (also published as: *Destitution in the Highlands*) – serialised in the *Scotsman*, January–March 1847 – Edinburgh, 1847

Burt, Edward, *Letters from a Gentleman in the North of Scotland*, London, 1815

Burton, 'Emigration in its Practical Application to Individuals and Communities', reprinted in the *Scotsman*, 1851

Carlyle, Thomas, *Past and Present*, London, 1845

Carruthers, Robert: *The Highland Notebook, or sketches and anecdotes*, Inverness, 1887

Fullarton, A. and Baird, C.R., *Remarks on the Evils at Present Affecting the Highlands and Islands of Scotland*, Glasgow, 1838

Grant, Elizabeth, *Memoirs of a Highland Lady*, 1797–1827, Canongate ed., Edinburgh, 1991

Grant, James, *The Romance of War*, Edinburgh, 1845

Jack, T.C., *Scottish Newspaper Directory and Guide to Advertisers*, Edinburgh, 1855

Johnson, Samuel, *A Journey to the Western Islands of Scotland*, 1775, Penguin ed. 1989

Knox, Robert, *The Races of Men, A Fragment*, London, 1850

Mackenzie, Alexander, *The Highland Clearances*, Inverness, 1883

MacKenzie, J., *Letter to Lord John Russell on Sir John MacNeill's Report*, Edinburgh, 1851

Mackinnon, W.A., *History of Civilisation*, London, 1846

Maclaine, T. *Population of the Highlands of Scotland*, Edinburgh, 1857

MacLauchlan, T. *The Depopulation System in the Highlands*, 1849

MacLeod, Donald, *Gloomy Memories of the Highlands*, 1840–41, Glasgow, 1892

MacLeod, Donald, *The Sutherlandshire Clearances*, Glasgow, 1856

MacLeod, N., *Letters to the Rev. Dr MacLeod regarding the Famine and Destitution in the Highlands and Islands*, Glasgow, 1847

Malthus, Thomas, *An Essay on the Principle of Population*, 1798

Marx, Karl, *Capital,* London, 1867

Miller, Hugh, *The Cruise of the Betsy,* Edinburgh, 1858

Miller, Hugh, *My Schools and Schoolmasters,* Edinburgh, 1993

Miller, Hugh, *Sutherland As It Was and As It Is,* Edinburgh, 1843

Mitchell's Newspaper Press Directory & Advertisers' Guide, London, 1846–1858 (irreg.), 1869–1907

Mulock, T., *The Western Highlands and Islands Socially Considered,* Edinburgh, 1850

Pennant, Thomas, *A Tour in Scotland and Voyage to the Hebrides,* London, 1790

Pinkerton, John, *An Enquiry into the History of Scotland preceding the reign of Malcolm II, or the year* 1056. 2 vols, Edinburgh, 1789, 1814, incl. *Dissertation on the Origin and Progress of the Scythians or Goths*

Porter, G.R: *Progress of the Nation, 1836–1843*

Robertson, Alexander, *Barriers to national prosperity in Scotland, an inquiry into some of the immediate causes of modern social evils,* Edinburgh, 1853

Robertson, Alexander, *Where are the Highlanders?,* Edinburgh, 1856

Ross, Donald, *The Glengarry Evictions,* Glasgow, 1853

Ross, Donald, *Real Scottish Grievances,* Glasgow, 1854

Ross, Donald, *The Russians of Ross-shire or Massacre of the Rosses in Starthcarron,* Glasgow, 1854

Ross, Donald, *The Scottish Highlanders: Their Present Suffering and Future Prospects,* Glasgow, 1852

Russell, A., *The Highlands: Men, Sheep and Deer, Edinburgh Review,* vol. 106, 1857

Scrope, G.P., *Some Notes of a Tour in England, Scotland and Ireland,* London, 1849

Sinclair, Alexander, *Fifty Years of Newspaper Life, 1845–1895,* Glasgow, 1895

Sismondi, S. *The Celtic Tenure of Land,* 1856

Sismondi, S., *Political Economy and the Philosophy of Government,* 1857

Skene, W.F., *Celtic Scotland,* Edinburgh, 1880

Skene, W.F., *Sketches of Highland Character,* Edinburgh, 1873

Smiles, Samuel, *Self-Help,* London, 1859

Somers, Robert, *Letters from the Highlands,* Inverness, 1848

Southey, Robert, *Journal of a Tour in Scotland in 1819,* London, 1929

Spencer, Herbert: *Social Statistics or the conditions essential to human happiness,* 1851

Stewart of Garth, David, *Sketches of the Character, Manners and Present State of the Highlanders of Scotland with details of the Military Service of the Highland Regiments,* Edinburgh, 1822

Thornton, William Thomas, *Overpopulation and its remedy; or an inquiry into the extent and causes of distress prevailing among the labouring classes of the British Isles,* London, 1846

Tregellis, E.O., *Hints on the Hebrides,* Newcastle, 1855

Wilson, J.G., *Poets and Poetry of Scotland,* London, 1876–77

Secondary Sources

Aspinall, A., *Politics and the Press, 1780–1850,* Home and Van Thal, 1949

Barnard, F.M., *Herder's Social and Political Thought, From Enlightenment to Nationalism,* Clarendon Press, 1965

Bell-Fialkoff, Andrew, 'A brief history of ethnic cleansing', *Foreign Affairs*, Summer 1993

Blum, J., *The End of the Old Order in Rural Europe*, New Jersey, 1978

Bolt, C., *Victorian Attitudes to Race*, London, 1976

Boyce-Curran, *Newspaper History*, London, 1978

Briggs, Asa, *The Age of Improvement*, London, 1979

Bryson, Bill, *Made in America*, London, 1995

Bumsted, J.M., *The People's Clearance, 1770–1815*, Edinburgh, 1982

Cameron, A.D., *Go and Listen to the Crofters*, Stornoway, 1986

Chapman, M, *The Gaelic Vision in Scottish Culture*, London & Montreal, 1978

Checkland, Olive: *Industry and Ethos: Scotland 1832–1914*, London, 1984

Checkland, Olive, *Philanthrophy in Victorian Scotland*, Edinburgh, 1980

Clayre, Alasdair (ed), *Nature and Industrialisation*, Oxford, 1977

Clyde, R.D., *From Rebel to Hero*, Edinburgh, 1995

Coppock, J.T., *An Agricultural Atlas of Scotland*, Edinburgh, 1976

Cowan, R.M.W., *The Newspaper in Scotland – A Study of its first expansion, 1815–1860*, Glasgow, 1946

Craig, David, *Scottish Literature and the Scottish People 1680–1830*, London, 1961

Craig, David, *On the Crofters' Trail*, London, 1990

Dahlgren, P. and Sparks, C., *Journalism and Popular Culture*, London, 1992

Devine, T.M., *Clanship to Crofters' War*, Manchester, 1994

Devine, T.M., 'The Emergence of the New Elite in the Western Highlands, 1800–60', in: T.M. Devine (ed), *Improvement and Enlightenment*, Edinburgh, 1989

Devine, T.M., *The Great Highland Famine: Hunger, Emigration and the Scottish Highlander in the Nineteenth Century*, Edinburgh, 1988

Devine, T.M., 'The Highland Clearances', in: *New Directions in Economic and Social History*, eds. Digby, A. & Feinstein, C., Basingstoke, 1989

Devine, T.M., 'Highland Landowners and the Potato Famine' In: *Perspectives in Scottish History*, 1988

Devine, T.M., 'Highland Migration to Lowland Scotland, 1760–1860', in: *Scottish Historical Review* LXII (1983)

Devine, T.M., 'Landlordism and Highland Emigration', in: Dickson, Tony (ed), *Scottish Capitalism*, London, 1980

Devine, T.M., 'Temporary migration and the Scottish Highlands in the nineteenth century', in: *Economic History Review*, 2nd series, vol.32, 1979

Donaldson, William, *Popular Literature in Victorian Scotland: Language, Fiction and the Press*, Aberdeen, 1986

Donaldson, William, *The Jacobite Song*, Aberdeen, 1988

Ferguson, J.P.S. (ed), *Directory of Scottish Newspapers*, Edinburgh, 1984

Ferguson, W., *Scotland 1689 to the Present*, Edinburgh, 1968

Flinn, M.W, *Scottish Population History from the Seventeenth Century to the 1930s*, Cambridge, 1977

Gaskell, P., *Morvern Transformed*, Cambridge, 1980

Gifford, Douglas (ed), *The History of Scottish Literature*, Vol.3. *The Nineteenth Century*, Aberdeen, 1988

Gray, J. (ed), *Scottish Population Statistics*, Edinburgh, 1952

Gray, M., *The Highland Economy, 1750–1850*, Edinburgh, 1947

Grigor, I.F., *Mightier than a Lord*, Stornoway, 1979

Hamilton, H., *The Industrial Revolution in Scotland*, Oxford, 1932

Harrison, B., 'Philanthrophy and the Victorians', *Victorian Studies*, 1966

Hazard, Paul: *European Thought in the Eighteenth Century* 1946

Herd, Harold, *The March of Journalism: the story of the British Press from 1622 to the present day*, London,. 1952

Hobsbawm, E.J., *Industry and Empire*, London, 1968

Horsman, Reginald, 'Origins of racial Anglo-Saxonism in Great Britain before 1850', in: *Journal of the History of Ideas*, XXXVII, July-September 1976

Houghton, Walter E., *The Victorian Frame of Mind*, Yale University Press, 1957

Houghton, W.E. (ed), *The Wellesley Index to Victorian Periodicals, 1824–1900*, Toronto, 1966–1989

Hunter, James, *A Dance Called America: The Scottish Highlands, the United States and Canada*, Edinburgh, 1994

Hunter, James, *The Making of the Crofting Community*, Edinburgh, 1976

Hunter, James, *On the Other Side of Sorrow: Nature and People in the Scottish Highlands*, Edinburgh, 1995

Huggett, F.E., *The Land Question and European Society*, London, 1975

Lovejoy, A.O., 'The Meaning of Romanticism for the Historian of Ideas', *Journal of the History of Ideas*, II (3), 1941

McCrone, David, *The Making of Scotland*, Edinburgh, 1989

McCrone, David, *Understanding Scotland: The Sociology of a Stateless Nation*, 1992

MacDonald, D.F., *Scotland's Shifting Population*, Glasgow, 1937

MacInnes, John, *The Press in Scotland*, in: *Scottish Affairs* no.1. Autumn, 1992

MacInnes, Allan, 'Scottish Gaeldom: The first phase of clearance', in: *People and Society in Scotland*, Vol.I. 1760–1830, eds. T.M. Devine & R. Mitchison, 1988

MacInnes, Allan, 'The Crofters' Holding Act of 1886: A Hundred Years of Sentence?' in: *Radical Scotland*, Feb./March 1987

MacKenzie, W.C., *The Highlands and Isles of Scotland: A Historical Survey*, Edinburgh, 1937

MacKenzie, W.M., *Hugh Miller: A Critical Study*, London, 1905

MacLean, M. & Carrell, C., *As An Fhearran: From the Land*, Edinburgh, Glasgow/ Stornoway, 1986

MacLean, Marianne, *The People of Glengarry: Highlanders in Transition, 1745–1820*, Montreal, 1991

Macleod, James Lachlan, 'Race Theory in Nineteenth Century Scotland', paper presented to the annual conference of the Association of Scottish Historical Studies, in April 1994

Macmillan, 'Sir Charles Trevelyan and the Highland and Island Emigration Society', in: *Royal Australian Historical Society Journal*, XLIX (1963)

Mechrie, S., *The Church and Scottish Social Development*, Oxford, 1960

Meek, Donald E., *Tuath is Tighearna/ Tenants and Landlords*, Edinburgh, 1995

Mitchison, R., 'The Highland Clearances', in: *Scottish Economic and Social History*, 1981

Mosse, George L., *Toward the Final Solution: A History of European Racism*, London, 1978

Muir, Edwin, *Scottish Journey*, London, 1935

Nairn, T., *The Break-Up of Britain*, London 1977

Norrie, William, *The Progress of British Newspapers in the Nineteenth Century* – Supplement to Sell's *World Press Guide*, London, 1907

Orr, Willie, *Deer Forests, Landlords and Crofters*, Edinburgh, 1982

Phillipson N.T. & R. Mitchison, eds, *Scotland in the Age of Improvement*, Edinburgh, 1970

Pittock, M.G.H, *The Invention of Scotland: the Stuart myth and Scottish identity, 1638 to the present*, London, 1991

Prebble, John, *Culloden*, London, 1967

Prebble, John, *The Highland Clearances*, Penguin edition, London, 1969

Prebble, John, *The King's Jaunt: George IV in Scotland*, London, 1989

Pringle, T.R., 'The privation of history', in: Cosgrove, D. & Daniel, S. (eds), *The Iconography of Landscape*, Cambridge, 1988

Richards, Eric, *A History of the Highland Clearances*, London, 1982

Rosie, George, *Hugh Miller: Outrage and Order*, Edinburgh, 1981

Royle, Trevor, *The Mainstream Companion to Scottish Literature*, Edinburgh, 1993

The Scotsman: The Glorious Privilege: The History of 'The Scotsman, Edinburgh, 1967

A.W.B. Simpson, 'Entails and Perpetuities', in: *Juridical Review*, 1979

Slaven, A., *The Development of the West of Scotland, 1750–1980*, London, 1975

Smout, T.C., *A Century of the Scottish People, 1830–1950*, London, 1986

Smout, T.C., *A History of the Scottish People, 1560–1830* London, 1985

Smout, T.C., 'Tours in the Scottish Highlands from the 18th to the 20th century', in: *Northern Scotland*, Vol.V., 1983

Stromberg, N.R., *European Intellectual History Since 1789*, New Jersey, 1986

Thomson, D.C., *An Introduction to Gaelic Poetry*, London, 1974

Turnock, D., *Patterns of Highland Development*, London, 1970

Wallerstein, Immanuel, *The Modern World System: Capitalist Agriculture and the Origins of European World Economy*, San Diego, 1974

The Waterloo Directory of Scottish Newspapers and Periodicals, Vols. 1–2

Watson, Adam: 'Depopulation and clearances and non-enforced emigration in the north-east Highlands', in: *Northern Scotland* Vol. 10, 1990

Weber, Max, *The Protestant Ethic and the Spirit of Capitalism*, London, 1930

Whyte, I., 'Before and after the improvers: Scottish agriculture and rural society from the 17th century to the 20th century', in: *Scottish Economic and Social History*

Withers, C.W.J., *Gaelic Scotland: The Transformation of a Culture Region*, London, 1988

Womack, P., *Improvement and Romance*, Basingstoke, 1989

Youngson, A.J., *Beyond the Highland Line*, Edinburgh, 1973

Index